I Am
the
Storm

I Am the Storm

Inspiring Stories of People Who Fight
Against Overwhelming Odds

JANICE DEAN

HARPER

An Imprint of HarperCollins*Publishers*

HarperCollins books may be purchased for educational, business, or sales promotional use. For information, please email the Special Markets Department at SPsales@harpercollins.com.

FIRST EDITION

Designed by Nancy Singer

Library of Congress Cataloging-in-Publication Data
Names: Dean, Janice, 1970– author.
Title: I am the storm / Janice Dean.
Description: First edition. | New York, NY: Harper, [2023]
Identifiers: LCCN 2022029071 | ISBN 9780063243088 (hardcover) | ISBN 9780063243217 (ebook)
Subjects: LCSH: Sexual harassment. | Self-preservation. | Self-actualization (Psychology) | Struggle. | Conduct of life.
Classification: LCC HD6060.3 .D43 2023 | DDC 331.4/133—dc23/eng/20221025
LC record available at https://lccn.loc.gov/2022029071

23 24 25 26 27 LBC 5 4 3 2 1

For those who continue to fight.
Never give up.

You may have to fight a battle more than once to win it.

—*Margaret Thatcher*

Contents

Introduction

For almost twenty years, viewers have seen me as the "mostly sunny" meteorologist on television. (I even wrote a book about it!) But like the weather I forecast, life isn't always clear skies. The storms roll in, sometimes without any warning. And it's what you choose to do with those moments that can change the outcome. Sometimes the roughest conditions teach you the hardest lessons, but it can also prepare you for the future and help build a stronger foundation to stand on.

I've had plenty of bad weather that threatened to destroy me. A home invasion in my early thirties made me reevaluate where I was living, and helped me decide to move back home to heal. It forced me to look at where I was headed and start over to make better choices. A few years later, a diagnosis of multiple sclerosis threatened to sidetrack my career and hopes for a family of my own. After a few months of feeling sorry for myself, I surrounded myself with encouraging people (and a good therapist) who told me not to let a chronic illness get in the way of my dreams. Despite a few people advising me to keep my MS a secret, I decided it was more important to be honest and share my illness to help others.

Being bullied in school as a kid and having a couple of abusive bosses at work also helped shape the person I am today. Sometimes the best course of action is to walk away from the abuse, which I did in 2003 when I worked for the notorious shock jock broadcaster Don Imus. Not long after I moved to New York for what should have been the best job of my life, I had to look for something else. And that brought me to Fox News, where I've worked for almost two decades.

In 2016, I was one of the women who came forward about being sexually harassed by Fox News CEO (now deceased) Roger Ailes. The harassment happened early on in my career, and I was able to navigate the situation while still having an exciting, productive job. I just figured the boss was a lonely guy looking for an affair. I brushed off his suggestions and provocative questions and reminded him I was in a relationship. This wasn't the first time I'd had to deal with this kind of behavior, and it's not exclusive to powerful CEOs in broadcasting. Back then, there wasn't much I could do about it. Most companies were set up to protect those in power.

When Gretchen Carlson filed her lawsuit against Roger after being let go from Fox, many of us had to decide if it was worth coming forward to tell our stories during an investigation. My friend Megyn Kelly's name was leaked in the press for confessing that she too was harassed and propositioned by Ailes, and that's when we found the courage to share our own experiences.

None of us thought Roger would be fired, and we would be punished. But, on behalf of other possible victims, a silent army of us risked our jobs and livelihoods to tell our embarrassing, dark stories to a roomful of lawyers. The action was swift. Gretchen won her lawsuit and Roger was let go.

It's important to point out that all of this happened before the #MeToo movement. Sometimes I wonder if maybe my small part helped pave the way for the brave women who came forward about former New York governor Andrew Cuomo's alleged sexual harassment.

I've been asked which was harder: going against one of the most powerful CEOs in broadcasting or a dynasty politician? I will say this: Had I not had the challenge of risking my career to tell the truth about a very powerful boss, I don't think I would have had the courage to stand up to a Cuomo.

It began in the spring of 2020, when my husband lost both of his parents. They contracted the coronavirus in separate care facilities within two weeks of each other. It changed our lives forever, and gave me a new purpose: to find out if their deaths could have been prevented.

Michael and Dolores Newman were both born in New York City. Fondly known to family and friends as "Mickey and Dee," they lived in a four-story walk-up in Flatbush, Brooklyn, for more than fifty years. They would have celebrated their diamond anniversary, marking sixty years of marriage, had their lives not been suddenly cut short.

Sean's parents were declining in health and were having trouble getting in and out of their apartment. For many years we urged them to find a place that had better access, but we could never convince them. There were aides who would visit, but Mickey was suffering from dementia and Dee's health was making it tough to take care of him. It was time to find a place that could help look after both of them. Sean and his sister Donna drove around with Dee looking at assisted living residences, and found one close to us that would take both her and Mickey, but we had to get Mickey in better shape. He was in a nursing home/rehab for various ailments, and his dementia was getting worse. We hadn't even packed up their Brooklyn apartment when COVID crashed into our lives. The Newmans had never been apart for more than a couple of days in their fifty-nine-year marriage, but they ended up both dying alone.

Mickey's death was in late March. We were all in quarantine, and prohibited from visiting him. It was hard to get regular updates on his health. On a Saturday morning, we got a call saying that he wasn't feeling well, and was running a fever. Three hours later he was dead. We didn't find out he died from COVID until we saw his death certificate.

Sean had to tell his mom over the phone that her husband had died. It was the hardest thing he's ever had to do. Two weeks later, Dee got sick and was transported to the hospital, where she was diagnosed with COVID and died a few days later.

At first, we didn't blame anyone for their deaths. We knew the virus was particularly dangerous for the elderly, but we were advised to have them stay put. We later found out there was no proper personal protective equipment (PPE) or ways to test incoming patients. More important, our family was never informed of the March 25 executive order that the governor and the New York State Department of Health were enforcing. More than nine thousand COVID-positive patients would be put back into nursing homes instead of the other facilities that the federal government had provided. I remember that a few days before Mickey died, an aide told us he was being moved to another floor to make room for incoming residents. At that moment we didn't think anything of it, but now I believe it was to bring in infected patients.

When I finally found out about the governor's deadly mandate, it was too late. Sean's parents were gone. We were unable to have wakes or funerals for them. Many bodies were stored in refrigerated trucks because there was no room for them at the morgues. My sister's childhood friend Frankie, who owns a funeral home, offered to keep them together until we could bury them several weeks later.

As we were mourning their loss, I was trying to find out more information on what was happening inside nursing homes. Why were we told to stay at home and as far away from the virus as possible while the most vulnerable were like sitting ducks with the deadly coronavirus flooding their residences? Some local reporters were starting to ask questions, but Cuomo seemed to be getting a pass. And when he was asked to comment, he deflected the blame.

Meanwhile, the New York governor's star was on the rise. The media was in love with this "New York Tough" talking governor. His daily briefings were televised on national TV and he was embarrassingly fawned over during interviews on all the major news networks.

Cuomo's brother, Chris, the prime-time anchor on CNN, was frequently hosting him on his program despite ethical concerns. Many of the segments were peppered with jokes and comments about Andrew's love life.

The insensitivity of it was infuriating, especially for those of us who lost loved ones and were trying to find answers for their deaths.

I do remember the day my grief turned to rage. I saw the Cuomo brothers laughing on CNN with their giant cotton swab props. They were joking about Andrew getting a COVID test and how big his nostrils were. I couldn't believe this comedy routine was happening; these guys were making fun of the fact that they had access to COVID tests—something most people couldn't get, including nursing homes.

I've always said that, had Andrew Cuomo admitted his mistakes early on, apologized, and told us he would spend the rest of his career making sure this never happened again, I would've forgiven him. Instead he celebrated himself, blamed others, and went to great lengths to cover up his egregious errors.

I wrote an opinion piece May 22, 2020, about my in-laws' tragic deaths and went on Tucker Carlson's show on Fox News to share our family's story. With a lump in my throat and a broken heart, I was no longer the meteorologist warning of incoming weather systems. We were grieving relatives who wanted answers.

As New York's death toll was dramatically rising, Cuomo continued his national media tour, never being asked the nursing home questions I so desperately wanted the answers to.

In August 2020, King Cuomo announced his next crowning achievement: a memoir he somehow found the time to write in the middle of a pandemic. While thousands of families were faced with the fact that they would never see their loved ones again, he was auctioning off a $5.1 million book to the highest bidder.

The book deal was shocking enough, but then, not long after that, Hollywood decided to give him an Emmy Award for his daily COVID briefings.

Andrew Cuomo was a ratings hit while real lives and livelihoods in New York were being crushed to death.

I kept speaking out as much as I could on local New York television and radio stations. It was tough getting liberal media outlets to cover my story, and when they did, they would focus on where I worked instead of the incredible tragedy that happened to my family. Social media became a very important weapon for me, where I could tweet news articles and call out reporters and members of Cuomo's administration about what was happening in New York. I traveled thousands of miles throughout the state to attend rallies with other grieving families and a handful of politicians who were brave enough to go against his vindictive, brutal political machine.

A friend who knew the Cuomo family well warned me early on to "watch my back!" Those who tried to cross him would feel the wrath of his team, who were all well versed in attacking, smearing, and making phone calls at midnight screaming at their targets. I was feeling the pressure.

In December 2020 I almost gave up the fight. Exhausted and feeling the weight of trying to work, raise a family, and be an advocate was taking its toll. Sean was reminding me it might be time to take a break. Was this really worth it? One of the biggest triggers for MS is stress, and at this point, I was a ticking time bomb for a relapse. I also knew how hard it was for my family to watch their mom (and wife) being consumed by something that might have seemed like madness.

Just as I was about to step away from the Twitter keyboard and put away my rally signs, New York attorney general Letitia James released a report in January 2021 on the nursing home tragedy. The headline was that Andrew Cuomo's administration "severely" undercounted virus deaths. Then, in a stunning conversation leaked to the *New York Post*, Cuomo's top aide, Melissa DeRosa, admitted that they were purposely hiding the nursing home data so the federal government wouldn't find out and use it against them politically.

The FBI and federal prosecutors in Brooklyn announced they were investigating Cuomo's coronavirus task force with a focus on his administration's handling of nursing homes early in the pandemic. The stories of bullying and abuse were suddenly seeing the light of day in newspapers, on social media, and even on the Cuomo-friendly cable channels.

This was also around the time when a woman named Lindsey Boylan decided to tweet about her worst job ever: working for Andrew Cuomo.

After months of favorable press and puff piece interviews, the tide was turning against the three-term governor from a New York dynasty.

Eleven women would come forward with stories of sexual harassment and assault, and there were more investigations being announced about the then governor's abuse of power. The tangled web of high-powered Cuomo connections was also about to unravel.

In August 2021, Andrew Cuomo resigned in disgrace, along with the key members of his administration. In September, his health commissioner, Howard Zucker, submitted his resignation, following bipartisan pressure criticizing his role in the state's COVID-19 pandemic response.

Then in December, Chris Cuomo was fired from CNN for helping advise his brother during the sexual harassment investigations, and for his own alleged #MeToo issues. In February 2022, Jeff Zucker, the president of CNN, and his longtime girlfriend, Allison Gollust, a top CNN executive (and former communications director for Andrew Cuomo), were forced to resign after an investigation showed they were also advising the former governor during the pandemic and using CNN to boost his profile. Ms. Gollust would feed questions to producers and hosts while the governor was being interviewed.

There was a media machine built to prop this man up and try to silence people who were trying to speak out. I was one of them.

Had you told me that I would be spending over two years of my life trying to shine a light on a tragedy that happened to more than fifteen thousand elderly, thanks in part to the reckless leadership from one of the most powerful politicians in New York history, I would've said you were confusing me with someone else. There's no doubt this fight brought out a fire inside me I haven't quite felt before.

While all of this was happening, I found others who were doing the same thing: finding their voice to speak up about issues that were affecting their own families. A lot of this passion was taking place during the pandemic when people were at home, experiencing life under quarantine, not being able to go to work, see their kids in schools, travel, or say good-bye to loved ones before they died. That kind of dynamic made us angry about what was happening in the world, and begged the question: How can we change things for the better?

I also found myself wondering: What fuels an individual's passion to go up against a much stronger opponent? That kind of storm was brewing inside myself, and I wanted to talk to others who had the same powerful perseverance despite the odds against them.

I remembered back to the biblical book of Samuel we learned about as young kids in Sunday school: the young man named David, who, with only a sling and a pouch full of stones, stepped forward to face the mightier Goliath. The Philistine champion's smaller, weaker opponent was told he didn't have a chance in the battle. And just when it looked like David might be finished, he launched one of his rocks toward a vulnerable spot on Goliath's head that was unprotected by armor. It knocked him out, and miraculously, David was able to end the monster for good.

What I've found out is that there's a David in all of us. From soldiers fighting wars, parents who stand up for their kids, a fireman who risked his life to make sure others would have health care, and a horse trainer who beat the odds to keep doing what he loved to a young woman who delivered a forecast that changed the world.

The common threads through all of these moments are resilience, hope, and perseverance. The question is, how long are you willing to fight for the truth, and if no one else rises to the challenge, do you stand alone?

It's that moment when fate whispers to the warrior and says,

"You cannot withstand the storm,"

And the warrior whispers back,

"I am the storm."

I Am
the
Storm

Prologue

Did you know that one of the most important weather forecasts in history originated from one of the most remote lighthouses in the Atlantic? The crucial information about the atmospheric conditions gave two days' warning of a storm that was brewing 500 miles away, and helped decide whether a precisely planned invasion two years in the making would go ahead.

This true story has always fascinated me as a meteorologist, but when I found out that it was a young woman that relayed this historic information, that's when it became much more interesting.

Maureen Flavin grew up in the southern part of County Kerry, Ireland. She had just turned eighteen, had finished her secondary school exams, and was looking for work. She saw an opportunity as a post office assistant that was located in Blacksod, at a hard-to-get-to lighthouse in the southern end of the Mullet Peninsula. Her nearest relative, Uncle Edward, owned a pub next door and had no family of his own. He announced that he would leave his niece the pub if she wanted to stay there.

Maureen said she wasn't interested in owning a pub, and even dreamed about traveling to America since she had family that had immigrated to the Northeast. After taking two and a half days to travel to Blacksod (which nowadays would take just a few hours), Miss Flavin decided to accept the job as the new post office assistant.

Maureen enjoyed the work but didn't realize how involved it would be. A big part of her duties involved documenting the weather.

According to the *Irish Independent*, "Blacksod was the first land-based observation station in Europe where weather readings could be professionally taken on the prevailing European Atlantic westerly weather systems." During World War II, the Republic of Ireland was neutral. But it did allow the sharing of weather information with Great Britain.

Maureen spent quite a bit of her time writing down the atmospheric conditions. She really didn't understand what for, but she was diligent about her work and getting it right. Things started to get a bit more hectic as she was being requested to send more data every hour.

It was on her twenty-first birthday, on June 3, 1944, at 1:00 a.m., that Maureen was on duty documenting the information. One crucial instrument that has been used to study weather since the 1600s is a barometer. It measures the atmospheric pressure, which gives us clues about the conditions we're going to experience. A drop in air pressure usually means there are clouds, rain, and/or windy conditions approaching. Alternatively, if the barometric pressure rises, that means the atmosphere is pushing away the unsettled weather and bringing in a drier, more stable air mass.

On that day, Maureen's research was showing that the air pressure was dropping rapidly. That meant there was something out there in the Atlantic, a nasty storm that would hit the Irish coast, move over the United Kingdom, then down over the channel into Normandy, France. Miss Flavin compiled the report and then sent it to Dublin. That information was then forwarded to Dunstable, England, where the meteorological headquarters were stationed. Captain James Martin Stagg was the chief meteorologist for US General Dwight D. Eisenhower and was helping plan the Allied invasion. Stagg saw Maureen's hourly updates and decided to bypass the Dublin office for information. He then had someone call the Blacksod post office directly.

In a recorded interview in 2014, Maureen recalled that crucial phone call:

"A lady with a distinct English accent requested me to Please Check! Please Repeat!"

Stagg and his staff saw what Maureen was sending them: a drop in the barometric pressure indicating a strong area of low pressure.

Maureen was getting nervous about all of these requests, so she called someone she knew who was more experienced: Ted Sweeney, the son of the woman who ran the post office (and the man she would marry a few years later). Maureen asked Ted to check her work. He said it looked correct, so she went ahead and sent the information to Dunstable. The Supreme Headquarters Allied Expeditionary Force (SHAEF) in England was forwarded her weather reports, which were checked and double-checked.

When asked if her forecast was accurate, Maureen said it was.

Maureen said that when it came to the invasion, there were things they could put in place, but one thing they had no control over was the weather.

"They had it all worked out to the nearest detail, but our weather report put the first spoke in the wheel."

The rest is history.

General Eisenhower decided to postpone D-Day by one day, so instead of going ahead on the fifth, Operation Overlord (the code name for the invasion) took place on the sixth of June. Ted and Maureen had no idea of the gravity of their reporting. If it weren't for their accurate prediction, Allied forces would have gone ahead on the fifth and the invasion would have been a disaster.

It wasn't until decades letter that Maureen Flavin Sweeney realized how crucial her observations were.

"There were thousands of aircraft and they couldn't tolerate low cloud. We're delighted we put them on the right road. We eventually had the final say!"

Although Maureen didn't know how important her reports were, she took her work very seriously and always wanted to do a good job.

The trajectory of history would be very different if not for Maureen Sweeney's hard work determination, and the precise weather report she delivered.

Maureen Sweeney will turn one hundred this year on June 3, 2023, just a few days before the seventy-ninth anniversary of the D-Day invasion. She lives in Belmullet, County Mayo, Ireland, not far from the lighthouse where she used to work.

Her story inspired me to write *I Am the Storm*, and when I interviewed her son Vincent, I came to the conclusion that one person really can change the world. It doesn't happen overnight, and sometimes it takes a lifetime for the history to be written.

And just as I was learning more about the Sweeney family, Vincent revealed that they knew something about mine.

You could say Mother Nature had something to do with it, but then you'll have to read on to find out why. . . .

1

"I Don't Want Anybody to Be One Day Too Late"

The Mother vs. the Opioid Crisis

While I was writing this book, several people recommended I watch the series *Dopesick* on Hulu about the opioid crisis in America. It paid particular attention to the prescription pain medication OxyContin, which was developed and patented in 1996.

Living in New York, I had followed the story through news reports about the wealthy Sackler family settling thousands of opioid-related lawsuits, but the TV program revealed how their company, Purdue Pharma, knowingly took advantage of the doctors who treat pain and the patients who suffer. The deaths and damage this has inflicted on tens of thousands of families is unforgivable.

According to the National Institute on Drug Abuse, addiction is a "chronic, relapsing disorder characterized by compulsive drug seeking, continued use despite harmful consequences, and long-lasting changes in the brain. It is considered both a complex brain disorder and a mental illness. Addiction is the most severe form of a full spectrum of substance use disorders, and is a medical illness caused by repeated misuse of a substance or substances."

More than 100,000 people die from drug overdoses a year in the United States, with opioids factoring in 7 out of 10 of their deaths. In 2022, overdose deaths were up by 30 percent, and unfortunately, going through a pandemic made things worse for those living with this Goliath known as addiction.

Shelly Elkington of Montevideo, Minnesota, believes that her daughter Casey's struggle with opioid addiction led to her suicide in 2015. After Casey's death, Shelly wanted to help other families living the same nightmare they went through. This fight has not been easy for her or her own family, but she keeps going to try to prevent this from happening to others.

I begin our conversation by asking Shelly to tell me about her daughter. She says it's her favorite place to start.

"You know, Casey was just like anybody's daughter. She was fun and energetic, and she could be difficult as a teenager. We had lots of great times together. She was athletic, and one of the most determined people I've yet to meet in my life. We had a great friendship. She was very much about family, and I know I was really important to her. She was strong-willed, but she had so much energy about her. And then she got sick."

Casey was diagnosed with Crohn's disease in her first year of college. Crohn's is a type of inflammatory bowel disease that causes swelling of the digestive tract. That inflammation can bring many symptoms, including fatigue, weight loss, and extreme, debilitating pain.

It was hardest for Casey during her first year in college. She watched her friends go out and do all these fun things, while she had to deal with this frightening, long-term illness. At the beginning, Casey was doing well on her own, but then having to endure multiple surgeries was an incredibly tough journey that changed Shelly's daughter significantly.

The medication began when she was recovering from the surgeries and living with Crohn's. Every time she ate, she was in pain.

"For so long you're trying to figure out what's wrong, so the treatment for that probably wasn't wrong. And I'm very cautious about this part of the story because I don't place blame on her doctor, necessarily. He was treating her for pain, which was appropriate at the time."

Shelly says that back then, the doctors were sold a bad bill of goods and didn't really know how addictive these drugs are. After Casey went in for a big surgery, she had already been on high dosages of opioids.

"Treating the pain from that was almost impossible, so it began a couple of years before her death. It was in 2013 when she started getting the regular prescriptions."

The pain meds were oxycodone. (Oxycodone/OxyContin have the same active narcotic ingredient. The difference is in how the tablet releases the medication. OxyContin tablets release oxycodone continuously throughout the day; oxycodone is immediate.)

Casey was also prescribed fentanyl patches (used to relieve severe pain in people who are expected to need medication around the clock for a long time). Shelly says that as a parent, all you want to do is make your child feel better, and you don't care what it takes. Back then, Casey was trying to be independent, living in Fargo, North Dakota, and going to college. She came home for a while after the surgery, and did well. Eventually, Casey wanted to go back to school, and was driven to try to do that. But living with a debilitating illness was wearing her down.

"She weighed eighty-five pounds. She was so tiny taking all these meds, and it dawns on you that something's wrong. The drugs are now becoming a little bit different than they're intended to be."

Shelly says that at one point Casey was in the hospital and the doctors were giving her the drugs through an intravenous line. It wasn't working. Her doctors were struggling because they realized they couldn't give this tiny girl any more medication. It was becoming too dangerous.

"She's crying and having procedures done with no pain relief, and I'm crying because I just don't want her to hurt anymore. And I think that was the time I knew we were in trouble. Really big trouble."

When Casey was discharged from the hospital, Shelly remembers one of the doctors saying they needed to talk: The opioids had created something different. Casey had built up a tolerance and was now dependent on them.

"The last thing she wanted was for anybody to take them away from her."

I ask Shelly where she gets her strength to do this. How long after Casey's death did she realize that she wanted to use this tragic situation to be a force for good? She says her daughter died in August 2015, and a few months later, in December, she saw something about an opioid issue happening in her state and she submitted a comment. The Minneapolis *Star Tribune* called her because they had read what she wrote and wanted to do a story.

"And that was kind of my first time I'd ever been asked about any of it. I think that's what moves you—from that immense grief sitting alone in your house, to all of a sudden a couple of years later, being at the State of the Union because you've been an advocate. It's not sadness and it's not anger. It's this combination of trying to prevent other people from having to go through what you're going through."

Shelly recalls one of the last times she talked to her daughter. It was after her son Zack had called to say he thought Casey was in trouble. He was scared for her and knew she needed help. Shelly reached out and announced they were going to do something.

"And she's crying, and she says, 'It's not my fault, Momma.' And I'll never forget that because what that told me was she was afraid to ask for help. How embarrassed, how humiliated and ashamed she must have felt. And I thought: How many other people must be going through life like Casey and how many parents like me are feeling helpless not knowing what to do? So honestly, that was it. That was the drive and then channeling grief into that work."

Listening to Shelly tell this story brings tears to my eyes because I can relate to that feeling. I remember my sister-in-law, Donna, telling me that one of the last things her mom (my mother-in-law), Dee, said on the phone when she was sick with COVID in the hospital was that she was scared. It's something you never forget, and it's what fuels the desire to channel it into advocacy. You can let it eat you up and make you sad or depressed or angry. For me, I admit, it has become a bit of an obsession. I'm not sure if it's healthy, but it has gotten me through several years of never giving up by wanting justice for my family.

Shelly says she's been called a zealot, and had to look up the word.

"I was, like, I'm not sure that was a compliment, but I'll take it."

I asked Shelly to talk about her husband, Tim, through all of this, because my husband, Sean, seeing me on social media, doing hundreds of interviews, driving to rallies, often asks me, "When does it end?"

She says her spouse, Tim, is very low-key, and can relate to this.

"He never went with me to any of the events I was attending. Maybe once or twice when I asked him to. He's not one to be in the spotlight, and never one to be interviewed. Tim just really supported me, and asked, 'What do you need?'"

Afterward he would pack a lunch and make sure her car was safe, asking her to call him every time she arrived to her events.

"He was just a great husband and a great support person who I knew loved me and missed Casey terribly. And he knew I needed to do this. Looking back on it, I feel his grief."

Tim was alone quite a bit while she was pounding doors and making noise. She says he was a quiet griever, but at the same time, a tremendous support system.

"But the day he said to me, 'Hey, are you sure you're safe?' That was something I'll never forget."

I tell her how much Tim sounds like Sean, and I'm weeping a bit. They both express their concern for us, and then they pack our lunch so we can go out and try to change the world.

Shelly admits that her way of grieving was channeled by driving to St. Paul two or three times a week, sometimes in a blizzard, to fight the fight while her husband was at home.

"I'll never forget when I really started to get worried about what I was doing and who I was fighting against when the weather was bad and I shouldn't have been out on the road. Tim looked at me and said,

'Are you safe? And I don't mean from the weather, but are you safe? Are you afraid of what might happen? Are you afraid of what they can do?'"

But Shelly says she couldn't get into that headspace. Instead, she decided that no matter what, she had to try.

"I got in that car and I got louder than ever because that was our last push to get a bill passed that we had been working on and I thought, Not today. The fight doesn't end today."

But since then, Shelly has realized it's one battle and then it's on to the next one. It's a cycle that entwines itself into a world she didn't know a lot about: politics. That's when she found herself getting more overwhelmed and then suddenly starting to cry when the grief rushes in.

However, she's also found that in this world of being an advocate, there are many who stand by you.

"You find out quickly there are people helping you every step of the way. Not everybody can do what you do with your voice and the advocacy you're doing. Not everybody could do what I do, but they're still there, holding you up. And that's really how you keep going. It's the people that have gone through this same thing saying, I'm here for you. Let's do it."

When Shelly first started speaking out about what happened to Casey, she met a couple named Bill and Judy Rummler. They had lost their son Steve to a heroin overdose after years of a crippling addiction to opioids and created a foundation in his honor. That's when Shelly began networking through the Rummler family, and they took her in and held her hand. She wasn't alone anymore.

I ask Shelly if she ever feels like she's making a difference. There are times when I think I've helped bring awareness, but I'm not sure anything has really been fixed. Sometimes it seems endless. And when it comes to the David vs. Goliath aspect, there's no real decisive moment when this David wins the battle. It's a lifelong crusade that makes people around us ask, "When is it over?" And "When do we stop trying?"

But when there are victories, like legislation for emergency responders to carry naloxone (Narcan), there is the hope that people will be helped. Shelly pushes every day for that, but there are those moments of, When do we finally rest?

Shelly asks me if we can spend a minute on Casey's death because sometimes people get it wrong, and she wants to be very clear about what happened. There's a lot of assumption that Casey died of an overdose, but she didn't. Her cause of death was suicide, which leaves Shelly and her family in a tough place emotionally and in their advocacy because her death was also investigated as a homicide.

"The last three months of her life, she was out of touch with us, and for the most part, she was with heroin dealers. There's a lot of speculation around her death that we don't know. So sometimes in advocacy, I don't always feel like I fit in. But I want people to know that these deaths matter. People do take their own lives, and people have their lives taken by others as a result of this."

Shelly says that for Casey, as long as she was only using the meds that were prescribed to her, she felt she was doing nothing wrong. And that's how she convinced herself it was fine.

"She got very creative, but as long as they came through a pharmacy, it seemed normal. But Casey got to a point where it just wasn't okay anymore. She did end up with people that were using heroin, because I'm sure somebody told her at one point, it's cheaper and it's easier to get."

I ask Shelly how she dealt with this period when her daughter wasn't contacting her. Once your child becomes an adult, you have to let go, but how do you cope every day knowing she's sick and you just want to help?

"I remember my husband, Tim, saying, 'Have you heard from Casey?' I tried to find somebody who might know where she is. And the last time I did see her, Casey had to go to her doctor, and I thought, This is the day we are going to get her help."

Shelly picked up her daughter in St. Cloud, Minnesota, and drove her to the appointment. Casey didn't speak to her in the car, and her mom felt like she didn't know who this person was. They went into the doctor's office, got her meds, and filled them at the pharmacy. And then Shelly asked Casey to come home, because she needed help.

"And she said, 'I'll come later. I need to get my stuff. I need to get my car.' It was always something."

Shelly told Casey she would pay for a hotel room because during that time she was living in someone's garage.

"And I just remember her hugging me harder than she's ever hugged me, almost like she knew she wouldn't see me anymore."

The last three months before Casey died were very frightening. Shelly says they had gotten information from an ex-boyfriend that she was hanging around dangerous people, and was with someone who had been released from prison for domestic assault.

"There were a lot of people in her life that normally weren't. We never had these kinds of concerns about who Casey was with. It was just the last few months of her life, and that's what makes her death such a mystery to us and hard to navigate."

After Shelly had talked to Casey on the phone, she wanted to bring her to rehab. She had a doctor who had helped during one of her surgeries and now had a clinic specializing in suboxone, one of the medications used to treat opioid addiction, but back then it wasn't well-known.

"I didn't know what suboxone was. I had to google it. And I'm a nurse. I said, this seems like a really good option for you, Casey—something that could really help you. She agreed to do it. They had sent all the paperwork, and she had called me the day before. That appointment was on August twentieth of 2015. She died on August nineteenth."

Shelly says that's the hardest part for her, and when it comes to what drives her, it was that day.

"I don't want anybody to be one day too late."

Back in 2015, we didn't know the magnitude of opioids. Getting off of them is not as simple as quitting cold turkey. These powerful pain medications actually change your brain chemistry and once someone is addicted, you are dealing with a different person. Shelly says we have so much more work to do when it comes to awareness, resources, and building more clinics. In their community of Montevideo, there is now a suboxone team of doctors that you can call, and they will get an induction started. There wasn't that avenue back when Casey needed it.

Still, the success rate of getting off the drugs is not great. It's about 20 percent.

"So what other systems do we need to be looking at to make this better for people? It's such a cost on our society, and not just the horrific loss of losing your beautiful daughter. That's the ultimate price, but the literal cost. The taxpayer cost."

Shelly says just getting awareness of opioids into the education system has been a Goliath battle. The pushback from schools is alarming in some communities.

"I have a great friend who does this work where she's going into schools and educating kids. You wouldn't believe the pushback she gets. They don't want her to come in, and that was before the pandemic. Kids are slipping through the cracks."

It's in every city and every town in America. I live in a close-knit community on Long Island filled with hardworking, middle-class families (many Irish Catholic and Italian families with both parents still married), good schools, and wonderful friends. I know several people in my community who have been touched by opioid addiction and death. It's heartbreaking. And unfortunately, there is a stigma attached to this that makes it even worse trying to raise awareness. No one in our society is immune from this crisis.

"This is why Casey didn't ask for help. She saw people who were addicts, and that was somebody else. Because society told her it was never going to be her. So then when something's wrong, imagine how hard it was for her to admit it. That's tough stuff."

I ask how we start talking to our children about this. My boys are eleven and thirteen. I've taken them both aside and said, We know you're good boys. We like your friends, but you still always need to come to us if you're in trouble. You have to keep us in the loop even if you're scared to talk to us. It only takes someone giving you half a pill that could end your life. You have no idea what's in that pill, which could be laced with fentanyl, a synthetic opioid eighty to one hundred times stronger than morphine. Am I being too harsh by scaring them? How do you preemptively help them with a potential situation?

"If you were to ask me, I would have said exactly that. And keep conversations going because having children in that age group, their friend groups change significantly through these ages. And you need to see what's going on with their social media. This is their main line of communication. A lot of things get bought and sold online or things get set up through that process. Even if you kind of address it like gossip in school, sometimes that can start a conversation. You just need to get them to talk."

I ask Shelly if she's an optimistic person despite all of this. Oftentimes it's the people who have gone through some of the darkest times who see the light more clearly.

She says she is.

"I am so grateful for the twenty-six years I had with her. I wish I had more. I do, but I can't change that. I cannot change the outcome of what happened. So, I really do wake up with as much gratitude as possible."

This fight has always been about many people and many moms. Shelly says they all look out for each other. And it may be a cliché, but life really is short.

"When you go through something like this, all of a sudden you realize, I'm not going to waste time. I'm going to fight. We don't have a lot of time on this planet and we need to make it count."

I ask Shelly what her next goal is. Being an advocate has its small victories, but sometimes the ghost of Goliath rears its head again, and you feel your three steps forward have moved backward. She says it's something you have to be prepared for. You work hard, you drive through a blizzard, and sometimes the car won't start. But you ask yourself, Am I okay? Am I safe?

And you try again.

For Shelly, the grief still comes when you least expect it. There is no right or wrong when it comes to dealing with it. Also, always being out there raising her voice and demanding change can sometimes be a distraction instead of opening up those channels of healing.

Therapy has been a big part of Shelly's life to help her mental health. She needed someone to talk to while her daughter was chronically ill and she was worrying about her son, too, who she felt was being reckless because of what they were all going through. She remembers a moment when she told a therapist she was so worried about one of her children dying. It was consuming her.

"And I'll never forget her saying, 'You'll live.' Wow. And it sounded harsh at the time, but she was right. You do. You live. I have hundreds of people I know and have met in my life that are proof of that. And we all 'live' in different ways, but we all still make it. So I think that checking in on my own grief and knowing when I need help is really important."

Shelly says she's back in a therapeutic relationship now, but there are also people she can reach out to anytime. They call themselves "the moms" because that's who they are to each other.

"And sometimes you won't hear from somebody for a while and you know, that's just their time. They need to check out for a bit. And then they're back and we're supporting each other again."

I am curious about how politicians factor into Shelly's life. Are they a force for good? I have met many leaders in my nineteen years working at Fox, and more recently during my fight for those who died in nursing homes. There are good ones who want to get involved for the right reasons, and then there are ones who just want to get their name out there.

Shelly says she asks a couple of questions when meeting lawmakers: Will they help others and do they have the ability to make a difference? Even if they are using her story to benefit themselves, that's the nature of politics. There are some really good folks, though, including two people who helped her pass legislation. They came together from a place of grief, and on different sides of the aisle, because both lawmakers had lost a child.

"And I'm going to tell you that it was the most amazing experience of my life working with these two. They are still both two of my dearest friends. Representative Dave Baker and Senator Chris Eaton. The work that got done would never have happened without their help, and their personal stories. I remember testifying, saying when you are asked to identify your daughter at a morgue, they don't ask you if she's a Republican or a Democrat."

It's easy to lose hope when it comes to trying to change laws or legislation to help a cause. But it can happen in small steps. Nobody is going to get everything they want, but there has to be compromise. And you don't learn this overnight. The right politicians will guide you through, because it's never going to be perfect, and there's always going to be more to fight for.

"My friend, Representative Baker, would call me up and say, 'Okay, Shelly, here's how this works.' He was so good about making sure I understood the process because I was still emotional. He would coach me on what we need to do to get through a committee. Grassroots politics is interesting because you're almost too innocent to know what you're up against. . . . So maybe that's why we do it."

If there's one thing I've learned in this fight, it's that we can be very powerful as family members who have gone through a tragedy. I've met so many wonderful people who went through the same thing we did. And, having this shared experience, you stand up for each other and those who are no longer with us. Those voices come together as a chorus.

Some of the best ideas about opioid resources have come from those who have lived through it, including family members who work tirelessly to expose the horrific consequences. They are the ones that experienced drug addiction in their own homes.

The series *Dopesick* has done an excellent job shining a spotlight on this epidemic and has made the country more aware of how the OxyContin crisis began. In 2022, there was a settlement hearing where the court allowed people who lost loved ones or who themselves were addicted to the dangerous drug to address members of the Sackler family.

Twenty-four people were able to speak during a Zoom session to David, Richard, and Theresa Sackler. Their stories were heartbreaking and infuriating.

An advocate who struggled with his own addiction to opioids, named Ryan Hampton, told the three Sacklers, "You know what you did. I hope that every single victim's face haunts your every waking moment and your sleeping ones, too. I hope you hear our names in your dreams. . . . I hope you hear the sirens. I hope you hear the heart monitor as it beats along with failing pulse. . . . You poisoned our lives and had the audacity to blame us for dying. . . . Richard Sackler, you are the abuser, you are the criminal, and you are the culprit."

Shelly is good friends with Ryan. She says she watched the testimonials and found them emotional, but also very necessary.

"I really thought that it was important for the Sackler family to hear and understand the grief and what people need to go through to manage this, the rest of their lives and the rest of our lives. Whether it made an impact for them, I don't know."

Shelly says the fact that this family had monumental wealth before this and after this is important to remember. These people still go about their lives free from responsibility while society is focused on the users. But this case against the drug companies is very much about deception. And despite how much there is against them, they are still not being held legally accountable.

"There's a lot of people in jail right now for small crimes, drug crimes, and people who are users who have substance use disorder. Those individuals are entrapped in a legal and criminal justice system for years, losing their families, their jobs. But yet this uber wealthy family that made billions of dollars, not millions, billions. They're not going to jail."

Shelly texted Ryan after the testimonials and thanked him for what he did on behalf of all the families that have gone through opioid addiction. She was grateful for the opportunity to have this story covered in the news. But one big settlement isn't going to make this go away. Shelly wants the focus to be on the stigma, because we still think of those suffering with substance use disorder as the bad guys instead of the people that lied to us saying the drug wasn't addictive.

"I was with Casey many times when she filled a prescription for oxycodone and OxyContin. I remember thinking, This can't be right. This is making her worse. She deteriorated from that day forward."

It's also important to remember that it's not just the Sacklers. They're an easy target to make into an evil billionaire family. The distributors and third-party folks between insurance companies are also enablers. The pills themselves are inexpensive to make and to sell.

"You can get thirty oxycodone for five bucks. That's part of the insurance. Then there's the benefit managers. All those folks have a place in this madness and it's all about the money. So this six billion dollars or whatever the final number is [for the Sackler family], we can't continue to feed this wheel that isn't working. We have insurance capping out people at fourteen days of treatment trying to get clean. And there is no way that works."

The insurance companies need to help those who are trying to get into facilities to get off the drugs, too. Shelly says that once patients get in, they do great with three meals a day and mental health care. But as soon as they leave, there's the risk of serious setbacks.

"All of a sudden, they're out with very low serotonin levels" (serotonin is a chemical that the body produces naturally and helps regulate mood; people who feel depressed may have low levels) "and are subject to relapse. So, I think my passion lies in fixing the system. As a business owner, I'm accountable for outcomes. And I just feel like the treatment industry is also a part of this problem. They're not accountable for the outcomes."

As for the Sacklers, many people would like to see the receipts and where the money goes from here on in.

"Why is it there is jail time for felonies like drug selling and causing deaths? Why aren't people like the Sacklers not held criminally responsible? There's certainly enough evidence there."

Shelly says we need to visualize these people and companies that have manufactured and created this epidemic as drug cartels.

"They should be held legally accountable. We're using the criminal justice system to manage a disease. And we don't do that with any other disease. We just do it with this one."

Not only should there be liability for these types of crimes, but there also has to be awareness. The public has to know what's happening to keep the pressure on. That's where we come in. Those who have lived it. The storytellers are a very important key to this.

"Because every time we tell our story, it reduces the stigma. And the more that we can reduce the stigma in this country, the more people will begin to ask for help."

That means having drugs on hand to "reverse" an overdose or treat those who have opioid use disorder to reduce the severity of withdrawal symptoms.

"I've met people at midnight who need suboxone. I don't care. I'll get it for them. Because you can't recover if you're dead. So, if we can keep people alive, then there's going to be a chance they can get help."

In 2018, Shelly was invited to be a guest at the State of the Union address for her work in bringing attention to the opioid crisis. She was invited by Senator Amy Klobuchar, who was also using her platform to bring attention to the epidemic. Shelly says it was an honor being there, sitting in the center, staring right at the president during his speech. It was great to be part of, and it shouldn't matter who you voted for. This was a moment when people on both sides of the aisle were listening, and it makes a difference. But it's still not enough.

"I'm fortunate to have resources that allow me to go to the State of the Union and take off of work, because not everybody has the ability to do that. So I will use that privilege where I can, however I can."

Shelly tells me she had a dream about Casey the night before our interview. Her daughter was sick in bed, and Shelly was at home taking care of her. That's something that happened quite a bit when Casey was first diagnosed with Crohn's and had numerous surgeries.

I ask how that felt. Did it make her sad after she woke up from seeing Casey or did it feel like Casey was still alive and here with us on earth?

"I was grateful afterwards. I always am. We used to talk every day. And that's the part you miss the most. The 'Hey, what's up? Do you have twenty bucks?' There's a lot of good memories."

Shelly says she loves it when Facebook memories pop up on her computer or her phone and she sees her daughter smiling back at her. It doesn't make her sad. It gives great comfort.

"Because they're always so sweet. Just an 'I love you' random moment. And it just makes my day."

Before we hang up, I tell Shelly how much I've enjoyed talking to her despite the difficult topics. I feel like I've known her much longer, in a way that's hard to describe. Maybe sharing stories of grief connects us in ways we never imagined. Because that's the way we keep the memories of our loved ones alive forever.

2

"We Settled In for a Fight"
The Visionary vs. MTV

During the pandemic, I started listening to podcasts while I walked thorough our neighborhood to get some exercise. Instead of it being a chore, I looked forward to it, and if I found something interesting, the hour of counting steps flew by. One day I was listening to my friend Megyn Kelly's program (one of my favorites), and she had on a fellow broadcaster (and former MTV VJ), Adam Curry. Their conversation was friendly, entertaining, and informative. I walked the whole hour and a half, which for me is the sign of a really great podcast.

Not only did I enjoy the fact that Adam had some wonderful stories about his days at MTV interviewing rock stars and had equally famous eighties hair, but I also learned that Adam was one of the pioneers of what we know as podcasting today. His life from growing up in the Netherlands to finding his way onto MTV is quite a journey. Fame can be a Goliath for many who achieve it, especially so young. But what struck me the most about Adam is his ability to foresee incredible opportunities that others didn't. His whole life has been about taking chances, and betting on himself. When others tried to take advantage of him, or his ideas, he fought back.

We began our chat discussing our matching big hairdos back in the eighties. Adam admits it was his signature look back then, and if you google "Adam Curry," there's a whole treasure trove of pictures to admire. It wasn't an easy thing to achieve. My own big-hair days consisted of constant perming, highlighting, and cans of hair spray. Adam's first wife was the one who came up with his teased-to-perfection look, and reveals it was a production to create that level of poufiness.

Looking back on all of it, he appreciates those days introducing Ozzy Osbourne and interviewing Paul McCartney, but it wasn't as glamorous as one might think. More important, though, the tools he needed for fighting various Goliaths in his life were there from the beginning.

"Many of my extended family are either military or, more likely, intelligence. My uncle is Donald P. Gregg, who was [Vice President George H. W.] Bush senior's national security advisor during Iran-Contra. And then he was ambassador to [South] Korea, where, if you recall, the embassy was under attack. People were throwing firebombs over the wall. He was ambassador then, but most notably, he was very high in the CIA."

Adam's maternal grandfather was Albert Schauble, who came from Schwartzwald, Germany. He emigrated before World War II and actually fought as an American citizen in the US Army's 741st Tank Battalion. He landed at Omaha Beach on D-Day.

"He was a Signal Corps guy, and I didn't know him as well as the rest of my family, but there was some influence there, and something about the mystique of that has always been with me from early on."

Communication and understanding technology would shape Adam's entire career. Born in Arlington, Virginia, he moved with his parents to the Netherlands when he was seven. At age thirteen, he was building FM transmitters and making his mom drive around the block to test them. He was sixteen when he was hired for his first radio job, and that's where his heart is. One of his proudest achievements was getting his ham radio license a decade ago. This makes me laugh out loud because my husband, Sean, got his ham radio license before the pandemic, and is also extremely proud of it. I suggest that ham radio might save the world one day.

"When we hit snowmageddon a few years back, here in Austin, the first thing I did was run to my ham rig. Local radio becomes very important when there's a big local event. Let's face it, turning on NPR and listening to Terry Gross in the middle of a power outage is not helpful. The local radio stations communicate more information than most news outlets or even the government itself. Ham radio is where it's at. And how far can it reach? Oh yeah, I just communicated with the International Space Station."

I explain to Adam that I feel blessed to have a job in television, but there's something so intimate and powerful about listening to a voice telling you a story without the pictures attached. Your imagination fills in the blanks and there's nothing to distract you. It's exciting that the podcast is bringing that experience back for those of us who love to listen.

Adam enjoys seeing the evolution we've gone through from radio to the podcast. Considering his part of history developing the medium, he should be proud of how it all turned out.

"I was in New York in 2018, sitting in the yellow cab with the heater blasting and the windows open. It used to be that the cabdriver would be tuning into the AM radio fading in and out. But now he was listening to a podcast. That was awesome. That's the stuff that makes me go, Oh wow, you know the crazy thing we did eighteen years ago?"

So how did Adam come up with the unbelievable idea of the podcast?

He says there's two parts to the story. The first came when he sold his stake in a company that he took public. His wife was Dutch and had followed him to America for twelve years, but having grown up in Amsterdam, they moved back for a bit before heading to London. That's where he was introduced to the cable modem, a network device that delivers internet over a cable TV line.

"So now you have this magical phenomenon where you didn't have to dial up anymore. You had a dedicated computer that was on the internet all the time. It wasn't fast by any means, but it was incredibly cool."

From an entertainment perspective, Adam knew that we would one day be broadcasting online. But the experience back then was far from easy. You'd have to click and open up a player on your computer. That wasn't fun.

"But I realized, like the evening news, most of that is all pre-produced and it's sitting there waiting to pop on at six o'clock when you sit down and watch it. So, I thought, What if there was a mechanism that would know you're waiting for something, whatever that something is, whether it's a TV show or a radio show—and your computer is scanning at regular intervals, when it sees that there's something new, it downloads it? Then it notifies you, and therefore eliminating the entire waiting process."

At the time, Adam found out about a guy named Dave Winer, who was building RSS for blogs. (RSS is a type of web feed that allows users and applications to receive regular updates from a website or blog of their choice.)

"So he's an interesting dude, but he wasn't easy to convince. I flew to New York because I saw this would be the way to do it: We could have an attachment to a blog post. And then the software that aggregates (reads the blogs on your computer) will see that, and will download the file or folder before you listen to or watch."

Adam realized that the RSS just needed changes to the code to get the audio files instead of text files. It took him several times to convince Dave to try it, and did so by programming in his own software to demonstrate what he meant.

"And then when I showed it to him, he said, 'Yeah, I'll put it in, but only under the promise, you never, ever touch my software again.'"

Adam and Dave were the only ones in the world using the technology, sending things back and forth from Amsterdam to San Francisco. Then, in October 2001, Apple announced the release of one of the biggest music game changers in history, the iPod, which also gave us iTunes, the software that allowed you to download and listen to music on the device.

It was like time traveling back to when Adam was seven years old and his grandmother gave him his first transistor radio. He knew this was different than anything else in recent years.

"This is not a digital Walkman, this is not a jukebox, this is a radio receiver. So then I set about with my coding skills, creating an Apple script that would look for my RSS feed. And if there was a new file attached to it, it would download it."

Back then you still had to connect your iPod back to the computer for it to download. But it would trigger an update, and then put that show into a playlist like an album. After that, you could grab your iPod, put your earphones on, and listen.

"And I went, 'Holy crap!' I immediately created a show called the *Daily Source Code* and started blogging about it."

Suddenly software developers from around the world were paying attention.

By then, Adam was publishing his files on a Mac Drive (which would now be considered the iCloud). It was a simple thing, not for sharing files, but for storing stuff for yourself. Adam later learned that the folks at Apple saw that he was using these files in a way no one had ever done before. They could track how much bandwidth he was using, and Steve Jobs, the CEO of Apple, wanted to see "what this guy was doing."

In the mid-2000s, people were taking notice of Adam's exciting adventure, and he was being asked to talk about this new way of communicating.

"I got a call, asking if I had some time to meet with Steve Jobs. And I said, 'I don't know, let me check my calendar.' But it turned out to be a one-on-one personal meeting for an hour where we talked about all kinds of stuff. I've met a lot of interesting people, but meeting Steve Jobs is right up there with meeting Quincy Jones."

Jobs asked if Adam could put podcast functionality into iTunes. He agreed.

"There were a couple of thousand podcasts back then, and we had an open-source index. Looking back, Apple became the de facto on-ramp to podcasting because of this."

In 2005, Jobs previewed Apple's podcasting efforts by playing *Daily Source Code* at All Things D [Digital], a huge tech conference.

There's video online of Jobs in front of an audience playing Adam's podcast and talking about a cool new thing being integrated into iTunes, which would work on your iPod.

"And lo and behold, Apple started promoting all kinds of mainstream stuff—the NPRs and BBC, highbrow mainstream stuff, which I hadn't thought about."

That was the genesis of the podcast.

"Anybody can use it. Anybody can publish. No one owns it. There's no one you can go to and say, hey, turn that guy off. If you publish a podcast feed, you're publishing it on the internet. Anyone can do it. It's fair game to get that feed and subscribe to it or do whatever you want with that information. You don't need a third party. That's how podcasting grew with a big assist from Apple."

Pretty awesome from the guy who used to introduce Metallica videos during MTV's *Headbangers Ball*.

I ask Adam about his big David-and-Goliath moment with MTV back in the day. He says he can give the history of what happened, but says he should start with what he's supposed to say first: "So I have an official line, which is the lawsuit between MTV Networks and Mr. Curry has been settled out of court. Neither party has any further comment. But I can certainly tell you all the history behind it because it's fun and it's well documented."

MTV started in 1981. Many of us remember that moment pretty clearly, with the astronaut planting the flag with the MTV logo on the moon. The first video ever aired was the Buggles' "Video Killed the Radio Star." And for those of us who loved eighties music, seeing our favorite bands on-screen for three or four minutes acting out or lip-synching with their music was life changing. It truly did change the way we consumed music.

MTV recruited Adam after someone saw him hosting a fan favorite Dutch pop music program called *Countdown*. They brought him to New York in 1987 with the next wave of new VJs. Adam liked the gig, but he didn't really connect well with management. He thinks it's because he had too many aspirations other than the job they were paying him to do.

There was a new hobby that was occupying his time in the mid- to late eighties called computers. He was fascinated with modems and games and had to put his Sinclair ZX80 and Commodore VIC-20 into the closet because he realized they were distracting him in an unhealthy way. His obsession was interfering with his day job.

Adam also knew about this thing called the internet before most of the world was clued in. He remembers his dad being interested in computers early on, and saw these huge, clunky pieces of equipment as the future. He had a Mac Plus with the online service CompuServe. America Online, or AOL, hadn't even started yet.

"I got a huge twenty-megabyte external hard drive with a SCSI cable," he recalls. "If you can remember that big honking cable with big connectors. Got a modem, and very quickly, I was reading some of the computer forums about this thing called the internet."

Adam discovered there were groups filled with college kids who had access to mainframes and computers that were connected to the internet, posting all sorts of amazing stuff about music he was interested in.

"There was another program called Gopher, which was invented by the computer science lab at the University of Minnesota. It was like a hyperlink thing: You have to be on a menu and then you could use the arrow keys and request the document. But the cool thing was that document might not be on the computer you were accessing. Instead, it was finding it from another computer at a different university clear across the country."

This was fascinating: Adam could link from one document to another, and even set up his own. He began writing about all of this exciting new technology on a Gopher server, and realized he needed his own server to put all of this on. There were only a few people online who did this kind of thing.

"There were these guys in Virginia above a Chinese restaurant at a company called Digex. Crazy bearded guys setting up something called 'hosting' and they told me I needed a domain name first. So that's when I said, 'How about MTV.com?'"

While Adam was registering MTV.com, he decided to grab a few more domain names he thought would be cool to have, including Curry .com and Diaries.com, which he says still has, and will never give up. He also decided to grab Elvis.com, which became an important lesson later on. . . .

Adam figured that the kids who were watching MTV were probably also into computers, so he began telling his fans, "Look for the server MTV.com on your computer and send me an email. Adam@MTV.com."

He approached his bosses several times to tell them what he was doing. There was no money involved. It was just something to enhance his show and connect to his viewers.

"And around this time, I got an email from a kid in college out of Champaign-Urbana, Illinois. It said: 'Adam, I see you guys at MTV .com, love the Gopher server, but check this out: If you install this server, you can use this piece of software called Mosaic. And then you can have a multimedia experience to this new thing called HTML.'" (HTML, or hypertext markup language, is the code that is used to structure a web page and content.)

The email was from Marc Andreessen, who co-created Mosaic, the first widely used internet browser. Marc later went on to create Netscape Communications with Jim Barksdale, one of the biggest Silicon Valley billionaire investors. Adam was now being helped by major league World Wide Web talent.

Meanwhile, he had another conversation with the MTV brass to make sure everything was still okay with using the handle MTV.com. And they still didn't think anything of it.

"The legendary words were, 'Oh yeah, no, that's cool, man. You do whatever you want. We're not interested in the internet. We have AOL keyword.'"

Adam soon realized the internet was about to explode, and his days of introducing rock videos and Aqua Net were over.

"I remember driving in on Route 3 from New Jersey through the Lincoln Tunnel. It was a beautiful day, and I'm like, What am I doing? I'm going to go in to work, and then I'm going to go home and do this other stuff that I really love on the internet until three in the morning. I should be doing this full-time."

He and his wife had saved up enough money to try his new project for a year.

"So I just went in and did the Top Twenty countdown. The number one video was Beck, 'I'm a Loser.' And that's it. I'm out of here. I said, 'The future is on the internet and I'll see you there.' And I walked out and I never looked back."

That day began a clean slate to do what he really loved and believed in. The future was bright. Until a knock on the door at 7 a.m. on a Saturday a week later. MTV served him papers suing over the ownership of MTV.com.

"And my first thought was, Well, why didn't you fucking ask me for it? If you asked me for it, I would have given it to you. But now you're being a dick."

Adam decided to countersue because they had told him several times it was no problem while he was using it and promoting it. And for the first time in his life, he hired a publicist.

"I said, this is David and Goliath. I need the right stories in the *New York Post*—local stuff to really mess with their heads. I got a great lawyer, Joe Donnelly. And we settled in for a fight."

I ask Adam where he got his fearlessness from, because a lot of young men at that age would have been scared out of their minds when a behemoth company was coming after them.

He knew he had truth on his side. This was about ownership. And nine-tenths of the law is possession.

"I had consensus and agreement and permission. So, this was really just me saying, 'Hey, you stabbed me in the back.'"

The Lanham Act is what they were suing him under. It protects brands and trademarks from consumer confusion.

"It was about usage, which means, could the consumer be confused by going to MTV.com and seeing music-related stuff and Adam Curry? Of course. No one can disagree with that."

But, he argues, he could have used it for anything, which was his point.

"I wasn't necessarily in disagreement with what they were saying, even though I was saying, 'Hi, I'm Adam, I'm a DJ. This has nothing to do with MTV. I'm doing it with their permission.' And that's literally what I did. That was under verbal agreement with multiple people."

Adam says the absurdity of it is that he registered thousands of names along with MTV.com early on, when no one cared. At the time, there wasn't even a website to register through. It was a guy who knew a guy, and it was just in fun.

It didn't take long for there to be a settlement. Adam says it was just a few weeks. And he wasn't afraid, because he knew where he stood morally.

"I went in there and said, 'You're not going to get this from me. And you're going to have to pay me because I knew there was going to be a big legal bill.' I did want to win. You don't countersue unless you're pretty sure you're going to do it and go all the way through."

He had the moral high ground. And they knew it. It was just so unnecessary. Because had they just asked, he would have given it to them.

And remember Elvis.com? "I had Elvis.com for the longest time. I also had King@Elvis.com. I published that and people were emailing me."

Elvis fans were writing Adam thinking that Elvis Presley was still alive. He says he appreciated those beautiful emails talking about how much the King meant to everyone. Then he tells me that one day, he got a call from Elvis's daughter, Lisa Marie Presley . . .

Noooooo! I gasp.

She asked if she could have the domain name.

"Yup. And of course, I said, 'Lisa Marie, you can have Elvis.com.'"

He didn't ask for a cent.

I tell Adam this is truly the meaning of life. If only MTV management could have asked nicely for their website name. How hard would that have been?

He agrees and says that his wife, Tina, works for many charity organizations. The number one reason people don't support nonprofits or any cause is that they're not asked. And when you ask someone in a friendly way, you'd be amazed what happens.

"It doesn't take a lot to be polite."

It's one of the things my husband and I try to do with our kids all the time. Teach them manners. Please, thank you. How is your day? May I have my MTV.com, please?

This wouldn't be the last time Adam decided to fight back. This time, on behalf of his family. In 2006, a Dutch tabloid reprinted photos of his daughter from his blog without permission. He sued them successfully for violating portrait rights and for copyright violation over the improper use of personal photos online.

"That was the first legal defense of the Creative Commons copyright, and I'm really proud of that one because it took me to prove that this is real and does work, and it can work under international legal standards. And it did."

His victory on the copyright claims demonstrated and set the precedent that Creative Commons licenses are enforceable in court under copyright law.

Over the years, Adam has had great triumphs, and he's also had disasters happen, too. There was a time in the late 1990s when several of his business ventures failed. A partner and good friend whom he invested with emailed him one day out of the blue to confess that he was a total fraud and wanted in the United Kingdom for grand theft auto and drug trafficking. Soon after that, Adam was hemorrhaging money and trying to pay all of his employees. At one point, he decided to sell a reality TV show to pay the bills featuring his family living in a Dutch castle. When I asked him if he'd ever watch it again, he says it would be too difficult. Thankfully, he says he owns the rights, and there are no plans for syndication.

Looking back on those moments, Adam says they are all important, because when a storm moves through, sometimes it sets up a new path for a more important journey.

"When everything fell apart, I knew two things: I'm never going to worry like I did at that moment because something will eventually happen. And then what I really learned was that when shit collapses, the view should be clearer for you. Like, let me look around. What do I see over here? Is there something I can do?"

I ask Adam about living with Tourette's syndrome, something I found out about him while doing research. He says he started developing the tics and twitches at the age of eight and his father had light tics as well.

"Whenever I got nervous, I would learn how to cover it up with a little shake of my head or pushing hair out of my face. Maybe that's why I didn't cut my hair and why it's always been long. I was trying to hide it."

His parents had him tested and nothing really came back conclusive, so he just learned to live with it.

"It was kind of difficult going into school, especially fifth grade, because it just made me even more weird. It was obvious I was ticking and twitching. And then that social awkwardness gets really trippy when all of a sudden I'm on TV. There were many times I thought maybe I wasn't well suited for this."

When he'd watch interviews of himself, he would see the twitching and get upset, but his first wife told him to stop focusing on those moments. It made him special, and different than everyone else. It made him interesting.

"I hadn't considered that. That helped a lot. And then throughout the years, I wasn't really doing a lot of TV anymore, and anyone who knows me, doesn't make a big deal about it."

In March 2020, Adam was invited on the insanely popular *Joe Rogan Experience* podcast. If you haven't seen it, Joe interviews his guests on-camera for sometimes hours without breaks. Adam knew his tics would show up. So, he decided to just get ahead of it, and just come out and tell Rogan and his audience.

"I said, 'Joe, I've got a little bit of Tourette's—I start to blink my eyes and twitch. You know what that is?' And that actually made it better for me, although when I'm really focused, I twitch more because the brain is firing in some peculiar way. Even when I'm doing my own podcast, and I'm talking about something, or trying to explain, I will squeeze my eyes closed. I just have a different way of communicating."

After that episode with Rogan, Adam says it opened up a lot of things for him both personally and professionally. It was a relief to be honest about something that he had lived with his whole life.

"And funny enough, in the span of just a few years, I've learned that the more you talk about it, the less it becomes a thing. I just flipped the switch, and now I'm very open about it."

Adam says he gets emails from parents worried about their kids, asking if he has any thoughts or suggestions on how to deal with Tourette's. His advice is to just keep talking about it, and if the kid has a really good tic, just say, "Hey, that was a good one!"

The best thing is to embrace it, not hide it. And nine times out of ten, the parents will email back to say it helped; to not make it shameful.

I tell Adam that when I was first diagnosed with multiple sclerosis, I was told by so many people, including one of my bosses, to keep it a secret; not to talk about it with anyone except my family and maybe a few close friends. At first I was terrified of how the illness was going to affect my life and my livelihood, anticipating a wheelchair in my future. But after I got over the shock of the diagnosis, and knew I had the support of friends, family, and eventually my workplace, I decided to share my experience in hopes of helping others. I went behind that one terrible boss's back to ask another supervisor if I could take a camera crew out with me to my doctor visits, MRI appointments, for a lifestyle piece. I wanted to take the stigma off living and working with a chronic illness, and it's still one of the best decisions I ever made. Because not only am I not hiding something, I'm leading by example.

The other thing I've learned in close to thirty years of broadcasting is that perfection (or the pursuit of it) is not relatable to others. In other words, the more you admit your flaws or setbacks, the more human you become to others. People feel like they really know me instead of just the person on a screen telling them the forecast. My other piece of advice to others choosing a career is do things that you most love to do; that way it never ever feels like a "job" or "work."

Adam says that's something he lives by, too.

"Find out what you really love doing, then find someone to pay you to do it. That's it. That's the secret to life in a nutshell."

And we can't forget about the ham radio license, either. Because when the apocalypse hits, it's the hams that will save the world.

3

"I'm Going to Be Happy No Matter What"

The Long Shot vs. the Front-runners

I t's a horse race, and anybody can win."

Those wise words were said to me by Eric Reed, trainer for the 2022 Kentucky Derby winner, Rich Strike.

I've covered a lot of fun events working in morning television over the years, and my favorites have involved animals. There have been multiple visits to Punxsutawney, Pennsylvania, to see the groundhog make his famous prognostication of an early spring or six more weeks of winter. I've interviewed best-in-show winners Wasabi the Pekingese, Rumor the German Shepherd, Uno the Beagle, Trumpet the Bloodhound (and their humans) at the Westminster Kennel Club Dog Show. But, by far, the most exciting event I've ever been invited to cover is the Kentucky Derby at Churchill Downs in Louisville, Kentucky.

Sometimes referred to as the "Run for the Roses" because of the beautiful blanket of 554 roses placed on the winning horse, the race takes place the first weekend in May, and is the oldest American sporting event. It has never been canceled since its inaugural race in 1875. The race was rescheduled in 2020 during the pandemic, but still took place during the Great Flood in 1937, the Great Depression, and both world wars. I've had the chance to personally meet some of the winners, including Triple Crown winner Justify in 2018.

One of the first dates I had with my then-boyfriend (now husband) Sean was at the Belmont Stakes back in 2003, when a New York–bred horse named Funny Cide (the first from New York to win the Derby) had a shot at the winning the Triple Crown after a twenty-five-year drought. For a horse to win this rare achievement, they must place first in the Derby, the Preakness at Pimlico in Baltimore, and then the Belmont Stakes in Elmont, New York.

Funny Cide was derailed by a stallion named Empire Maker, who had finished second in the Derby and skipped the Preakness to train and rest up for Belmont. New Yorkers came in droves to see their possible colt hero win a Triple Crown. It rained all day, and I don't recall the race that well, but I do remember a muddy track, plenty of drunk, disappointed New Yorkers when their horse didn't win, and having to throw out my brand-new sandals that were ruined by the numerous puddles I stepped in and the spilled spirits.

Sean and I joke that this date began the journey of my horse racing coverage, and my love of sporting fancy hats: the bigger, the better. And when the sound of the trumpets blare as the horses come out to their posts, and the thundering noise of hooves coming out of their gate—there's nothing quite like it.

After two years of a pandemic, divisive political races, wars, and inflation, we needed a feel-good story that might give us some hope in 2022. Not unlike 1980's US hockey game against the Soviets, when we believed in miracles, this win came from a horse, his trainer, and a jockey nobody had heard of until the announcer exclaimed:

"Oh my goodness! The longest shot has won the Kentucky Derby!"

The horse was Rich Strike, and the odds were 81-1. That meant if you bet $2, you won $163.60. This was one of the greatest upsets in Derby history since 1913, when Donerail had odds of 91-1.

I watched the most exciting horse racing moments of my lifetime in the media tent set up for our broadcasts. It was directly across the track, where I could clearly see the enthusiastic and packed-to-the-rafters crowd waiting for the starting gates to fly open. I wish I could say that I placed a bet on Rich Strike, but I was rooting for the horse called Messier, named after hockey legend Mark Messier. As the stallions galloped by our vantage point, Rich Strike was starting to move ahead. By the final stretch, the horse was in the middle and then surged past the favorites Epicenter and Zandon. In an aerial view that was posted on social media after the race, you could see how much traffic this horse had to get through to make history.

My producer, Sam, was able to secure an interview with Eric Reed, Rich Strike's trainer, the morning after his Derby win. I knew right away that I had to include his incredible journey in this book. It's a story not only about the horse who stole the show, but also Eric's own amazing life overcoming odds and tragic circumstances. He tells me it's taking some time to let it all sink in, and realizing how important "Richie" is to the world.

"He's a good horse, and he won a big race, but it's the history part of the race I can't seem to wrap myself around. The local police came by and they've got two cars here, 24/7 for security. He's going to have this for the rest of his career. Everywhere he goes. They follow him in and out of places and in the barn. Real security."

Eric jokes that when the officers came after the race, he thought they were just there to say "Hello" and "Congratulations." But their job was to protect the now valuable winner of the Kentucky Derby.

Eric's love of horses and being a trainer started very early in life. He grew up watching his father, Herbert, who started out as an exercise rider and later became a trainer.

"I used to go to the barns with him when I was six years old. I mean, that's just the way it was. I was a daddy's boy and I hung out with him. The more I was out there, the more it influenced me. Not so much the trainer part at that time. It was just, Man, I want to be like him, because everybody loves my dad."

Herbert (or Herbie, as he likes to be called) told his son training horses was a hard life, and you had to put in seven days a week. Going to school was more important, and they'd worry about the rest later. But Eric knew what he wanted to do, and his dad was with him when Rich Strike crossed the finish line first. It's hard to put into words what that meant to him.

"The race is obviously the greatest moment of my history as a trainer and in the business. You have your children and nothing's ever greater than that . . . maybe your wedding. But this is probably the biggest moment of my life, because I got to be with my dad. I was so happy just to get into the Derby and say that we had a horse here, and he was going to see that. I wasn't thinking about all this other stuff. When it happened, it was like nothing is going to top this, ever."

When the race was over, his dad tried to talk, but he started to cry instead. Eric says he's never seen him get choked up like that.

"I said, 'You don't have to say anything, Dad.' And he said, 'I love you, boy. We saw that.' He said, 'I don't know how you knew this horse was that good, because I don't think anybody else would have thought he was that good.'"

Eric is from Lexington, Kentucky, and has lived there his whole life. He doesn't remember how many horses he's trained—probably in the thousands since he started back in the 1980s.

One day after turning eighteen, he walked in to help get his dad's horses ready at 4:30 in the morning, something he did every day.

"And there was a box, a saddle, a bridle, two big tubs, and two buckets sitting by the door. I went and started getting everything ready. My dad got there and I said, 'We don't need all this. All the equipment is outside the barn.' And he said: 'Well, you wanted to be a trainer. Now you're a trainer. We're going to give you two horses and I've got some stalls at Ellis Park [two hours away]. You need to be ready when the van comes to get you.'"

Eric thought he was joking and asked where was he going to stay. Herbert said, "That's up to you. You're a trainer now."

I ask Eric to take me through a typical day at his barn. He says you have to be up really early and prepare the horses before the sun comes up.

"The first thing you do is clean out the stalls and make sure all the horses are happy and healthy. There's a set list, which is how they decide who's going to train that day and what order. You write down the distance and the kind of work out they need to do. The first horses are at the track between six and seven depending on the weather, and they go all day until the last horse is finished their training."

The biggest win Eric ever had before Rich Strike was the Grade 2 Lexus Raven Run Stakes, held at Keeneland in Lexington, with Satan's Quick Chick in 2009.

"That was one of the top tracks in the country, and by far our biggest win. And then probably the biggest race I ever had, which wasn't really a win, was when I went to California with a filly—another long shot, and almost beat the great Zenyatta, who had never been beaten, and had never been tested. That was the first time anybody ever got that close to her. We almost pulled a major upset in 2012, like we did this year. We just came up short."

Eric says the road to finding Rich Strike began when one of his clients, Richard Dawson, wanted to buy some horses and didn't want Eric to spend a year or two training them. Rick wanted to try to get some action early.

Eric went to a claiming race, at Churchill Downs, where he was allowed to purchase the horse right out of a race for a set fee. He originally had a different colt picked out, but he kept looking over at the other horses and Rich Strike kept popping up, despite having run dead last in the only race he ran in his life. But Eric knew that just because Rich Strike came last didn't mean he didn't have talent—especially if you knew his potential running on the dirt.

"My guess—my gamble, or whatever you want to call it—was that they ran him on the turf because he trained so good on the dirt leading up to that race. It was strictly a guess and a gamble and it was right."

Rich Strike liked dirt.

Getting into the Derby was another long shot. Another stallion had to bow out for him to get into the race. There's a point system, and the top twenty horses with the most points get to run at the Derby. There's a 9 a.m. deadline for all the horses on the Friday morning before the race. Rich Strike was 24, and ran in the Jeff Ruby Stakes a few weeks before the race. He rose to number 22 and now had a better shot. A lot of things can happen to a contender before Derby Day.

The Lexington Stakes ran two weeks later and bumped Rich Strike down to 24. Team Reed wasn't feeling quite as good. They now had three weeks to get him qualified. Eric heard that a couple of horses were going to be scratched (taken out) and they were back at 22. Then another defection had them sitting at 21 all week. By 7:30 a.m. on Friday, they trained Richie and gave him a bath. They walked him, and Eric looked at all his guys, knowing they were on pins and needles. Their hopes were fading fast every minute that clicked by. At 8:30, everyone was looking at their watches and moods were starting to change. There was a man assigned to their barn in charge of giving race information throughout the day, and at a quarter to nine, he came walking across the parking lot.

"This man became a good friend of mine after we met. He held his arms out, shook his head, and had a little tear in his eye. He said he was so sorry, it's just not going to happen. And I said, okay. I was ready for it. But I wasn't. . . ."

Eric then had the job of letting the Team Reed know that Richie didn't make the cut. Then he told Herbie.

"I said, 'We got close, Dad, but we'll go on to New York next week and we'll worry about the Belmont Stakes.'"

Suddenly, Eric's phone rang at 8:58. It was Chief Head Steward Barbara Borden, calling to inform him that he was in. Eric says he could hardly breathe to get the words out and had to take in three big gulps of air. Then he might've screamed, "*Yes!*"

"Everybody was looking at me and they knew something was happening, but they didn't know what. And then she said, 'You're in. I'll see you in the paddock.'"

Eric turned around and screamed. He likens it to being at a funeral and three minutes later it turns into a frat party. That's the kind of emotion that they were all going through at the time.

Hall of Fame horse trainer D. Wayne Lucas was the one who decided to scratch his horse Ethereal Road before the official cutoff. He didn't have to do that. He could have waited for 9 a.m. and called afterward and the Derby would have had nineteen horses instead of twenty. Eric says he doesn't know why the horse was taken out, but he spoke to Wayne after the Derby win to thank him. His influence is enormous in the world of horse racing, with four Kentucky Derby wins alone.

"Wayne's been an ambassador to the sport for many, many years. And I think he had made the right decision for his horse. I don't know the exact reasons, but when I spoke with him he was so kind and gave me a lot of good advice. He paved the way for two winning horses because his horse won the Kentucky Oaks the day before the Derby. So, I mean, it's hard to imagine one guy influencing both those races so much, but he did."

I ask Eric how he knew Rich Strike was a contender. On paper, he was definitely 80-1. But he sensed many things about the horse that no one else knew about, and that's why his team tried so hard to get in. Even though they didn't think they would win, the horse belonged in the race.

"The only way you're ever going to know is when you get a chance to triumph. And we had to get in just to triumph. But we were right in our assumption. He is a great horse."

Eric says Richie has a unique running style. His jockey, Sonny Leon, knew the colt well, and that's when the magic happened.

"We've tried a couple of races to get him going early and it didn't work. He still ran well, but he didn't care for it. And when he trains in the morning, he's that way. It takes him a while. And then once he grabs a bit, he's ready to go. Sonny knew that our best chance to win was to let him break and somehow work his way to the inside to save some ground. He's not traveling so many more feet than everybody else in the race. And then as he got to the middle of the backstretch, he had to start making some decisions. And that's where the tactical part of Sonny won the race for us. He's a masterful rider. People don't know him because he's not on TV all the time, but he's won a lot of races. He's won a lot of stake races, and he's the guy that wins three or four races a day at his tracks."

A horse is important, but the jockey also needs to be commended. Eric says they knew he had the ability, and they had all the faith in the world in him. The horse knew Sonny, and Sonny knew the horse.

"I think that's what happened. He saw the moves he needed to make, and the strategy was always to get to the inside. Then pass them all before you get to the wire."

A race like the one we saw with Rich Strike is very rare. Eric says he's never seen anything like it, and he's been watching races since he was a little boy.

"I think it's one of the best rides ever at the Kentucky Derby. If you watch the video from above, it looks like an arcade game. That's what I first thought when someone showed it to me. I thought it was animated because I couldn't believe a horse could actually be running that fast as he's zigzagging."

Rich Strike was clearly the best horse. He passed the two favorites, and they were finishing strong. Richie ran right by them.

Afterward, there was a lot of backlash on social media about Rich Strike's behavior. The horse was still very hyped up and rambunctious. Video went viral of Richie biting the outrider as he was trying to calm him down after the race. I tell Eric that this is typical of how things work in the media. People love an underdog story, but there're also those on the other side who would like to create a controversy and bring the heroes down. Rich Strike's behavior is not unheard-of. That's why there are special leather protectors around the horse's necks and legs, because they've been bitten before.

The job of the outrider is to soothe the horse right after the race. When passing the finish line, he goes around the turn and meets the outrider as he tries to slow the horse down. The adrenaline is flowing and the horse has to unwind before getting to the winner's circle to be photographed. Along the way, as the outrider is doing his job, the jockey will typically talk to the reporters and the fans so they can enjoy the excitement from the rider and the happiness of the win. But it didn't turn out that way for Sonny, his jockey, because Richie saw the outrider's pony and thought he was supposed to race him, too. After all, he had passed sixteen or seventeen horses just a few minutes before.

"And when they [the outrider and horse] tried to get a hold of him, Richie didn't understand why. He didn't like it, and he tried to bite the guy, like 'Let me go, I got to run!' And that's when it got out of hand. Richie kept biting. He savaged that man's leg, his arms, and his horse. It was becoming a brawl between two horses and the outrider was in the middle."

Eric explains that if the outrider had let his horse go, and Sonny fell off Rich Strike, then the winner of the Kentucky Derby would be running loose on the racetrack. He could have injured himself severely or fatally. He could have turned around in the other direction, running backward, through the mob of people standing on the track that were waiting to see the winner, the trainers, owners, and jockeys with their horses. It could have been an absolute catastrophe had Richie gotten loose.

"Even though that rider was injured and bleeding, he never gave up on calming my horse down. He led him back and everything worked out. But if he had let go of him and said the heck with it, it could have been really, really bad."

I ask Eric to take me back to before the big win. What does he remember most? He says he was proud for his father to be able to see this moment. As everyone was walking over before the race, he looked at the grandstand and remembered that for the first time in two years, Churchill Downs had a full crowd.

"I said, 'Look, Dad, we've always been those people watching these horses. Now they're all watching us.' He said, 'Can you believe it?' And I said 'We're going to soak this all in as we walk over.'"

When they got to the paddock before the race, Rich Strike was calm despite all the loud music and hollering. They got his saddle on and let him walk around a bit. Then they headed to the gate.

Once the race started, Eric saw everything until the middle of the second turn, and then he couldn't find his horse on the screen. He asked his friend Ken Tyson where he was.

"I couldn't see him. By then he was on the inside, fifth or sixth. The weight was off at that point because I just wanted some respect for the horse—he wasn't going to be last. He wasn't even going to be mid-pack. He was going to run fifth or sixth, and I was so happy about that."

Then Richie sped up. Heading around in the middle of the stretch put him in third or fourth.

"I remember telling my dad, 'We're going to hit the board!'" meaning place at least third. "And then a few minutes later, my friend Ken Tyson says, 'Oh my God.'"

And then he said it again.

"Oh my God."

That's when Rich Strike pulled out in front.

"I grabbed my father. I said, 'Daddy, we just won the Kentucky Derby,' and I fell down."

Eric says he doesn't know why his legs gave out on him. But he remembers looking at the sky, and then all of a sudden people were piling on top of him and he was looking at the face of his father, who thought his son was hurt.

"They jerked me up and it was like a dream. Had this really happened? I never even saw Richie when he crossed the finish line. I didn't see that part. I just knew that he had made the lead and it was close and that we'd won."

I'm curious when Eric finally saw the footage of Rich Strike winning the race. He says it was in the press box, and he kept watching the television while the reporters were asking him questions. Someone asked if he saw anything different on the screen in a replay. Eric replied:

"No. He wins every time!"

I asked if being a famous Derby horse trainer has hit him yet. Eric says he wasn't ready, and he still isn't, but he's had a lot of friends looking out for him. One thing he has realized is that he can't be everywhere at the same time for everyone. He never wants to turn anyone down for an interview.

"I want to give everybody, no matter who it is, their chance to do their job and ask me a question. But I got so exhausted, because I was working on four hours' sleep two days after the Derby and I was willing to do whatever it took to accommodate making sure everybody that needed a comment to keep their paycheck and their fan base in this little town going, so they got their story."

A friend of his who managed musicians in the past took him aside and said he couldn't continue at this pace. It was unsustainable. He told Eric he would take over and start managing his appointments, emails, and interviews. That has been very helpful. But the highlight during all of this excitement is that he and his dad got to go fishing together. That brought back some normalcy.

"We got to spend some quality time together. And naturally, we shared a lot of tears. And a couple of fish. And he's living the dream, too. He's had people interview him, and he's got a great story of his own to tell."

I ask Eric to tell me his father's story, which turns out to be one of the most incredible moments of our interview.

"My dad's mother died when he was six. He had a younger brother and sister. They lived in a tiny one-room cabin with no electricity and no running water. There were about fifty people that lived on that little hillside. It was 1952 when his mother—my grandmother—passed away. He was at the funeral, and his mother's sister lived close to their house, and they took him and his brother and sister home afterwards."

The kids were in the cabin waiting for their dad (Eric's grandfather) to come home. He never came back. After they buried their mother, he walked away. For three days and nights, Herbie, his brother, and his sister lived in the cabin with no food or water. No electricity, and no adults. They just waited for him to come home.

Herbie, at six years old, finally decided to try to find someone and get something to eat. No one knew that their father had left for good. A relative finally came to their house and took Herbert and his brother. Someone else took their sister. The family they stayed with was very poor, and their own kids were starving.

"They would shoot blackbirds and eat them for dinner. That's how they were feeding each other."

Young Herbie heard them say they had to take the kids to the orphanage. They couldn't feed everyone.

On Christmas Eve, Herbie grabbed his little brother and they started to run to town. He didn't want to go to the orphanage, so they hid in the back of a chicken truck. In the middle of the night, the chicken truck started up and drove off with the boys in the back. They ended up in Versailles, Kentucky.

"There's a six-year-old with a four-year-old brother. Didn't know the town they came from. Didn't know anything. They hopped out and a sheriff was there. And Mac Miller, the horse trainer, was there with him. My dad said, 'Please don't put us in an orphanage.'"

Eric says his father and brother were raised by three or four wonderful families. Herbie quit school in eighth grade and started betting on racehorses at the track, and then became a horse trainer. He's has been around the world twice, and now owns a bed-and-breakfast and many rental properties.

"My dad is a very successful person with no education, no family, and very easily could have gone down the wrong path at any time. He raised me and my brother in the greatest home that any kid could have. So that's why it means so much to me to have him here enjoying this moment."

I tell Eric he has quite a story to tell, and his whole family must be so proud of him. He says none of them think they deserve it.

"We're just appreciating it, and can't believe what's happening. With all the tragedy and crazy stories, this horse came out of nowhere, and he's made us all happy again."

I ask why he thinks he's not deserving of this moment.

"I don't believe anybody deserves anything. You get what's given to you by God, and you make the best out of it. You can work hard, but you still might not get there, or you might get everything. But you've got to just try. I think everybody's given a spot in life, and I've always said that if you work hard, and you treat everybody nice, that's what counts. You just do the best you can."

Eric says everyone is going to make mistakes. That's part of life, too. But enjoy it. Be happy.

"I know my glass is three-quarters full, even if there's not a drop in it. And that's how I want to be. It's too easy to be sad or grumpy and bitter. I'm going to be happy no matter what. That's how my dad is and that's why I love him so much. I don't know if I ever deserved this. I'm not proud of everything that has happened in my life, but I sure do appreciate it."

There was a time when Eric almost gave up being a trainer and the family business. An enormous tragedy happened when he was living his best life and had everything he ever dreamed of: a beautiful property with three barns full of strong, healthy horses that were all winning races. There was financial stability and he didn't have to worry about when the next paycheck was coming. But that all changed one stormy, horrific night when a lightning strike started a ferocious fire.

"I remember the glow over the farm in this driving rainstorm that had come through with all the lightning. The sky was orange, and I told my wife that we lost it all tonight. 'Whatever you do, don't run in and do something foolish and get killed. Because this is over. It's over.'"

I can tell that Eric is getting emotional as he tries to describe it. One of his crew members jumped out of bed and tried to save their ponies.

"He had no shoes, no clothes of any kind. He ran out into the cold rain and into that burning barn. And he got burned, too. But he kept trying to take those horses out. To save their lives. He was such a hero that night."

When the sun came up, Eric knew it would be the worst day of his life. They would find all the horses that didn't make it.

"No one should ever have to see something like that. Twenty-three bodies lying in that barn all burned. What was once this great, beautiful, historic garden was now a piece of tin roof and ashes and cinder block. That's when I said, 'I can't do this. I'll never train another horse again.' It was the end of the road for me that day."

His crew started finding the other horses. They thought there were only four or five that had survived, but they had thirteen, and sent some immediately to the clinic with burns on their ears and legs. But they were alive.

"My dad calls me and he says, 'I don't know what to tell you. I can't tell you anything.' He said, 'Just take care of those horses, because they'll take care of you.'"

Eric took his father's advice. And there were terrible days. Investigations, insurance, the cleanup, and the rebuilding. But he took care of the horses. And when the first one that survived went to the track a couple of days later, he started to heal. And then to see how everyone rallied around him and his family to help.

"That's when the real healing came from. I know on TV and in the news you hear a lot of doom and gloom. And there's a lot of hate out there, but there was so much love that I saw after that day. It saved me. And that's why I'm still here."

I tell Eric that being in the weather business, you see a lot of natural disasters like hurricanes, tornadoes, and wildfires that tear through and change lives and livelihoods forever. Those incredible tragedies make you question God and your faith. But then, after the storm has passed, you see the absolute best in humanity. Like Mr. Rogers used to say, "Look for the helpers. You will always find people who are helping."

People drove in from Georgia, Alabama, South Carolina; strangers he didn't know, just wanting to lend a hand.

"They would bring blankets and hay and buckets. The trainers and my friends, people I went to school with. They all came to feed my crew and help my family. And I knew if I quit, then those horses died for nothing. My career was for nothing. But it was a hard decision, because I had given up. That's no doubt about it. I had given up."

When I first met Eric, the day after his incredible Derby win, he showed me his gold fingernail and his gold toenails. It was a tradition that began with his youngest daughter, Martha, after a big race in California—the first long-shot horse that almost won against an unbeatable filly.

"Before I flew out there, my twelve-year-old daughter told me she wanted to paint my toenails for good luck. 'Nobody will see them because you have shoes on, but you'll remember me while you're gone because I'm going to miss you.'"

Eric let her do it, and when his filly ran so well and almost shocked the world by beating the favorite, he came home and told her it was good luck. And now, before every big race, their crew, along with friends and family, paints their toes gold and their right pinky finger. That was ten years ago. Martha is twenty-two now, and she painted her dad's toes gold before the Kentucky Derby.

If you follow horse racing, you are well aware of the controversy that has surrounded one of the biggest trainers in the history of the sport, Bob Baffert. In 2021, Baffert was banned from the Kentucky Derby after his horse Medina Spirit tested positive for a corticosteroid that was used as an ointment for a skin condition. Some say that if Baffert had been in the race, Rich Strike might never have had a chance. I ask Eric if he wants to comment on any of that since it was certainly a moment that has cast a dark cloud over the racing world. He says he doesn't know the whole story, or what went on.

"Here's what I do know about Bob Baffert. When I had my barn fire, the next day, Mr. Baffert was on the phone with me. Bob Baffert offered me horses to train. He offered to send me clients so that we would survive and not be without income. He asked what I needed—to let him know, and he would take care of it. The man didn't know me other than saying good morning once when I was in California. That's how he treated me. He didn't have to call me. I'm not the first person to have a barn fire. But he treated me really well. I just know the person he was to me, and he was exceptionally kind to myself and my family."

After our interview, it was announced that Rich Strike was not going to race at Pimlico for the Preakness. Many people expressed disappointment in that decision, but after talking to Eric, and seeing how adamant he was about keeping the horse healthy and not risking injury, I wasn't surprised that he thought of the horse first instead of the glory of trying to win the three jewels in the Triple Crown.

"He's America's horse now. We're sharing him with America, but he's still Richie to me. I just hope he makes people happy. We're special because of Richie. He's the one that brought all the sorrow back to joy. He's changed a lot of lives. And now I get to say we have the Kentucky Derby winner. Right here on this farm."

I tell Eric how happy I am that I've met him, and that I was able to write his story about a horse named Rich Strike, who, against all odds, rose to the challenge and with grit and determination came out ahead. The long shot gives hope to all those who think they didn't have a chance at something. Because in the end, it's the courage to enter the race that counts the most.

4

"What Is the Point of Being Here If I Can't Tell the Truth?"

The Assemblyman vs. the Party

The first time I met New York assemblyman Ron Kim in person was in August 2020, when my husband, Sean, myself, and my sister-in-law, Donna, drove to Albany to try to push legislation for an independent bipartisan investigation into the state's nursing home deaths.

Ron, a Democrat from Queens, and New York State senator Jim Tedisco, a Republican from upstate, were cosponsoring a bipartisan bill to introduce the idea of a panel with subpoena power to perform a top-to-bottom review of the deaths that we now know were purposely being underreported by the Cuomo administration at the height of the pandemic.

Ron also wanted answers about the nursing home tragedy that took the lives of thousands of our elderly loved ones, and for him, it was personal. His uncle died after contracting COVID in a Queens nursing home, and he was hearing from his constituents early on about the horrific conditions that were happening inside the states' facilities.

Through tragedy, Ron and I became not only good friends but also advocates speaking at many rallies and in joint TV and print interviews. We've also enjoyed each other's company with our spouses over dinner and drinks. When he heard that Sean learned how to surf in Atlantic Beach, Long Island, he told him he'd love to join him when the weather gets nicer.

I know we'll be friends for the rest of our lives.

And if it weren't for Ron Kim, Andrew Cuomo would probably still be governor. It was not easy to go against his own party and a powerful boss to try to bring justice for our loved ones.

Having gotten to know Ron over the last few years, this chapter is an important one about battling abusive bullies and standing up for what's right.

Ron came to the United States from South Korea with his family when he was seven years old. He didn't speak any English, but his parents had a tremendous opportunity to live in America. His mom and dad wanted what many immigrants desired: prosperity in the United States.

They ran a grocery store for ten years, but small businesses like theirs were having a tough time competing with the bigger chain stores. They had to file for bankruptcy and start over again.

Seeing his parents going through these highs and lows is what fueled Ron's desire early on to be in public service. It also opened his eyes to those in power who didn't have to work very hard to get there.

"There's the promise that in this country, if you work hard enough, if you put in the blood, sweat, and tears, you have a fair shot of succeeding. But I think the problem is many people are waking up thinking that no matter how hard they work, they can never be someone like Andrew Cuomo, who was born on third base and given all the privileges in the world, thinking that they could bully and shoot down at people. I think that for me, what I want to get across is it takes an extraordinary coalition of people like ourselves with political will and courage to punch up at people like Andrew Cuomo."

I ask where that will comes from. Is it from seeing what his parents went through? Ron says that from a very young age he saw how hard his mother and father worked. Twenty-four hours a day, seven days a week. No vacation. Their young boy was in a new country, not speaking a word of English, and was bullied in the school bathrooms and on the playground. He didn't want to burden them with his problems. When Ron finally told his mom about how he was teased and hurt growing up as a kid who was different than everyone else, she burst into tears.

"She broke down because all that time she just thought they were protecting me. But even as a kid, I was trying to shield them from my stress. I mean, that's very common, I think. The immigrant struggle should be embraced and celebrated because at the core, that's what makes this country great. That we allow people to pursue their passions and believe that if they put in the time and effort, they can be a part of the middle class and have upward mobility."

The part about Ron being bullied is familiar to me. I was also bullied in school about what I looked like and my weight. I was a fat kid for many years growing up. It got to the point where I would cry to my mom that I didn't want to go to school. I wonder if, because we didn't have it so easy being young, maybe now as adults we can stand up for ourselves to make up for all the times we didn't have the wherewithal back then.

"Yeah, one hundred percent, and I think the unique thing about you and I in this fight is that it's easier when we've been abused in the past, and now we find ourselves in positions of power to fight back. Many in politics spend their careers shooting down at people. That's what Andrew Cuomo did. I think what makes our journey unique is that we didn't fall victim to that kind of thinking and mind-set."

Ron tells me a story about when he was younger. His dad would give him a lot of advice, and one of the biggest lessons he remembered was never pick a fight with someone weaker than you. There's no honor in beating up someone that you can take.

"And that rang true, because in high school I was in football. I went on to play college football—I was a class jock: I knew those guys well. But I would always try to sit down in the cafeteria and be friends with people who weren't in my core group—the ones who weren't included because they were nerdy or whatever. I always felt like I had a duty to stick up for them because that's where I came from. I was the outsider. The immigrant kid who came to school with smelly food and was made fun of. So I always felt compelled to stick up for the kids who weren't popular."

I ask Ron to tell me about his uncle, Son Kim, who inspired this fight for justice.

"He was the patriarch of my dad's family. There were three sons; he was the oldest. My dad was the middle brother. And they were planning on a fourth son because of the way they were named in Korean—after north, south, east, and west. But they ended up having six daughters, so they never got that far."

We both laugh. Ron says it was an "incomplete brotherhood" in the Kim family. He never met his grandfather. Times were tough back in South Korea in the 1950s. There were wars breaking out and his dad's father was addicted to alcohol. He died at a young age, and that set the stage for his uncle, the eldest son, to take the lead and provide for the family. And because of that sequence of events, his uncle Son became the father figure. He was the one the family invested time and effort into getting into college, but not just any college. Ron says Seoul University was the "the Harvard of South Korea." The entire village was so proud of that achievement. Son then pursued his studies in the United States, and was accepted into New York University dentistry school in the 1960s. Back then, it was hard for him to find a practice as an immigrant professional, so he joined the US Army, became a captain, and served for many years. Uncle Son was the one who brought the Kim family to America. He sponsored all their visas to immigrate.

"So it was him that set up the foundation for us to be part of this borough of Queens. My uncle, my aunt, they all came here at the same time. And if it wasn't for his patriotism, his drive, and his studies, we wouldn't be here."

Ron says that because his uncle was a veteran, a retired Army captain, he should have had the best retirement benefits. For many years he was suffering from dementia. He needed twenty-four-hour care. His family decided it might be time to get him into a care facility to provide help. Ron's dad would visit with his brother once a week before the pandemic.

Looking back on it, knowing what we know now, of course we would have done everything in our power to get our loved ones out of harm's way.

"But you just assume that this is America, this is New York. How can we not trust that the system will take care of our seniors?"

Ron says there was a disconnect in that moment. We all thought they were in the safest place they could be.

"I shouldn't have to worry about him in that facility. That's the kind of subconscious assumption that I had. And literally within days it was out of control. He died in the end of April [2020] without any clear communication about what was going on. They just said that he had a fever and he deteriorated rapidly in a matter of days."

This is what happened to thousands of families, and as a result revealed a weak spot in the system. Ron gave the government the benefit of the doubt.

"I trusted him [Cuomo]. And then the health commissioner, Howard Zucker, comes into our conference room and spent three hours with us. I trusted him, too. So as you can imagine, this level of betrayal I felt when not only did I experience a failure personally for my family, but for thousands of other families who were gaslit from April, May, June, and, you know, all the way till now, it's beyond infuriating. I went out of my way, putting my credibility and reputation on the line because there were other, more progressive Democrats that didn't trust Zucker and Cuomo. And I defended them. So I feel like the fool, and betrayed."

I ask when Ron started to become suspicious of what was happening in the nursing homes. One of his constituents in Queens was trying to rescue her mom out of a facility, and he was trying to help her with it. Somehow he was able to extract the truth from the director at the care home that there was a severe underreporting of people dying there.

"The director told me they had no control of how to do it, and people were exposed. There was no staffing and the seniors didn't have PPE. I mean, it was like a death camp in there."

As Ron starts describing what he was hearing during that time, I hear the anger rising in his voice. He was talking with the administration almost every day and began to realize that the inspectors and lobbyists were the ones controlling the message of how they were going to spin this to the public instead of trying to help.

"Cuomo's people were worried about their reputation and the PR nightmare they had to deal with instead of trying to do whatever they could to save lives."

Ron was in communication with the governor's office when he found out that Cuomo and company had introduced language into a state budget bill giving legal protections to nursing homes in the event of future lawsuits regarding their COVID-19 practices.

This explained a lot about how these facilities were behaving.

"I couldn't believe how rude and confrontational the nursing home directors were to my constituents. These are family members sitting outside, saying 'I need to make sure my mom is safe,' and they're yelling at them. That's when I realized these facilities had lobbyists behind them."

The nursing homes were given legal immunity that shielded them from criminal and civil liability. And not only that: they apparently didn't have to report what was going on inside. Outside people were barred from coming into the residences to act like a watchdog.

"They could literally get away with murder inside its facilities and they had a get-out-of-jail-free card."

Ron began putting the puzzle together, and started fighting back, trying to repeal the blanket legal immunity the Cuomo administration had put in place. Ron believes Cuomo went to one of his lobbyist donors and they wrote a bill for him without considering the families or the workers.

"I'm not against the nursing homes, the good ones, the honest operators that are out there, and I'm not against the concept of providing some sort of protection to save their businesses. But the way that it was done was very shady. There should have been discussions."

Ron says they could have waited until the COVID restrictions were lifted and life was seemingly getting back to normal. It should have been done publicly, with the family members, and the workers, where everyone participating gets to see the evidence of how much was done to save people's lives.

"And at the end of the day, if they did everything they could, but they still lost lives, then we, the public, can recognize that and work out a solution. But that's not what they did. They quietly snuck that in, retroactively, took away Sean's parents' rights and other people's rights."

Ron says this is something we need to be outraged about. We need to know that our parents and grandparents have some recourse and have certain rights that no one should be able to take away from them.

"But Cuomo took that away retroactively, and that's why these facilities felt like they could do whatever they wanted and not be punished."

There needed to be proof of this, so in April and May, Ron and his staff spent nights writing, researching, and publishing reports on legal immunity in nursing homes. A few outlets, like the *Guardian*, Associated Press, and some of the Albany media, were starting to pick up on what he was doing, and there was traction. Ron and his team were telling the truth, and he felt there was enough to start repealing the bill and holding people accountable. But then, all of a sudden, Cuomo started issuing his own reports and self-audits that showed deflated nursing home data.

"He used his power as a platform to go on these press conferences to say 'it's not that bad, look at these other states . . .' That was taking away our ability to legislate with urgency. And that ultimately led to a compromise—only a partial repeal of that bill in July, because we no longer had the public sentiment or narrative on our side to fully get rid of this bill and hold these facilities accountable."

Ron says the partial repeal to the bill in July wasn't good enough.

"And I think around that time afterward, that's when I met you and people that were willing to listen and hold as many public events to tell the truth about what was going on."

It reached a point where Ron says he almost gave up.

"I remember dropping off a hundred-page report to the United Nations claiming there's a crime against humanity in the state of New York and no one wants to hold this governor accountable. We are submitting an official request to investigate this through a higher court."

This is also the time when Andrew Cuomo's celebrity began to rise: the press conferences, the fawning interviews, and the regular visits to CNN, appearing on his brother Chris's prime-time program.

I remember how hard it was back then going up against the Cuomo machine. There were emails and texts from people telling me to be careful. Why was I on Twitter every day yelling about nursing homes and the cover-up? My mother was afraid, friends were uncomfortable, and there is a point where you have to decide if this is all worth it. The Cuomo family are vindictive and will stop at nothing if they feel threatened.

Ron says he felt it, too. People told him to back down, to stop talking about nursing homes and going after Cuomo. Two thousand twenty was Ron's reelection year, with a competitive primary and general election. His opponent was raising plenty of money and campaign consultants were telling him to stop rocking the boat. He was told he was going to lose because Cuomo was polling at 80 percent, and his district liked Cuomo.

"I was like, what is the point of me being here if I can't tell the truth? People died and I made promises to these families and I don't care. I don't care if I am going to lose this election. I don't care if I am going to die on this hill. I am prepared to leave because there's no point of me being a lawmaker if I can't tell the truth."

Those convictions resonated with his constituents during the election. Ron won his primary with 70 percent, and at the general election 83 percent.

"I felt emboldened, despite making a lot of enemies in my own party and establishment. I had a clear mandate with my voters in my constituency. And despite the polling and how they feel about Cuomo, they still sided with me and my fight for accountability and truth. I felt confident that I can continue this battle."

I ask if there's something that gives Ron courage to keep going up against Goliath. Because everyone else was telling us Cuomo wasn't going anywhere. He was too powerful. But like the saying goes, one truth is stronger than a million lies.

"Right, because by definition, it could only be one truth, and I think people like Cuomo spend their lives defending different versions of the facts and different versions of untruths. That's how they maintain power, versus people who have been victimized by the system. We're in constant pursuit of the singular truth. And without it, how can we actually have a system that works?"

I think Ron Kim is a rare kind of politician who chose his career for the right reasons. He didn't get into it because of a family name or his bank account. He wanted to fight for what he believes in and the people he represents. There needs to be more Ron Kims getting into the arena. This should transcend political ideologies.

I ask Ron to tell me about the phone call from Cuomo in February 2021. This was when the dam really started to break with the governor and the nursing home death toll cover-up. Attorney General Letitia James had released a report in late January that confirmed everything that we had suspected: Cuomo, his administration, and the Health Department were cooking the books and undercounting the nursing home deaths by about 50 percent. A few weeks later Cuomo's top aide, Melissa DeRosa, admitted in a closed-door meeting with Democrats that they hid the nursing home data so the feds wouldn't find out.

The *New York Post* had the exclusive that hit Team Cuomo like a ton of bricks:

Gov. Andrew Cuomo's top aide privately apologized to Democratic lawmakers for withholding the state's nursing home death toll from

COVID-19—telling them "we froze" out of fear that the true numbers would "be used against us" by federal prosecutors, The Post has learned.

The stunning admission of a coverup was made by secretary to the governor Melissa DeRosa during a video conference call with state Democratic leaders in which she said the Cuomo administration had rebuffed a legislative request for the tally in August because "right around the same time, [then-president Donald Trump] turns this into a giant political football," according to an audio recording of the two-hour-plus meeting.

"He (The President) starts tweeting that we killed everyone in nursing homes," DeRosa said. "He starts going after [New Jersey governor Phil] Murphy, starts going after [California governor Gavin] Newsom, starts going after [Michigan governor] Gretchen Whitmer."

In addition to attacking Cuomo's fellow Democratic governors, DeRosa said, Trump "directs the Department of Justice to do an investigation into us."

"And basically, we froze," she told the lawmakers on the call.

After the story broke, Cuomo and company went into damage-control mode. They began calling, demanding loyalty, especially from the lawmakers who were in that closed-door meeting, including Ron Kim.

"It was close to eight o'clock, which is usually bath time for my three young girls. It's a phone call from his office: A generic 518 Albany number. I get calls from his staff once in a while, so I'm thinking they probably have some issues with the report that came out from the *New York Post* about DeRosa's comments, and they're trying to fix it. So, I'm thinking, All right, well, let's pick this up . . ."

Cuomo's secretary was on the phone: "I have the governor on the line for you. . . ."

Ron says he stopped what he was doing and signaled his wife to take care of the girls as he tried to walk away from them into another room. There was complete silence for a few seconds, and Ron didn't know if anyone was on the line. So he asked, "Governor, are you there?"

In his gruff "New York tough guy" accent, Cuomo said, "Mr. Kim, are you an honorable man?"

Ron says the first thing he thought was, What a bizarre way to open a conversation. But then he quickly realized that this was who this guy really was.

"I mean, this was very coded language, you know, asking me to read between the lines of what he was saying. I'm sure he was fed up with me and my staff, biting his tongue for months and now he wants me to know he can ruin and destroy me by telling the whole world that I'm a bad person."

The governor wanted Ron to write a statement that would "clarify" what DeRosa had said in that meeting. Cuomo wanted him to write that his top aide did *not* admit to obstruction of justice. He wanted him to lie and state she *did not* say she "froze" when asked to share information with the Justice Department.

"So basically, long story short, what he was saying is that even though you witnessed the crime, you have to lie and tell the press that you did not see that crime."

That was the moment of truth for Ron. After a sleepless night and a few days thinking about what had happened in that phone call—the demanding of loyalty and the lies the governor wanted him to write—it was clear. Andrew Cuomo had crossed the line.

"It's one thing if you're calling me to just curse at me or yell at me or be a playground bully. That's politics. There's a lot of very toxic men in politics who would do that. But for Cuomo to leverage his power, to get a lawmaker to lie and cover up the lies, that is beyond just bullying. It is a violation of multiple laws. And he should be held accountable. And that's when my wife and I came to the conclusion that we have to fight back."

Ron says that night his wife was very hurt and was afraid about what was going to happen next. There was a moment where she thought maybe he should just go back and do what Cuomo wanted him to do.

"I think that's how everyone in that position would say as a knee-jerk reaction. You have to protect your family and forget everything else. Forget the constituents, and the nursing homes because it's easier that way. But then, the more we talked about it, if I did what he asked me to do, his vindictiveness would put me in a much more vulnerable position where he could actually really hurt me. So no matter how you slice it, the only thing we could do is push back and fight."

Reflecting back on it a bit more, Ron says you get one shot with something like this.

"It's King Cuomo and you can't miss. You have to do whatever you can to go full steam ahead. There's no backing down."

This is an important lesson about being a David in front of a Goliath: You can't think about what's going to happen next. You just have to just keep one foot in front of the other, stand tall, and try not to look around you, because if you focus too much on the possible fallout if you fail, you may never go through with it.

What happened in the weeks and months after that phone call made Ron Kim an opponent. He says all the interviews on television, like being a guest on *The View*, and talking about what happened took a lot of energy.

"I know that I can't screw this up. You can't deny the incredible power that he had. It is David and Goliath. If we were in a cave together, he somehow would have made it dark. He would have found a way to stab me in the back while I'm not looking. So, at every moment I had to be assertive and aggressive and keep punching up. If you're going to fight you have to be willing to lose. You have to know the risks and accept it."

I ask Ron what accountability means for him.

"Accountability means the whole truth of the mistakes and how those mistakes led to massive deaths of our most vulnerable seniors in this state. And we're so close to getting it right because throughout

America's history, it's very hard to properly write the truth of these moments. People in power most often control the narrative. It never happens in terms of a guy like me, an immigrant kid from Queens of Korean descent, taking on Andrew Cuomo and being able to actually tell my story in a book you're writing. This is America's most elite political family. You know, he gets to rub elbows with all these celebrities in the Hamptons. I'm sitting eating dim sum in Flushing, Queens."

Ron says he's optimistic about seeing this through, because in the end, it's not about politics. It's about what's right.

I ask what kind of future Ron hopes for when it comes to his three little girls. He says he wants them to have passion in their lives and happiness. To find something that makes them want to be the first to show up and the last to leave. He says we also have a responsibility to make their world better for them to grow up in.

Before we end our conversation, I ask Ron to tell me the story of where his name comes from. I remember hearing him mention it one day when we were at a rally together. Ron's uncle Son, whom he lost in a New York nursing home in 2020, was the one who helped give him his name.

Son was a huge fan of Ronald Reagan, and when Ron came here with his family, he had a Korean name. Uncle Son said he should have a more American name, so he suggested Ronald, after President Reagan. He laughs and says that he used to tell his peers he was named after the New York Mets baseball great Ron Darling instead. But it proves he's had public service in his blood since he got here, even if he disagrees with some of Reagan's politics. In a time when everyone thinks democracy is failing us, Ron Kim thinks we're close to rewriting a chapter in American history. Together.

"It's about building something better with decent people that want accountability and don't care about political party lines. I think that's what excites me the most, that like our friendship, it's about our ability to go beyond what's in front of us, and to transform the political system. Together we can get democracy right, and that's the kind of stuff that can save this country again."

5

"I Can Choose My Career or My Values"

The Survivor vs. a Manipulator

The fall of Andrew Cuomo did not happen in one fell swoop. It took many things (and people) to finally get him to step down from a career in politics that began when he was a kid living in the governor's mansion with his dad, Mario, in the 1970s. Even though Andrew himself was a well-known name in politics for several decades, his star didn't really rise to meteoric levels until the COVID-19 pandemic. I was impressed by his calm delivery of the "facts" early on, and how he pledged to get us through it. I tweeted about how great I thought Cuomo was doing . . . at the beginning:

March 22, 2020

@NYGovCuomo is doing an excellent job for our state.

He's calm, presents facts, tells us we'll get through this. His social media is also helpful. Very grateful for his leadership.

April 14, 2020

I've said it before I'll say it again. Grateful for @nygovcuomo
and his leadership.

Then, however, in late April 2020, some of us began to realize that Governor Cuomo was not being truthful, and was putting people in danger. That's when some of us started speaking up.

Not surprisingly, we were in the minority. Our voices were being drowned out by the media fanfare and the celebrity lovefest. The Luv Guv was taking over America, with whispers of a presidency in the making. Every day was a challenge as we kept demanding answers and accountability as the powerful machine grew even stronger, with the mainstream media propping up their pandemic politician. The odds were not in our favor.

When our families were losing hope that he might be held accountable for his deadly decisions, there were new voices joining the chorus: those of brave women coming forward, one by one, to share stories of abuse, harassment, and mistreatment in their workplace, the Cuomo administration.

That, I believe was the true beginning of the end of Andrew Cuomo.

Charlotte Bennett was an executive aide and health policy advisor for the former governor's office. She was moved to a different position in November 2020 after complaining about her working conditions with Cuomo. She would later become one of eleven women to come forward about his sexual misconduct. Charlotte revealed her experiences in February 2021 to Jesse McKinley, a *New York Times* reporter, saying her powerful boss harassed her repeatedly as the pandemic was ravaging New York. Cuomo asked about her sex life and if she was involved with anyone on his staff. Because he knew that she was a survivor of sexual assault and rape, Charlotte said in the *New York Times* interview, Cuomo had a fixation on that part of her life.

She said in the interview: "The way he was repeating, 'You were raped and abused and attacked and assaulted and betrayed,' over and over again while looking at me directly in the eyes was something out of a horror movie."

Charlotte believed he was grooming her in those weeks, and the most unsettling moment came in June 2020, when she was alone with Cuomo in his office and he kept asking personal questions and sharing uncomfortable feelings with her. She disclosed the exchanges with her parents and close friends, and how it was becoming increasingly difficult it was to work with him.

I know firsthand how difficult it is to reveal embarrassing, disgusting behavior from a powerful boss. Reliving them brings back pain, anger, and shame.

I'm sure for Charlotte and the other women who came forward, it's horrifying to see their lives being dissected in the press over and over. Even though the criminal cases involving the governor's harassing behavior were dropped, it wasn't because of the character or credibility of the victims. Instead, it was based on whether there was a legally sufficient case to charge him criminally. Several district attorneys made it clear that the allegations and witnesses were credible. Many wrote in their findings that the legislature needs to change the current sexual harassment laws because they fail to properly hold offenders accountable and don't adequately protect victims.

Oswego County District Attorney Gregory Oakes wrote:

"If justice is to ever be obtained for the countless victims who are sexually abused and harassed in this state each day, the law must be revised."

There is no doubt that the stories of these women combined were damning enough that Andrew Cuomo had to step down. My own experiences with Fox News CEO Roger Ailes would never have brought down the most powerful man in cable news, but because other women came forward and had similar experiences, that established a pattern of behavior. Fox eventually did the right thing by letting him go. Ailes still received millions of dollars in an exit package, but his reputation was ruined and his career was over.

Charlotte tells me it still feels like she's walking around with a wound that's wide open.

Trying to get back to some normalcy after a tumultuous few years has been tough. When she disclosed the inappropriate behavior with the governor's chief of staff, she was immediately transferred to another job. Back then, Charlotte didn't want to bring on an investigation because she wanted to move on. But when she finally decided to say something, she felt lucky that a superior supported her. When Lindsey Boylan, a former aide to the governor, began to speak out about her terrible experiences, Charlotte's boss came to her and said that if she ever wanted to come forward, she would help.

I tell Charlotte I'm so glad that someone in her workplace was supportive, and that she still felt comfortable working there despite everything that happened. She says she feels a sense of relief, of still having a community that isn't begrudgingly supportive or "outright throwing me under the bus."

I ask, when was the moment that she knew Andrew Cuomo was being improper? Was it right from the beginning, or was it a slow realization? Charlotte says that when it first began, she didn't want to believe it was happening.

"Early on when you first meet him, it's kind of surreal. I'm serving New York and I'm serving the governor and wanting to see it in a positive light even though he is more and more inappropriate. It really was from the beginning. It's the person that he is. But you try not to see it. . . ."

My first experiences with Roger Ailes started out as joking and cringeworthy comments. I look back on it now and see he was testing me to find out how I would react to his behavior. But at the same time he was charming and funny, and you wanted him to like you. I also thought of him at times like a father figure, so it was a complicated dynamic. Still, at some point you have to decide that you're not going to put up with it anymore.

"It hit me like a slap across the face on June 5, 2020, when I could no longer do my job. It wasn't a friendly back-and-forth banter. I was trying really hard to interpret this as more like mentorship or a father-daughter type of relationship, but during this conversation, I left shaking and I knew that I was in danger. This was not going to go away and I couldn't do that to myself ever again: be in a room alone with him."

Charlotte texted her best friend right away to tell her what happened. This wasn't a surprise.

"She had been angry and frustrated with my workplace for a really long time. There was abuse and humiliation. Overworked, underpaid, and then the yelling and the fighting. How demeaning the whole job was."

Her friend told her to pack her bags and get out.

I mention to Charlotte how angry it made me to hear that she was the one who had to find a new position after Cuomo's disgusting behavior. Why did Charlotte have to leave her job instead of him? He should have been the one removed.

"Right? And after all the sacrifices I made and the work I put in. It was devastating."

There was no motivation for the new job she was now in, and found herself depressed and anxious.

"This man actively decided to ruin something I had worked for, and now he can go about his day while I had to look at his name on the building every time I walked in."

I asked if people knew what he was like. Was it evident how he treated others, especially women?

"When I did end up telling coworkers, no one was surprised. But there was no larger conversation about it. That was really upsetting."

It took Charlotte time to decide whether to come forward. It all began on February 24, 2021, when she "quote tweeted" Lindsey Boylan on Twitter. She wrote:

@_char_bennett_
For those wondering what it's like to work for the Cuomo admin, read
@LindseyBoylan's story.

Quote Tweet

Lindsey Boylan

@LindseyBoylan

Feb 24, 2021

Today I am telling my story. I never planned to share the details of my experience working in the Cuomo administration, but I am doing so now in hopes that it may make it easier for others to speak their own truth. https://medium.com/@lindseyboylan4NY/my-story-of-working-with-governor-cuomo-e664d4814b4e . . .

That's when the *New York Times* reached out and asked if she had a story to tell.

I ask how it felt after she sent that first tweet that set the ball in motion. She says it began an overwhelming sense of paranoia: feeling that people are watching and listening. If she talks too loud, someone will hear her. It was fear.

"The moment you open your mouth and you're suddenly being hounded by media and publicity. I was pacing, I couldn't read, and fairly quickly, I was shaking. Jesse [McKinley, the *Times* reporter who broke Charlotte's story] and I had multiple phone calls for many days and I was trying to send him screenshots of my text messages [to corroborate the story]. It took so much energy, and I felt like at any moment someone could show up at my doorstep. I had a plan that if I received a phone call from an unknown number, I would record it. I was always ready, standing by with a recorder in case it happened and someone from his office called."

At the end of February 2021, Charlotte's interview with McKinley was published. That was followed by an interview with Nora O'Donnell on the *CBS Evening News*. It sent shock waves across the country.

In a statement afterward, Cuomo denied Bennett's account:

When she came to me and opened up about being a sexual assault survivor and how it shaped her and her ongoing efforts to create an organization that empowered her voice to help other survivors, I tried to be supportive and helpful. Ms. Bennett's initial impression was right: I was trying to be a mentor to her. I never made advances toward Ms. Bennett nor did I ever intend to act in any way that was inappropriate. The last thing I would ever have wanted was to make her feel any of the things that are being reported.

This situation cannot and should not be resolved in the press; I believe the best way to get to the truth is through a full and thorough outside review and I am directing all state employees to comply with that effort. I ask all New Yorkers to await the findings of the review so that they know the facts before making any judgements. I will have no further comment until the review has concluded.

One thing I've learned about Cuomo (and many who are like him) is that even if he's guilty of something, and the charges against him are overwhelming, he will always believe that he is the innocent one, blaming everyone else, including those he wronged. He did it with nursing homes, never once apologizing or acknowledging any involvement, and instead pointed at God, Mother Nature, the *New York Post*, Fox News, the nursing home workers, and even the nursing home residents—for being old!

"Older people, vulnerable people are going to die from this virus," he said. "That is going to happen despite whatever you do. Because with all our progress as a society, we can't keep everyone alive."

He then blamed cancel culture and being Italian for the sexual harassment allegations. Goliath will never admit his mistakes, and will fight David to the death so he never has to.

Thankfully, a few people, like Attorney General Letitia James, weren't influenced by the governor or his administration. She released a report in August 2021 concluding that Cuomo had indeed sexually harassed several women in violation of the law. Cuomo responded via a televised statement and singled out Charlotte in trying to explain his actions:

I thought I could help her work through a difficult time. I did ask her [Bennett] questions I don't normally ask people. I did ask her how she was doing and how she was feeling. And I did ask questions to try to see if she had positive, supportive dating relationships. . . . I was trying to make sure she was working her way through it the best she could. I thought I had learned enough and had enough personal experience to help. But I was wrong.

Cuomo then directly addressed Charlotte and her claims against him:

I brought my personal experience into the workplace and I shouldn't have done that. I was trying to help. Obviously, I didn't. I am even more sorry that I further complicated the situation. My goal was the exact opposite. I wish nothing but good for you, and for all survivors of sexual assault.

Charlotte was in the car when she heard his statement.

"I'm watching the press conference from my iPhone. It was so devastating and it was so enraging and for him to have a platform to use it. And I just thought: this man is not right. He's wrong, and not only that, but he's mentally not in a good place, mentally not there, and I'm doing the right thing. I'm going to speak my truth. And nothing he can say will stop me."

I ask Charlotte where this strength comes from. She says she was raised by someone who was very similar to Andrew Cuomo, and that she has lived through an abusive relationship. She credits being in therapy for many years.

"I have this tool belt that I have acquired painfully my whole life. And it comes from a place of trauma, but I've tried my best to turn it into a force of strength, education, and knowledge. I trust in myself instead of the people speaking for him."

I ask Charlotte if she thinks sexual harassment is really about the sex, or is it about power and control over people? For a lot of these men, it seems to be about feeling they can do anything because no one is around to put them in check. They enjoy making women feel inferior, demeaned, and uncomfortable.

Charlotte thinks the former governor was trying to sleep with her, and that if the door had been open for that relationship he would have walked right through.

She found herself at a fork in the road, deciding whether or not to keep putting up with this behavior.

"I can choose my career or I can choose my values. He's forcing me to decide. He thinks his power will always triumph over goodness and the principles of trust, integrity, and doing the right thing. And I think he was lonely, and probably did want a relationship. But he was basically saying to me, 'All those things you've done and want in your life are silly. And I'll prove that to you because you'll lose your job. So, choose your job. Choose this administration over all of that.'"

I ask Charlotte if she remembers the last time she saw Cuomo before all of this blew up. She remembers it was a small gathering at a school, and he didn't look her in the eye or say a word.

"I was standing in a line with some other senior aides and colleagues, and he went over and hugged some people, so he had to hug me. It was a really awkward, uncomfortable hug, obviously. He never said anything to me, and I never saw him again."

And if she had the chance to face him now, would she say anything?

"I think, knowing him and knowing myself, I don't know if we can even have that conversation. I feel like I could sit down and be genuine and honest and straightforward. But we both know he's not capable of that himself."

I ask about forgiveness. Many say you have to forgive those who wronged you to be able to get past a hurtful situation in life. For me, I don't think I could ever get there.

"No. I won't forgive him because he doesn't deserve forgiveness, and honestly, I can't imagine him ever doing the work to understand what he's done wrong in his lifetime."

I tell Charlotte I feel bad for his family. Especially his daughters. They aren't responsible for their father's behavior, his wrongdoing or misdeeds, so I feel for them and what they have to carry in their life because of their father's incredible abuse of power. Charlotte says she can't imagine what this year has been like for them.

"And you know, whether or not they hate me, I don't really care. I just hope that they're okay and taking care of themselves. And in some ways, maybe they're trying to grapple with what the truth is. I feel like in his circle, they have always operated on a different set of facts. There are so many lies. And I just hope that a reckoning will happen. I feel for them. The girls. I've done a lot of work in my life to move forward. I can't imagine how hard it is for them. It's sad."

I admit to Charlotte that these last few years have been exhausting. I realize that at some point you have to let go, and hope that the truth prevails. We've done our part. But I'm having a hard time having faith that other people will help with the fight. Charlotte says the struggle will continue as long as he's out in public and in the news. But she says we owe ourselves grace, and to try to not let him take our energy.

"All that room that they're taking up in our brain, I refuse to give that to them and I will allow that space and energy for healing and for accountability, but he cannot sit in the back of my head and torture me. I won't allow it."

After Attorney General James released her report into Cuomo's sexual harassment allegations, it was revealed that the nonprofit organization Time's Up (a group that was founded in 2018 to help support victims of sexual harassment in the workplace) was actively trying to help Cuomo. Chairwoman Roberta A. Kaplan had to resign her position because of her role in trying to discredit Lindsey Boylan.

In September, the entire Time's Up board was dissolved, including several Hollywood A-list actors, largely because of the group's handling of the Cuomo sexual harassment investigation.

"These organizations don't have our back, so we need to find a way to stick together and also stand up for each other. It's hard enough going up against one institution, let alone one that's supposed to help women."

Charlotte says it's soul crushing seeing the betrayal from the places that are supposed to help us but instead are protecting the abusers.

"They [Time's Up] did everything in their power to undermine me, undermine Lindsey, all of the women and effectively sweep this under the rug. We know that Andrew Cuomo will protect Andrew Cuomo. But the other places that actually have that choice? We all thought they were doing the right thing, but they weren't. That was really painful."

As we wrap up our interview, I ask Charlotte if she watched the FX show *Impeachment*, about the Bill Clinton and Monica Lewinsky scandal. I remember following it all in real time, but now, decades later, it's interesting to see things from the perspective of Lewinsky. No matter what you believe and who you think was wrong, Clinton survived that scandal and is still getting a pass.

Charlotte says she thinks a lot about Lewinsky because even after all these years, how far have we really gone? We pat ourselves on the backs with #MeToo and seeing some of these guys go away, but many are still getting their golden parachutes when they're asked to leave.

"I find a lot of power in Monica Lewinsky and her presence, and I like that she is strong and has learned to navigate through all of this."

Also, Charlotte points out, there are so many similarities between Clinton and Cuomo. They are charming in their own way but are ruthless and always out for themselves.

And how fitting that one of the only people who reportedly kept telling Cuomo to fight the sexual harassment charges before he was forced to resign was the former president Bill Clinton himself.

"They will say and do what it takes, and ruin as many lives as necessary along the way. Our appetite as a society and as a country for these individuals is way, way too high. These people should not be invited to our party. They should not be invited to speak. They should not be on the news. And we have we have a lot of work to do."

As we're saying our good-byes, I tell Charlotte how proud I am of her. I'm so grateful we found each other even during a time of tragedy and pain in both our lives. She says that together, we're more powerful.

"And I really hope, moving forward, we all stay together for that reason."

6

"Some Part of Me Needed to Get This Out"

The Whistleblower vs. the Governor

I t was a tweet on December 5, 2020, that introduced me to Lindsey Boylan.

@avenaim
"Name the worse job you've ever had."

Lindsey wrote:

Most toxic team environment? Working for @NYGovCuomo

Those few words on social media started a tremor underneath the Cuomo empire that turned into a full-scale earthquake in the months to follow.

Cuomo's Goliath was protected by an army of enablers for many, many years, and it took a few Davids to help shine a light on the bullying, harassment, and corruption he and his administration took part in for more than a decade and a half in office, and likely decades before that during his entire political career.

I remember seeing Lindsey's tweet and feeling a range of emotions. My advocacy against Cuomo began in May 2020, and by December, I was becoming very discouraged by how the nursing home tragedy wasn't getting the attention I felt it deserved. But seeing Lindsey expose another potential abuse by the governor felt like a very big deal.

Lindsey and I began to communicate not long after her "worst job ever" tweet, and I consider her a good friend. She hasn't done a lot of interviews, and says whenever a news story breaks about Cuomo, her phone lights up with reporters asking for comments. She blocks unknown numbers because she never knows when the next call is going to come in.

After her explosive tweet at the end of 2020, Lindsey decided to publish an essay in Medium (an online publishing platform) in February 2021, describing the sexual harassment and abuse she endured for years working for Cuomo. She resigned in 2018 after he "forcibly kissed her during a meeting." She came to the conclusion that her boss was pursuing and trying to sleep with her.

After Lindsey came out with her accusations, it was reported that Cuomo's administration actively tried to smear and intimidate her.

Our conversation took place after Cuomo had just released commercials painting himself as a victim of cancel culture despite having resigned in disgrace. In his mind, this was all a political hit job instead of an investigation conducted by Attorney General Letitia James which concluded that Cuomo had harassed eleven women, including Lindsey.

A spokesperson for James wrote in response, "The only thing Andrew Cuomo has proven himself to be is a serial sexual harasser and a threat to women in the workplace—no TV ad can change that. It's shameful that after multiple investigations found Cuomo's victims to be credible, he continues to attack their accounts rather than take responsibility for his own actions."

Lindsey says she never had high expectations that any of the sexual harassment cases would be criminally prosecuted. But she's still very optimistic about how far we've come in this age of #MeToo.

"We're in a very modern era. And this is not Democrat or Republican. It's pervasive, and it just takes a cooler head and see how far we've come. I would venture to guess most women's mothers have had some version of these experiences. And, as terrible as it is, I feel really lucky that even the fact that he [Cuomo] felt he had to resign is something that would not have happened years ago. I mean, you can look at Eliot Spitzer (a former governor of New York who was involved in a prostitution ring) and all these other cases, but that had other entanglements. Just the sexual harassment alone, even just being taken seriously at all, is a fairly new thing."

I tell Lindsey I need to hear this perspective, because for me, every day that this guy keeps showing up and ignoring all of his atrocities makes me fear he's never going away. She agrees and says it's disturbing.

"I don't have to verbalize how alarming it is to see someone who has literally no moral compass whatsoever, and who has such evil intentions. I never really kind of thought about things in the context of evil, but I think he is an evil person."

Lindsey took a trip with her daughter to London before our interview, and while she was away she received several messages from reporters about the former governor. She says it feels like you can never get away from his abuse—even two years later. But she doesn't want to engage or be part of a conversation in the press that gives him back his power.

"I don't want to have anything to do with him at all. And I think it's a power that I have to say no to interactions. Even though there's so many people who try to beat us into these conversations, they're not genuine. And it's difficult to see things that are conveyed in a way that is not real and it's hard to ignore them. But I know this person. What he wants is to bait you into a war because it's really easy for someone who has no scruples to win a battle. I just don't want to be there."

I ask what it was like in the beginning when she met him. I've opened up about my interactions with Roger Ailes in the beginning of my career. While there were the times he was gross and inappropriate, there were also the times where he was charismatic, charming, funny, and kind. That's what was complicated and manipulative about his abuse.

Lindsey says that when she first started working with the Cuomo administration, it was right after the Trump election and he was billing himself as someone who was going to fight against that kind of approach in politics.

"And I think that's what lot of people were looking for, including me. We're looking for something to counter to how Trump pursued power."

At that point in her career, Lindsey says she knew who she was. Unfortunately, this wasn't her first rodeo experiencing sexual harassment in the workplace.

"I think like a lot of women, I've had many experiences, and you just view it as normal and that there's really no way around it."

Years ago, she talked to an employment lawyer who told her that she could have a claim about a coworker or a boss, but speaking up could derail a career. Was that worth it?

"So you self-censor. You go along. You stay in the environment. And I think for me, it was hard to really acknowledge that this was happening from the most powerful person in the state. But you saw it in plain view. Small things, like making sure there's no microphone for Cynthia Nixon (actress and 2018 primary rival) to speak at the Democratic convention. The little things that never require their touch or their signature or their handiwork."

Lindsey says that for many of us, this is the kind of unfortunate experience of being a woman in the workplace.

"I had been told in many ways, directly and indirectly, that when you speak up, it doesn't benefit you. And this wasn't just from the most powerful person in the state. This was coming from people in my party."

Lindsey likens the experience she's had in politics to training for the Olympics.

"I was competing at the highest level, and then to come and find out your coach or the person who's leading you is abusing all these powers. He's abusing women—and everyone who's close to the environment knows all about it."

Lindsey says it wasn't just the harassment. It was a visceral sense that if you spoke up about it, there would be real consequences.

"And yet because of all these experiences before this, I tried to suppress it because you don't see any good coming out of it, frankly. And if it were just about me, I probably never would have said anything, at least not in real time."

Lindsey envisioned herself being an eighty-year-old grandmother, finally telling someone what it was like working for Andrew Cuomo. "When you're finally old enough and it can't hurt you or anyone you love anymore."

But when she heard from a young woman named Charlotte Bennett, who said she was sexually harassed by the same man that abused her, Lindsey knew Charlotte was telling the truth. She finally felt compelled to speak up. There would be guilt that followed, knowing that had Lindsey complained about her abuser sooner, maybe this wouldn't have happened to Charlotte.

"I didn't even know this woman, but she was affected by it, and I didn't do something about it. Maybe that's part of the reason she had this unfortunate experience."

I ask Lindsey what gave her the courage to write the tweet in December 2020 about what it was like to work with Cuomo.

She says it was during COVID, when we were all at home, and that was a big factor. Most of us were not working in our usual office environments, and being home felt more like a safe space.

Lindsey had never really engaged on Twitter until she ran for Congress. By the fall of 2020, she was telling stories and promoting conversation on the social media site.

"And then someone had posted something about the worst job you've ever had. . . ."

That's when she responded.

"I didn't come out and say anything about sexual harassment at the time, but I did say something like working at Friendly's restaurant was much more respectful than working there."

After that tweet, Lindsey says there was a lot of outreach from former colleagues and people in state government who messaged her and said they were grateful for her comment. Many said they felt they could never say anything critical about Cuomo or the administration.

"Some part of me needed to get this out. I felt the need to communicate something about the experience."

Lindsey says the toxic work environment was an open secret. Even the people who have stood up for him publicly and supported him would complain.

"I remember very vividly we would have these terrible meetings with him, and one of his aides would say that she would prepare for them by taking her antidepressants. She didn't say that in a small group; there were a collection of people there. So, it was always known. It was always acknowledged that this was an abusive environment. There was really no way to escape that."

Despite all this, Lindsey admits it is quite amazing that there was some accountability that happened to him, and those around him. That should count for something.

"You and I have experienced the receiving end of those people. It's really not just about him, as monstrous as he is. It's also about the group of people around him."

One of those in Cuomo's inner circle was his top aide, Melissa DeRosa, who not only allowed this kind of behavior to go on but was the gatekeeper who manipulated information and did everything she could to hide things that were harmful to the governor's reputation. Melissa was the one who confessed that they were hiding the nursing home numbers. She also helped smear those who tried to speak up against Cuomo and was generally known as a mean girl.

DeRosa was also one of Cuomo's closest confidantes, and there have been reports that their relationship went beyond that of colleagues. Lindsey thinks that at one point, Melissa was one of his victims.

One thing I find very disturbing is that some of the most vicious defenders of Andrew Cuomo are women. There's a whole team of them who will say the most god-awful things on social media to attack and belittle those who criticize his leadership decisions or bring up ongoing investigations against their hero. Lindsey says the people that enabled Cuomo the most in his administration were a group of women.

I ask Lindsey when she told her husband about what was happening. One of the most painful moments in my life was telling Sean about my own sexual harassment experiences. I remember feeling so much shame around it. It's a whole journey you go through with your spouse when the truth finally comes out.

Lindsey says her husband knew some of the stories, but not the full extent of what truly happened.

"Because the more you verbalize it and the more you talk about it, the harder it becomes to deal with. And maybe if I had said something sooner, maybe I would have gotten myself out of that environment earlier. I don't know."

Lindsey says there are specifics she never wanted to share because she knew they would be very hard for her husband to take. It's difficult to talk about these experiences because you become accustomed to just getting through it on your own and don't want to burden anyone. Not to mention having to relive these incredibly embarrassing, shameful moments with a person you're married to.

Lindsey explains that this is a hard place for someone who loves you, and knows how much you love your job. It's a balance, saying you've got to get out of this terrible spot even though this is the place you've worked your whole life to get into.

I share a pivotal moment in my life when I was wrestling with whether it was worth telling the lawyers about my experiences with Roger Ailes. I was having second thoughts about giving a statement to the law firm investigating him. Was it really worth risking my job, that I would probably lose for talking about something that happened so long ago? I envisioned having to sell our house, move back to Canada, and being blacklisted in broadcasting. But that's the moment when Sean said it didn't matter. I had to go in and tell the truth about what happened. We would deal with whatever fallout happened afterward.

It was petrifying to be in a room with a bunch of strangers, telling them about these creepy moments that I had tried to bury so many years ago. But I did, and it worked out. I'll never forget how Sean encouraged and supported that decision to tell the truth.

Lindsey says that most people don't have any idea about how difficult it is to be engaged in these kinds of legal proceedings around sexual harassment.

"Being interviewed on the record for six hours in one sitting is extremely traumatic because they have to ask you every question. And I'm so glad you did it. You're very brave. And I just want to acknowledge that because I don't think people understand how hard it is to go through those kinds of experiences."

During the investigation into Cuomo's abusive behavior, Lindsey had her deposition taped on a Zoom meeting. Eventually all of the videos were put online by the attorney general's office. She had no idea they would ever be released to the public. I was shocked to see her interviews posted on YouTube. It feels like she was victimized again. Lindsey says she found out they were out there as she was returning from a trip.

"I get off a plane and realize that they've released all of the videos. I just started crying. I don't really cry very much—well, this year I have. But you kind of train yourself, particularly as a woman professionally, to not tear up or you just go to the bathroom. I just immediately was sobbing and dry heaving."

Lindsey stands by everything she said in her testimony, but it was the realization that now everyone in the world could see her reliving these painful experiences. Why was this necessary?

"People would send me stuff and say, 'Oh, I can't believe they're doing this to you.' And then you see the tweets and think, Oh my God, this person has clipped me crying on-screen."

Lindsey says this brings out the ugliness of the world *online*. The attorney general's office at the very least should have notified her that the videos of her being questioned were going to be released.

"I think that there needs to be a future world in which lawmakers and law enforcement officials can still achieve what they need to without outright traumatizing people more, and that's really what they did."

One thing people should remember is that the women who came forward to talk about the abuse they endured had so much to lose. There was no expectation that Andrew Cuomo would be held accountable. This is a common story for many of these David vs. Goliath moments, where you wrestle with whether it's worth risking what you spent your whole life working for, because it could backfire immensely.

"And you know that because you lived it, too. You've spoken up and you feel the heat every day, and of course, you wouldn't change a thing, just like me. I'm a very imperfect person, but there's no other way that this could have gone."

I ask Lindsey how she views the world of politics now. Is she jaded after all she's gone through? Many people are disturbed by what they've seen over the last two years from our nation's leadership. Lindsey says that at this moment, she's just trying to spend more time with her family and be grateful. But politics and knowing what's happening in the world will always be in her blood. It's a passion.

"Do I want to hear about the Cuomo circus? No. But there's no avoiding world news. It matters what happens with certain policy issues. I can't avoid still loving this field. And at the same time, I feel very differently about how I can impact that. Not dissimilar to what you're doing with your advocacy. I think storytelling is enormously powerful especially now."

But for Lindsey, there is less interest in tying herself to people who have not shown enough courage in order to make a life in politics work.

"I think that when I ran against Congressman Jerry Nadler, people said, 'How dare you run against a sitting member of your own party?' And I think that narrative about me has been around, and if anything has changed now, it's that I feel even less willing to kowtow to someone or anyone within my own party or beyond that is unwilling to do the same things that I've done to speak up and to help others."

Lindsey says she wants to continue to be a force for good. To be positive, and help women. How can she do any of that unless she puts herself on the line to actually do the work?

"While I'm very disheartened by the cynical nature of politics, I'm extremely heartened by the idea of helping people. I've probably never been closer to doing that, right now, which is what I've wanted to do my whole life. This journey has probably had more of an impact than anything I did in any campaign."

I ask about what she hopes for her daughter after all of this. What is she like and what does she want for the future? Lindsey's voice gets animated when she talks about her sweet girl, and says that no one's opinion matters more to her than that of her daughter.

"Her earliest memories were of her mom running for office, and then her mom finishing her time working for the governor. Even early on in life, kids are grappling with big ideas like how to deal with bullies, and how to include people. Basic things that people like Andrew Cuomo never really got in kindergarten."

It's important to show our kids how to confront a bully, how not to stoop to their level, and then to never lose hope, and never give up.

"Your kids force you to be your best self. You dust yourself off and you get back up again. I've had to really practice what I preach. Hopefully where I've fallen short, and where I failed and where I've had fear, I've tried to emphasize bravery and helping others. I think she's already a way better person than I am."

I tell Lindsey that's the same thing I'm doing for my own boys, having lived through this experience with them. Even though you want to protect your kids and shield them from the tough stuff you have to go through, these little humans are very perceptive and will learn from your actions.

When all of this advocacy was underway, and I was spending a lot of my spare time fighting for thousands of families against one of New York's biggest bullies, my youngest son, Theodore, was being tormented at his school by a cruel kid in his class. I was in touch with his teacher, and then the principal, to try to solve the issue. It seemed like every day there were tears. It was heartbreaking. Some days were worse than others, and Theodore just started living with the fact that every day there would be name-calling or mean things said.

Then, one day, my boy came home and told me that the bully had started to pick on someone else in the schoolyard. This time it was directed at one of his best buddies. Theodore explained that he suddenly got the courage to yell at the bully and tell him to stop it! Why was he such a mean kid all the time? Leave his friend alone! He was clearly proud of himself when he was giving me all the details. There were no more tears. Just a feeling that he was protecting his friend.

In that moment, I realized that my son had learned a valuable lesson, one that sometimes takes a lifetime to learn: it always takes courage to stand up for yourself, but it's even more brave and important to stand up for others instead.

7

"It's What You Do with Those Opportunities That Counts"
The College Kids vs. the Soviet Hockey Team

What is courage? Let me tell you what I think it is.
An indefinable quality that makes a man put out that
extra something, when it seems there is nothing else
to give. I dare you to be better than you are. I dare
you to be a Thoroughbred.

—*Coach Herb Brooks*

I looked at the scoreboard, and one thought ran
through my mind. I can't believe it, I said to myself
even as I hugged one teammate and the next and the
next. I can't believe we beat the Russians.

—*Mike Eruzione*, The Making of a Miracle

The David and Goliath comparison is used in sports all the time. An underdog team, horse, or player suddenly does something incredible to win. There was nothing more powerful than what Team USA accomplished in the little ski town of Lake Placid, New York, during the hockey semifinals of the 1980 Winter Olympics. The American team scored with ten minutes of play left, taking a 4–3 lead against the Soviets. Later, as the scoreboard counted down the final seconds, broadcaster Al Michaels famously announced:

"Do you believe in miracles? Yes!"

The odds had not been in their favor. Not by a long shot.

The Soviets had won four consecutive gold medals at the Olympics from 1964 to 1976. Many of their players had been on the team for more than a decade because of a loophole in the rules. "Professional players" were not allowed to compete at the Olympics, so none of them played "professionally," but they were all Russian soldiers who happened to play hockey as their military assignment. Their team was made up of men of all ages, and their goaltender, Vladislav Tretiak, was a machine.

Team USA's roster was made up of amateur college players brought together by a coach from Minnesota, Herb Brooks. His challenge was assembling a group of young players in just a few weeks. Thirteen of the twenty young men came from either Coach Brooks's school, the University of Minnesota, or Boston University, and they were bitter rivals. Brooks put together the men he believed would be able to handle incredibly tough training and crushingly high expectations.

To really understand how amazing this win was, you have to go back and look at the history of where we were as a country. It wasn't just the game. It was what was happening in the world that really gave people something to cheer about.

The United States was in the midst of the Cold War with the Soviet Union. The latter's 1979 invasion of Afghanistan prompted President Jimmy Carter to announce that the United States would boycott the 1980 Summer Olympics in Moscow.

There was a major recession, a gas shortage, and the Iran hostage crisis: fifty-two American diplomats and citizens had been taken hostage by Islamist radicals at the US embassy in Tehran during the 1979 Islamic revolution.

In other words, the whole world needed a feel-good story to bring us all together.

Forty-three years later, it's still considered one of the greatest moments in all of sports.

I talked to the man who scored the winning goal, the captain of Miracle on Ice, Mike Eruzione, to hear how this true story came to capture hearts and minds across America and around the world.

My first question to Mike was if he or his teammates knew what they were up against. Many Davids have no idea how big and strong Goliath really is.

He says they didn't have a clue, and they also didn't realize the whole world was watching. There were only three TV networks besides PBS, and the social media world we know today was nonexistent.

Mike says that getting picked for the team was a crapshoot, and he was invited to try out. There were sixty-eight young men who went to Colorado Springs, Colorado, to compete against each other, during a two-week period. Coach Brooks evaluated the players and selected twenty-six. Then, throughout the course of their six-month training, six guys got cut. Only twenty were allowed to go to Lake Placid, and not only was Mike chosen, but he was picked to be the captain. He doesn't exactly remember how it went down, but he didn't place a big importance on the title.

"I think many were captains of their college [teams] at one point and the rest were captains of their high school team. I always said I was a captain amongst captains. We had a great crew of leaders, a great group of players."

Mike started skating when he was eight years old. His family didn't have a lot of money, so he tried on his sister's figure skates, which happened to fit him. In Massachusetts, winters are cold, and they would pour water over the tennis courts down the street where he lived to make them into a skating rink. Every day, Mike would get up and go to the "rink" to join his friends and learn to skate.

His mother took notice and saved up enough green stamps to buy his first real pair of ice skates.

Mike's dad worked three jobs and his mom stayed home and took care of six children.

He loved all sports growing up—especially football, baseball, and hockey, and wanted to play all three in college because he enjoyed all of them. Mike says it's important for an athlete to be good at a few sports instead of specializing in just one.

"I think I was a good hockey player because I played baseball and football. Plus, there's the burnout stages these kids go through. If they play just one sport, it sometimes gets to be too much. There's no variety."

Mike had a chance to play on the 1976 Olympic men's hockey team, but he wanted to stay at Boston University to see if he could win a national championship. That didn't happen, but four years later the Olympics called again, and this time he couldn't refuse.

Mike knew Coach Brooks already because their hockey teams (Minnesota and Boston) played against each other. Brooks was very similar to Mike's coach in university: tough and in your face.

"They challenged you and constantly pushed the envelope to be better. Herb was very demanding, but he was very honest. We trusted Herb. We respected Herb. And as a coach, that's what you want from your players. I tell people he was like your dad. You love your dad, and sometimes you hate your dad because he makes you do things you didn't want to do and sometimes it hurts."

Part of Herb's success was his motivation. He put them together as the right players and the best players. They fit together like a puzzle. He pushed them hard, and because of that, they were in the best shape of their lives. The average age was twenty-one to twenty-two.

"We were just kids, playing and having fun and never looking at the big picture, just taking each game at a time."

If you've seen the movie *Miracle*, you might remember the scene where Brooks, played by Kurt Russell, runs the players ragged into the ice with his drills, to the point where the players are physically ill with exhaustion. I asked if that was a fair portrayal.

"We called them Herbies, he called it conditioning. We always thought it was punishment. But as it turned out, conditioning was the bigger part of it. We did them six guys at a time. And then we'd do them for fifteen minutes and then we'd stretch. We thought we were done, but we did it again and then we stretch and we did them again and we stretched and we did it again. Meantime, the other guys wanted to get dressed and come out on the ice and skate with us, but Herb said, 'Sit in the stands and just watch.' So we did them for a little while longer. I think it was Mark Johnson who smashed a stick against the glass and Herb said, "If I hear another goddamn smash against the glass, you'll skate till you die."

The lesson was learned.

Another big moment for Team USA was playing the Soviets a few days before the real Olympic game. After watching the movie, I wondered if Herb helped arrange that game to set them up to lose so that afterward they would know what they were up against.

Mike says the bottom line is Brooks wanted them to face the best competition heading into the Olympics. Also, at the time, his teammates weren't thinking about the Soviets, they needed to worry about three other countries first: Sweden, Czechoslovakia, and West Germany.

"The Soviets were never discussed once, until the day before, we were ready to play, and that's the only time we talked about the Soviets and then after we beat them, we never talked about them again because we had to play Finland."

It's important to add that if they lost or tied against Finland, there's a chance they wouldn't have even won a medal.

"So as great as a Soviet victory was, if we don't beat Finland, you and I aren't having this conversation right now."

On the morning that I'm interviewing Mike, the 2021 Summer Olympics are in full swing. The ratings were not great, and the biggest story was the gymnast Simone Biles deciding not to participate in some of the competitions because she felt she was not mentally prepared. I ask Mike if he still follows the Olympics. He says he does, and watches when he can.

"The Olympics are the ultimate sporting event. There's a lot of Super Bowls, World Series, and Stanley Cups. But the Olympics only come around every so often."

Gymnastics has been under the microscope for the disturbing amount of abuse that has gone on for years. Simone Biles was one of Larry Nassar's victims, the sports doctor who sexually abused the young women he was treating. After she went public, the spotlight was intense, and Biles decided to back out of some of the events because she mentally couldn't handle it. While there was a lot of support for her decision, there was also tremendous backlash for not powering through. I was curious what Mike thought about her situation. He was nothing but supportive.

"I have tremendous respect for Simone. I mean, clearly there's other issues going on in her life. And I think she was getting caught up in the emotions. I don't know her, but she is the greatest human as I've seen. But clearly, there's some other things going on in her head. She did the right thing for herself, and what was best for her. A lot of times, athletes usually don't do what's best for themselves because they let their egos get in the way. And she didn't."

I ask Mike if he ever had to do something like that: forge ahead regardless of the consequences or protect himself from harm.

He says that when you're that great, you have to have an inner drive that's off the charts, so what you rely on is the knowledge that you have as an athlete, the competition you've gone through, and the sacrifices you've made. All those things go hand in hand to help you get through difficult times because you prepared for them.

"But in [Biles's] case, it just got overbearing as an individual. I'm on a team sport and I have nineteen other teammates that I can rely on to help me. And even with all those surrounding you in a team experience, you're still an individual, an athlete performing by yourself, where as a hockey player, I get two linemates, two defensemen, and a goalie out there when I'm out there, helping me."

This is an important point, because although we focus on David vs. Goliath as just two individuals, there was an army behind them on both sides. One thing I've learned over the last few years of being an advocate is that you will always find teammates to help you play defense against the bully. Once you stand up for something that is important, others will pitch in to help and encourage you along the way.

I ask Mike about the famous line in the movie *Miracle* when his character says, "I play for the USA."

It is a big moment when his character realizes he isn't playing as an individual but as part of a unit. Mike says that was a Hollywood line, but it is crucial because it marks a moment in the film when "actor Mike" understands how important it is to play for the United States.

"One of the biggest questions going into the Olympics for a lot of people was, How will Minnesota, Massachusetts, and the Wisconsin guys get along? Because we competed intensely against them in college. But once our team was selected, we bonded right away, because when you put a jersey that says USA across the front, it's a whole different mind-set."

Mike says when you feel that honor, wearing the USA jersey makes the experience that much greater.

The fact that these guys didn't realize what they were up against, a Goliath, is very telling of the time they were in back in 1980. There wasn't social media or twenty-four-hour news channels. The pressure on athletes today is in many ways much more intense and comes from so many other places.

"There's more sports now, more athletes, more countries competing, and Lake Placid was a little village. It's like Pleasantville back there."

Mike says that none of them read what was in the papers or said on TV. Herb didn't let them do any press events. They would all hear the "USA! USA!" chants in the building, but he just thought that was happening to everyone.

"I remember calling my house and my sister answered the phone and she started screaming and yelling and I said, 'Well, obviously you're having a party. I'll call back.' And I hung up and she was so pissed off at me because I wouldn't talk to her or anybody else because I didn't know that people were excited about it."

It wasn't until after the games, when his team was invited to the White House, that's when it sunk in. It was a delayed reaction—knowing that the moment they all took part in had made such a tremendous impact.

After their gold medal win, it was time for Mike to move on. He was twenty-five and wanted to coach and teach. The computer company IBM approached him about being a speaker and doing appearances across the country. He made more money in two weeks doing ten events than his dad made in one year. It was a "no-brainer" to take this opportunity and run with it. He knew he was fortunate, and the last game he ever played on ice was a gold medal win. There was nothing he could do to top that. Had he stayed and played hockey professionally, Mike says he would've been just an average NHL player. But he still would have been a good teammate and person.

I ask Mike what he thinks Miracle on Ice would have been like today.

"It would have been absolutely insane. I can't fathom that it would've happened the same way. Especially what we're dealing with right now: the pandemic, and all kinds of social issues. But as a country, we're all looking for something to feel good about. And that's what took place in 1980. That 'something good' happened to us."

Mike has had people come up to him and start crying because that moment meant so much to them. Maybe it was the last time they remember being with a parent celebrating together or being so excited and feeling joyous. From a political aspect, beating the Russians reminded us what America is all about.

"This is why we have such a great country. We need a 1980 right now. But the pressure that's on the athletes today with social media, and the money they make. I mean, God knows what it would have been like today. It's a different atmosphere, a different culture of sports. The training is also very different."

Mike says that when he was a kid, you had to practice, but then you went to a bar and had a couple of beers. Today there are more demands and stresses.

I have to ask about the moment he scored the winning goal. What that meant. What it still means.

"When you play on a team, everybody's got to contribute. And I was fortunate to be in the right place at the right time. But we still had ten minutes to play after I scored! And, believe it or not, we played extremely well during that last ten minutes."

If you've ever watched a hockey game, ten minutes to keep playing and not have the other team score any goals is like forever. Those "Herbies" must have really helped keep their stamina. Mike says that conditioning paid out in huge dividends.

"We were trailing Sweden, we were trailing Czechoslovakia, we were trailing Norway. We were trailing West Germany by two goals. We were trailing the Soviets throughout the game. And then we were trailing Finland going into the third and found a way to win. What makes our story so impressive is how we did it, how we won and we weren't lucky. It wasn't a fluke."

Miracles are a catchy phrase, but it's still an athletic event, still a sport. They had all the right ingredients great teams have. Mike says that game was a moment in time that embodies everything we live for.

"Seeing the joy that we brought to so many people, the pride that we had as individuals and collectively as a group. Knowing what we did and what we accomplished. It made so many people happy and proud to be an American, and to wave the flag."

It still gives you the chills watching it. And over forty years later, Mike knows it was a big part of the journey to where he is now.

"I wrote about it in my book. The last line is I'm sitting in my backyard, looking around at my cousins and nieces and nephews and my grandkids and saying to myself, 'Boy, I'm glad we won.' That's the big thing. All I've been able to do, the places I've gone, the people I've met, the opportunities I've been given. It's because of that moment. You take great pride in knowing that."

But, he adds, while it's important to get the opportunities, it's what you do with those opportunities that counts.

Having kids and watching them play their sports has been a wonderful experience for Mike, as well as being a grandparent and seeing them grow and find their passions.

"I think that's all part of like the evolution of life. And not many folks have the fortunate moments in their life that I was able to have, so you just enjoy them, and you embrace them and, not every day is a great day. Nobody has a perfect life, but I can clearly look back on the last forty years with a smile on my face knowing I was part of something that was incredible."

And a gold medal is not everything. Mike tells his kids he doesn't want the awards in life to define them. He expects them to be good humans.

Just before we wrap up our conversation I ask the captain of the Miracle on Ice if he ever thought about getting into politics. He laughs and says Ethel Kennedy, widow of Robert F. Kennedy, told him once that he should be in politics, and he said no, he's too honest. Politicians tend to lie, and he thinks he would get himself into trouble. Right now he just wants to play with his grandkids.

"Watch them grow. Play some golf. Hang out with friends. Travel and speak. Enjoy life."

I tell him I'm grateful we had time to speak to one another, and that this winter, I'll be taking my kids to Lake Placid to show them a place where hard work and team spirit can make miracles happen.

8

"The Volume of One More Voice to Be Heard"

The Gymnast vs. the Culture of Abuse

Once I started writing this book and was trying to find other David and Goliath stories to share, I went on social media and asked if anyone had ideas or experiences they felt were similar. Don Orris messaged me right away and told me about his daughter.

Andrea Orris, a gymnast and coach, had posted an Instagram message in support of Simone Biles after Biles had bowed out of one of the competitions at the 2021 Summer Olympics. Miss Biles was one of dozens of women sexually abused by USA Gymnastics doctor Larry Nassar and has been painfully open about the trauma she has been dealing with. Nassar was sentenced to 175 years in prison in 2018 for sexually abusing women and girls as a doctor at Michigan State University and while working for USA Gymnastics.

Many people were supportive of Simone's right to disqualify herself after all she's been through. Others were angry, saying that as a world-class athlete she should have been able to compartmentalize her issues and overcome her anxiety to perform.

Andrea Orris was outraged at those who didn't support Simone's decision, and blasted the critics:

> We are talking about the same girl who was molested by her team doctor throughout her entire childhood and teen years, won the world all-around championship title while passing a kidney stone, put her body through an extra year of training through the pandemic, added so much difficulty to her routines that the judges literally do not know how to properly rate her skills [because] they are so ahead of her time. All of this while maintaining her responsibilities to her endorsement deals, the media, personal relationships, etc. And some people can still honestly say, "Simone Biles is soft. She is a quitter." That girl has endured more trauma by the age of 24 than most people will ever go through in a lifetime.

Andrea's post went viral, even being retweeted by Simone herself.

Her father, Don, said I should cover his daughter's fight as that of someone who has been trying to shine a light on the abuse of young gymnasts and standing up for all the young women who don't have a voice or a platform.

I asked if I could interview him first, because I've always been curious about what a parent goes through after finding out their child has experienced abuse in an industry that seems to be plagued with horrible behavior. Don lives in California and had just seen his daughter Andrea the night before our conversation. He tells me they were discussing all of the latest news that was coming out about the US Gymnastics team, Biles's decision to bow out of several events, and how he and his wife, Chris, will feel sorrow for the rest of their lives for not seeing their own daughter's suffering sooner.

Andrea became interested in gymnastics at a very young age. As she took it more seriously, the dedication and the need to put more hours into it became an even greater demand. Don and Chris enrolled her at the World Olympic Gymnastics Academy in Texas, which is owned and operated by two former Russian gymnasts.

While pursuing her dream of performing at the Olympics, the journey turned into a nightmare. Don says that everything you hear about the sport of gymnastics, all of the horror stories, are the truth. His daughter went through eating disorders, cutting (a form of self-injury where the person makes small cuts to their body), and suicidal thoughts. There was also mental, emotional, and physical abuse in addition to the injuries. Don says they didn't realize any of it was going on because Andrea was brainwashed into not sharing it.

"We got sucked into the whole idea that there are sacrifices that have to be made for her to achieve certain goals. It seems tough, but this is what's going to get her where she needs to go."

Even when things were getting harder, Andrea didn't want to quit or go to another gym. She kept telling her parents that this is what she needed to be doing. They later found out that this kind of thinking was part of the programming being done.

From the ages of eleven to fifteen, Andrea was homeschooled and was in the gym thirty-seven hours a week. When she was sixteen, she went to a private school that catered to athletes with incredibly strict training schedules. But in junior-senior year, she started to shut down.

She finally came to her parents and admitted she was having problems. The eating disorder was creating issues. Andrea had to take a year off from gymnastics because of heart inflammation and enlargement, and that jeopardized her college scholarship. In her freshman year, she was kicked out of school because her grades were so low.

Her coach at Illinois State University, Bob Conkling, tried to get her reinstated and said this was her last chance. Andrea wanted to quit, but she was told that she made the commitment to the scholarship. So, they told her, "Go through the season, and then you can leave." Coach Conkling was one of the good guys trying to help. The environment there was a healthy one, and her decision was to honor her studies and let the sport benefit her.

Don says that's when she started to turn it around. She fought through it and ended up being the Athlete of the Year, and had a very successful collegiate career. But she finally did say, "I need help."

I ask if Andrea confided in anyone. Her siblings? Friends?

Don says he thinks she did tell one of her sisters, but that she was mostly confiding with her teammates because they were going through the same things. Back then, summers in Dallas were hot and their coaches were sending the girls to a high school track in sweat suits with a twenty-pound vest they had to wear. Then they would run several miles on the track.

"That's the kind of stuff we look back on and we just cringe. It just destroyed her, her self-image, and self-worth. That's what leads to the issues."

He still regrets not being able to protect Andrea from all of it. That should have been his number one priority.

"Your first job as a parent is to protect your child. We do what we do based on what we know at the time. I failed miserably when she really, really needed me. And she still says that we had no way of knowing. That we didn't know what was going on. That it's not our fault. But as parents, it's our job to take care of them."

I ask Don about the beautiful Instagram message Andrea wrote in support of Simone Biles. Social media can sometimes be a pretty nasty place, but when it comes to raising your voice to show support, it can be a very powerful thing.

"She knows where she is coming from. She can relate to it. She knows the mental aspect of the sport."

Don says that even twenty years later, Andrea still suffers from something gymnasts sometimes get called the "twisties." It's a basic front flip skill, but if they get the twisties, they can't do it.

"The affliction is equated to a pilot losing the horizon where you become totally disoriented. You don't know where you are. That's what happens when you're in the middle of a two-and-a-half-rotation clip. That's what happened to Simone. Andrea knew what she was experiencing because she has had it happen, too."

Don explains that it's like a baseball player, when all of a sudden the muscle memory is gone and you can't make a simple pitch even though you've been doing it for twenty years. Something gets blocked in your brain and you can't make the simplest of throws because of that blockage. That's the equivalent of what happens with the twisties. The difference is that if you can't make the pitch, you walk the guy or the guy gets a hit off you. But in gymnastics, if you can't do the flip properly, you break your neck.

"And that's the serious nature of this. Andrea could relate to that. Simone Biles is the greatest gymnast probably in the history of the sport. She's doing things that other people can't even think about doing. She redefined the scoring process because they've never seen them done before. And to say she's weak because she came down with this affliction during the Olympics?"

That's why Andrea wrote the message on Instagram. To try to make people realize this is much bigger than an athlete quitting.

The fact that Andrea is a gymnastics coach is quite incredible for someone who spent so many years being abused by the sport. Andrea is trying to change the world by being someone who trains differently, treating her students with respect and kindness. Don says his daughter recognizes the skill and the reward aspects that go into practice, hard work and dedication. It was her ticket to a degree from Illinois State, where she met Coach Conklin. Don says that man saved her life.

"He was the right person at the right time in the right situation, and we owe him her life. And he's just a phenomenal human. We're a spiritual family and believe God has a plan. He put Bob in her life for a reason. And if that purpose is what she was doing now, well, I totally buy that."

Andrea's dad explains that we all become blurred versions of the important people in our life. We take a little bit from all those we meet on our journey. Those individuals help define who we are. Don thinks his daughter took from Bob's teachings, and then remembered the bad guys and how they taught. There was a balance.

"We learn from everybody in life. Sometimes it's really good stuff. We also learn some bad stuff, so that teaches us how to react when those situations repeat themselves. You take the good and the bad. You figure it out."

Don says his daughter's goal is to go back in and do whatever she can to fix this process, exposing the sport for what it is and making it better for the kids.

"God bless her, because at the end of the day, she wants the gymnasts to love the sport, which she also loves so much. But they've got to love it in the right way. She's thirty-three years old, and to this day, we'll get into emotional rants about stuff she went through back when she was fifteen. It never goes away for her. She's carrying this baggage for twenty years now."

I ask Don if this is really the beginning of change in the gymnastics industry. He says it's like shuffling the chairs on the *Titanic*. The sport has to be blown up completely for something different to happen.

"It has to be a total shift in philosophy and mentality. There has to be much more transparency to what's happening. You have to start going into the gyms at the local level and see what's going on. This stuff has to be exposed because we're damaging generations of children."

Around five million kids are registered in the United States for gymnastics every year. That's millions of kids potentially being hurt by this abuse. He gives his daughter tremendous credit as one person trying to fix it.

I tell him it's like a virus, and unfortunately, this kind of behavior from powerful people is everywhere. Perhaps in varying degrees, but it's there. And those who raise red flags and have a platform to do so will hopefully be the iceberg that brings down the ship.

I ask Don, as a parent, what he regrets. He says they should have taken a more forceful approach when they saw situations arise. He and his wife were right there by her side, but there is so much manipulation behind the scenes. They were blind to much of it, but they did tell her something wasn't right: You're depressed. Your grades are falling. At one point they thought Andrea was on drugs because her behavior was so odd and her personality used to be so easygoing, so carefree. They asked if she wanted to change gyms or quit, and Andrea kept saying no.

"We let her make the decision even though we were in a better position to know what was in her best interest. And we should have made the call and gotten her out of there."

What does Don think when he sees his daughter today? Despite all the challenges and pain she's had in the past, Andrea has channeled it into something so wonderful. He gets choked up a bit, understandably, and then explains: "I just love what she's become. All you want to do with your children is provide a better life for them. You want to give them the best possible opportunities. You're always looking to provide your children a pathway to achieve their goals and dreams. She struggled mightily in those teen years, and she fought through it."

Don says he admires his daughter so much because Andrea has come out on the other side of adversity without losing her love of God, her love of life, and the realization that she can make a difference.

Gymnastics can be a very ugly sport, and this mission that she is undertaking is incredibly brave. It's a monumental task that she won't accomplish alone. But Andrea is going to move the needle. Her dad is convinced of that.

I tell Don that I can't wait to talk to his daughter, and to not to be so hard on himself. He's a good dad, and a brave one for sharing his story with me.

• • •

Andrea Orris teaches gymnastics and is a fitness trainer. Her Instagram profile reads: "Here to smash the old gymnastics culture." Andrea is very vocal about changing things in a place she grew up in, and trying to be a force for good in a field filled with evil.

It began with social media, shortly after the release of a Netflix documentary called *Athlete A*, which tells the true story of the gymnasts who came forward and exposed USA Gymnastics doctor Larry Nassar's abuse. It also tells of the brave reporters who exposed USA Gymnastics' culture when there were many powerful forces protecting Nassar. After the film's release, more stories came out about the toxic culture surrounding the sport. Andrea says it opened up a forum to discuss the secrets that no one could talk about before.

Many of the gymnasts had experiences similar to hers, but Andrea's was extreme, and the more she began to expose the abuse, the more people started following her and sharing their journeys. It's also the reason Andrea decided to become a coach. To not only talk about it, but to do something about it.

"I'm just trying to do it from the ground level up and just show others that you can be a coach of a competitive gymnastics team without abusing the kids, and letting them have a say in their life, their sport and in their skills."

I ask Andrea to take me back: When did she first realize that what she was going through wasn't normal?

It started at the gym she belonged to when she was ten or eleven. When she first got there, it was amazing. She was speedily learning many difficult skills. At twelve, she was doing something on the bar called "blind change."

"It's where you swing over the bar and you do a half turn, and then you make a full three sixty around the bar. I accidentally fell over on the wrong side. I didn't make it over. My coach was like, 'Hey, come here, I need to talk to you.'"

Andrea now knows that a normal correction for that mistake would be in her technique, which could be fixed. But her coach told her she fell on the wrong side of the bar because she was gaining weight and her backside was getting bigger. She needed to lose five pounds from her butt.

He said it very nicely, in a helpful tone, and she legitimately thought he was trying to help and was concerned. He told her not to worry, there's ways to fix it.

"Start weighing yourself every day so you know where you're at." Then he said, "When you go home at night for dinner, it's a good thing to go to bed hungry because then you wake up in the morning feeling lighter."

The coach convinced her that when there's a competition, for three nights before, do not eat dinner. She was twelve years old at the time, and it made sense to her, but she knew her parents probably wouldn't agree with that. So she never told them. She would just practice late into the night after dinner.

"It was super easy for me to get away with it if I would just go home, and kind of dirty a plate and pretend I ate, and then put it in the sink. So it looked like I ate. And that's what started years and years of eating disorders."

The comments about her body and needing to lose weight became commonplace. It got to the point where her organs were shutting down because of starvation.

I ask if her parents had any idea. In my conversation with her dad, he admitted that they were in the dark for years. Andrea says it went on for a long time, and that her parents had no idea of the extent of what was happening. They knew she was self-conscious about her body, but didn't know how she was in fact starving herself and a bulimic. At seventeen, though, she was starting to misbehave and get into trouble. They all got into a big argument about something that had nothing to do with gymnastics, and her parents confronted her and asked what was going on. Andrea finally broke down.

"And I was just like, 'Okay: because I'm miserable, because I'm tired, because I don't eat. And when I do, I throw it up. And I just can't live like this anymore.' And I just freaked out and just told them. So they took me to see a specialist to try and get me help."

Andrea was admitted to an inpatient rehab program for her eating disorder. She didn't really want to do it, so when she turned eighteen, she checked herself out.

"I still had some issues," she admits. "It really didn't go away until I went to college, because my coaches there were very nice and very supportive. They talked about eating healthy and how to be a decent athlete, but they never, ever said anything bad about my body."

After a year of college, Andrea started feeling better. She began to realize a lot of this wasn't her fault. She started having all these disorders because her coach had encouraged them. But she could not articulate that at a young age.

"I just thought I was fat, so I needed to do this. It was part of the sport. I thought it was normal because I had no exposure to the outside world—being homeschooled and in the gym eight hours a day. I didn't realize other kids my age were bigger. I was only around people at the gym. They were teeny-tiny and muscular, so those were the only people I saw. I had no understanding of normal people my age, what their size is and what they ate."

Andrea's former coach is still very high-profile in the gymnastics world, and when questioned about his teachings in the past, he shuts down accusations quickly. Andrea says she would just rather move forward and continue to help others instead of dwelling in the past. That coach is still training and producing successful athletes, including Olympic medalists, so people are conveniently ignoring the rumors of abuse.

"It's very complex and deep, how trauma and abuse work," Andrea tells me. "These cycles continue and parents are blinded by wanting their kids to be successful to win medals at any cost."

Andrea says there's no question her coach did some terrible things. Does she want to ruin his life? No. But he is very powerful and has a lot of money and resources. It was also a long time ago. It's hard to go back and relive the pain. But she has teammates who remember what it was like. His abusive techniques have been mentioned by other athletes, in different articles. The eating disorders, the weighing of the gymnasts multiple times a day—the coach will just brush it off and say it was so long ago, and he remembers it differently, saying things like, "Maybe it was just her perception of things." Andrea says it's impossible to try to bring him down. She never specifically says his name when she talks about her past because she's worried about the retaliation. However, people in the community know. It's not hard to put the puzzle together.

Many years ago, when I first came to New York, I was working at a job that was abusive on so many levels. One of my managers would come into the newsroom and give me back massages in front of the others to try to help me "relax." I found it weird, but because it was out in the open, and since no one seemed to think it was odd, I let him do it. A few months later, right before I handed in my resignation, I was in this supervisor's office talking about work-related issues when he got up from his desk, came around, and started giving me a massage and telling me I was "tense." He then put his hands under my jacket and squeezed both of my breasts. It only lasted a few seconds because I pulled away from him, but I will never forget how violated it made me feel. When I wrote *Mostly Sunny* a few years ago I planned to name him. But then I decided not to. Maybe because it was so long ago. He was always a very kind person—this behavior totally shocked me because it was so unlike him. I just didn't have the power to do anything at the time, or anywhere to report him. Like the expression goes: you have to know when to pick your battles. I do know that this experience twenty years ago gives me the strength to fight back now.

Andrea says she can relate so much to this, and says it is her responsibility to tell her story and get the word out about the abuse she has gone through. But she doesn't feel it's her place to punish the coach who hurt that little girl so many years ago. Many people ask her, How do we hold them accountable now? She says that's not her job. She was the athlete. She was the one abused.

"I've done my part by putting it out there. And now it's time for someone above me or someone in the administration to do their job, to hold them responsible and say, 'This is how we're punishing this behavior.' That's not another burden of mine. We've been through enough. Someone else needs to decide what happens next."

I ask Andrea about her Instagram post defending Simone Biles. When she wrote it, she never imagined it would be seen by 17 million people. But she's really glad it got picked up because it started a conversation, and there needs to be more education about the sport and what happens behind the scenes.

"The abuse has been rampant for decades. And even after the whole Nassar scandal, it's still going on. What will bring this to a stop?"

When Simone Biles withdrew from the final individual all-around competition at the Tokyo Olympic Games, in order to focus on her mental health, it felt like an earthquake had happened.

Andrea saw the tweets about Biles being a quitter, and it got her back up. People were commenting that she was lazy, spoiled, narcissistic, or just couldn't finish.

"And I'm like, absolutely not. You guys are mischaracterizing this girl. I just felt a responsibility to defend her as a young athlete, as young gymnasts, because even though I know she's a grown, twenty-four-year-old woman, she's been in this system since she was a baby. And I just want to defend the little girl that was a victim to all of this abuse. They only care about her every four years. And yet they can see this snippet of what she's been through and judge so harshly."

Andrea typed out a brief summary on Instagram of Biles's track record, and what she's overcome.

"I just felt it as a responsibility, as someone who has been trying to shift the culture, that I had to stick up for this girl, for the sport. And still there's people criticizing her. But it is what it is."

Social media can itself be a Goliath. Everyone is a critic with their keyboard, and being anonymous gives people an excuse to be vile. It's especially awful because anyone can spout off their opinions and misinformation, all while we have young people who are so vulnerable growing up and seeing a different kind of abuse in the cyber world.

After losing both of her in-laws in the spring of 2020, when they contracted COVID-19 in separate long-term-care facilities in New York City, Janice became a voice for thousands of families demanding answers and accountability from the former governor of New York and the New York Department of Health.
(Courtesy of Craig Gordon)

Shelly Elkington has been a powerful advocate for opioid reform since her daughter Casey died, following a battle with addiction. Her important crusade keeps issues relevant to families looking for solutions.
(Courtesy of Shelly Elkington)

Adam Curry, known as a pioneer of podcasting, was one of the first to recognize the potential of the internet. His ingenuity and courage helped him overcome many obstacles, including a lawsuit against him by his former employer, MTV.
(Courtesy of Jeremy Poley)

Eric Reed trained the 2022 Kentucky Derby winner, Rich Strike, at the remarkable odds of 81–1. The true-life story of his surprising and thrilling victory inspired an entire nation.
(Courtesy of Janice Dean)

New York assemblyman Ron Kim, from Queens, has been one of the most vocal critics of Andrew Cuomo's handling of nursing homes during the pandemic, despite overwhelming pushback from his own party.
(Courtesy of Ron Kim)

The fall of Andrew Cuomo did not happen overnight. It took the bravery of women like Charlotte Bennett, who revealed to the *New York Times* that the governor had harassed her at the height of the state's COVID-19 pandemic.
(Courtesy of Charlotte Bennett)

Lindsey Boylan, a former aide to Governor Andrew Cuomo, published a lengthy essay accusing the governor of sexual harassment. She was the first whistleblower to come forward in a series of accusations that would eventually lead to the New York attorney general's investigation of Cuomo's disturbing behavior with several women in his administration.
(Courtesy of AP Images)

Mike Eruzione was the captain of the 1980 Winter Olympics United States national team that defeated the Soviet Union in the "Miracle on Ice" game, in which he scored the winning goal. Mike believes it was a team effort that led them to their historic victory.
(Courtesy of Mike Eruzione)

Andrea Orris has been involved in gymnastics since she was a little girl, and wants to be a helpful voice speaking out on behalf of other athletes. She believes the best way to change something is to lead by example.
(Courtesy of Andrea Orris)

Jennifer Sey is a former national gymnast and was Levi's chief marketing officer. She has fought several battles throughout her career to make sure she can speak out about injustices that have affected her and others around her.
(Courtesy of Jennifer Sey and Janice Dean)

Asra Nomani was one of the women leading the "mama bear movement." This diverse group of parents challenged the National School Board Association during an important election year.
(Courtesy of Asra Nomani)

Nurse Arlene Simmons was asked to help during the COVID-19 pandemic in New York in March 2020, when hospitals were overwhelmed with sick patients. With the money she made, Simmons transformed a building in her hometown of Milledgeville, Georgia, into a youth development center.
(Courtesy of Arlene Simmons)

Chef Andrew Gruel is an award-winning executive chef who founded the successful Slapfish Restaurant Group in California. He gained prominence as a relentless critic of arbitrary rules that put business owners at the mercy of hypocritical politicians leading his state.
(Courtesy of Andrew Gruel)

Doctors told Carlla and Brad Detwiler their son might not make it to term, and if he did, he likely would not survive. Despite the odds, even a slight chance of life was worth fighting for.
(Courtesy of Carlla and Brad Detwiler)

Ray Pfeifer was diagnosed with stage 4 kidney cancer after his time down at ground zero following 9/11. With federal benefits on the verge of expiring, Ray, in his wheelchair, led a small contingent to Washington, DC, in 2015 to challenge lawmakers. Long after his death, his brother, Joe Pfeifer, and friend Kenny Specht, a fellow FDNY firefighter, keep Ray's legacy alive.
(Courtesy of Joe Pfeifer and Kenny Specht)

Lieutenant Colonel Scott Mann is a retired Green Beret commander who joined Operation Pineapple Express, a volunteer group of veterans that has rescued over 500 Afghan allies from Afghanistan.
(Courtesy of Scott Mann)

Aaron Hale is a fourteen-year veteran of both the Navy and Army. His unit completed 1,100 counter-IED missions, destroying more than 20,000 pounds of enemy explosives. Despite being blind and deaf after an IED explosion, Aaron lives every day by his personal mantra: "Accept the challenge and overcome the odds."
(Courtesy of AP Images)

On June 3, 1944, twenty-one-year-old Maureen Flavin was the first person to forecast a strong Atlantic storm, which led to the Allies' changing their D-Day plans. Maureen's reading was used to pinpoint the short window of opportunity General Eisenhower needed to launch the invasion, thereby altering the course of the war.
(Courtesy of Vincent Sweeney)

Andrea is very glad that Twitter, Instagram, and Facebook weren't around when she was in college. I mention I had talked to Mike Eruzione about social media and how different his experience would have been in Lake Placid, getting ready to play the Soviets. He's forever grateful he didn't have to deal with that kind of pressure from the world around him. Andrea can relate.

"I was such a mess at that age. If I had the pressure of people commenting on my body and why I wasn't doing well—I couldn't imagine that. Everyone's a critic. The end argument that we're raising a generation of quitters and soft people? Simone Biles is the epitome of a tough, incredible overcomer. They totally mislabeled her and it was so unfair."

Coach Orris is trying to change those attitudes in young girls. She wants each of them to be proud of the body that God gave her. One kid at a time.

I ask what kind of red flags parents need to look for in a situation like Andrea was in. The first sign is when a coach does not want the parents to come to a practice. Another is when the coach is telling the parents what to do, and what's best for their child, instead of the mom and dad deciding themselves.

"When they're trying to control aspects of your life outside of the sport, I think that's a red flag. If you start seeing a general change in behavior or mood from your child, that's a red flag. Instead of blaming it on being a teenager or a bad kid, maybe there's something much deeper behind it."

When she was younger, Andrea says, she was bubbly, silly, and fun. All of a sudden, she was tired all the time. Irrational. She would lash out and cry for no reason. It's hard to identify, but when you start to realize that your kid's personality has changed, it's time to ask what's really wrong. Communication is important, including doing it in a loving and supportive way instead of accusing your son or daughter of acting up.

"Just being like, 'Hey, you know, I've noticed a change in you. I want you to know I love you so much and you can tell me anything.' Work on it together. I read this quote once that stuck with me so much: as a parent, when my kid does something bad, I want their first reaction to be, 'Oh my gosh, I need to go to tell my parents' instead of, 'Oh my gosh, my parents can't find out.'"

That quote hits me especially hard, because I feel like, as a mom, I want my kids to come to me right away. Never worrying that something they went through or did that would make them fearful to tell me what happened. I try to tell my boys every day that they can literally tell me anything. I obviously don't want them doing inappropriate things, or taking part in something that is wrong, but I want them to always feel like we're going to help them, no matter what. We love them regardless. Andrea feels the same way. Especially as a coach of young girls.

"I'm just like, 'Okay: Hey, if you have an injury or a mental block and you can't do your skills that day, come cry to me. Don't hide and cheat on your conditioning to try to get out of it because you think I'll be mad at you. Just tell me and I'm on your side. We're on the same team.'"

I tell Andrea I'm on her team as well. Cheering her on, and knowing she's making a difference, too.

• • •

As I was finishing the final edits on this book and was ready to submit the manuscript, I got a text from Andrea Orris, who wanted to fill me in on what was happening with her former coach, the one who had abused her when she was living in Texas. She said she was ready to name him. It was something she never thought she would do, so I set up another interview to include in her chapter.

Valeri Liukin is a retired gymnast and now a gymnastics coach. He is an Olympic champion and a USA Gymnastics Hall of Fame inductee.

Several gymnasts who had Liukin as a coach have come forward and accused him of shaming them about their weight, leading all of them to develop eating disorders and depression.

In 2022, he was named to head Team USA at an international competition in Germany despite being under investigation for verbally and psychologically abusing athletes, pressuring them to train on broken bones or while sick. Some of the girls were as young as ten.

The last time we spoke, Andrea said Liukin was lying low, and not really on the radar anymore despite still teaching high-level gymnasts at the gym he owned. But recently it came out that he was the front-runner to becoming the next national team coordinator, which in gymnastics is like the number one head coaching position of the United States. Andrea explains that people were confused because after the 2016 Olympics, when the whole Nassar scandal came out, Liukin was named to be the next national team coordinator, but after the Nassar fallout, he accepted a position to lead Team Brazil, and supposedly resigned from USA Gymnastics.

"He publicly said that the reason was because it was just too unstable of a future because of everything going down. It was rumored that he knew there were allegations against him. So, he went to work in another country. After a few years he came back, and there were reports he was supposed to be the next USA team coordinator again."

Andrea and the others she kept in touch with were confused, because everyone on the hiring team knew about this coach and his behavior. A few of the women went public with their allegations to a local newspaper, and Andrea was cited as an anonymous source. After that article was published, USA Gymnastics announced Liukin was no longer in the running. But he is still coaching.

This kind of stuff is infuriating for those who have been harmed by the actions of the abuser, especially if his peers are all aware of his past. Liukin's team, including his wife, are apparently messaging people on social media, telling them to take down their comments and trying to bully them. There's fighting and retaliation in the community.

Andrea says this isn't about a personal vendetta. She has moved on, and is happy with her life, but she just can't understand how people still support him, even while knowing what he is.

"I'm a thirty-three-year-old woman talking about this now, and this happened when I was twelve. I was a little teeny-tiny four-foot-eight, sixty-five-pound girl. And he was telling me I was fat. How is this okay? Defending an abuser just because he didn't do this to you?"

Andrea is still traumatized by what happened to her. She vividly remembers back to when she was just thirteen years old and a local magazine was doing an article featuring the gym she trained at and all her fellow gymnasts. There was a new ice cream shop, and the reporter wanted to have a fun picture showing the girls and their "banana splits."

"The girls were sitting in their split, holding ice cream sundaes, and he lined up my whole team, and in front of everyone told me, 'But girls like you can't eat ice cream, so you're going to go vault.' And he sent me back into the gym and he made me vault for over an hour unsupervised while the rest of my friends did the photo shoot. He did stuff like that all the time."

Andrea to this day wonders why she was the one he singled out. She definitely wasn't the only one, but there was always one girl he treated the worst.

Sometimes when you look at your abuser's past, there are clues to why they are who they are. It doesn't excuse the behavior, but it might help make sense of why it's happening.

"Valeri's childhood was very tough. He was born and raised in Soviet Russia and was sent to train when he was very young. I don't think he had a choice."

His family was very dependent on his success in gymnastics.

"So it was life-changing for his family for him to compete. Even though he was very successful, I'm sorry that he had that pressure on him. But he brought that way of life to the United States. And that's how he treats these little girls in the US. And I'm like: you can't do that here."

She says it would be one thing if Liukin learned from his mistakes, or was reeducated, trained to properly speak to young girls. But that has never happened. He's also never been remorseful or admitted wrongdoing. He just defends himself and pressures others not to say anything.

Andrea says her former coach has another side in front of others, where he is well liked, funny, and friendly. He had a job as a developmental coordinator for younger kids, where he was seeing girls three days every month and on good behavior. They liked him a lot, and there were many defenders whose word would go against the accusations. Right now, he's trying to do everything he can to get those friends to speak louder than the victims.

Andrea can't even watch gymnastics competitions anymore. She knows what goes into building the robot. There's a Dr. Frankenstein behind it.

I ask Andrea what it feels like to finally name her abuser. She was quoted in an article by the *Orange County Register* that reported Liukin's behavior and found women to speak out.

She says that coming forward has been a roller-coaster ride. At first it felt good, with great feedback and support, but now she's hearing that Liukin and his wife are reaching out to former athletes and asking them to write letters on his behalf about the good experiences they had with him.

There's apparently a petition addressed to USA Gymnastics that says something like, "It's a shame that we're letting the opinions of a few women tarnish everything Valeri's done for the United States in the past decades."

Now she's getting mixed messages from friends and former gymnasts, too, saying, "We support you, keep talking, however, he helped me get a college scholarship so I need to write something on his behalf. . . ."

I tell her this reminds me of the Roger Ailes period in my life, when he was first accused by Gretchen Carlson. Team Roger was still winning for a while, with plenty of support within the company, until more of us came forward.

Also, in a lot of ways this feels like our fight with Andrew Cuomo. Goliath always thinks he's right, and the public will often come to his defense without looking at the evidence against him. That's a tough battle, especially when the more popular person is a celebrity or someone who was born with or given a bigger platform than the one who was wronged.

Andrea says she's grateful for the support she's had, especially from the journalists who have been following the stories and amplifying them in the press. There have been complaints about Liukin since as early as 2011, with letters and documents from over ten years. Coming forward is not easy for anyone to do, especially where there's a powerful machine behind the abuser.

I can tell Andrea is feeling disheartened by all of this. She's been fighting for a long time. But I remember back to our first conversation, when she was the one giving me the pep talk about my fight with Cuomo. Sometimes you have to take a rest so that someone else can take over for a bit: take a break mentally and physically until you're ready to try again. In her own way, she's making a big difference in the lives of other little girls in gymnastics by coaching them with kindness and respect.

Andrea says that at first, she never wanted to name Liukin. She just wanted to encourage prevention and awareness.

"I don't want my responsibility to be getting someone out. I don't want to punish anybody and I don't think that should be on my shoulders. But then, when I heard he was telling people I was lying, I was like, okay, I do not have any confidence that things have changed."

We also can't forget that this isn't women he's abusing. They are little girls. Minors. The most vulnerable victims, who don't have the emotional capacity to fight back.

And even though we can sympathize with him, and see that he had a hard childhood, Andrea says it should not excuse this behavior with his athletes.

It shouldn't take eating disorders or mental and emotional manipulation and abuse to make the Olympics. Andrea points out that many people in US Gymnastics still think this method of coaching works. But is it winning if you're destroying people?

"Where are those gold medal gymnasts now? A lot of them are not involved in the profession anymore. Many of them are at home. They're in therapy. They're admitting their trauma. They're talking about how they were training eight-hour days, and now they can't even get out of bed because they're so tired, because they're so depressed. These are our Olympic champions. How did that happen?"

I tell Andrea that I've learned so much writing this book about everyone's battles. Are there any real winners? And when do you decide to stop? Those are questions only David can answer, and there's no right time. Sometimes you never see the results of what you were fighting for. The Andrew Cuomos and Valeri Liukins are always going to try to make a comeback, because that's all they know.

Andrea says that maybe we have to start thinking of it as not necessarily bringing people down, but instead as bringing awareness and educating people.

Maybe after reading this chapter a parent will ask more questions of their kid's coaches, or pay more attention to their moods or emotions. That makes a difference. Just like the butterfly effect: a tiny flap of a butterfly's wings over time can have a broader impact in the atmosphere around us.

Perhaps telling our stories is like planting a seed that will grow into something bigger. But sometimes that takes a lifetime. It's also important to take care of ourselves and our families, and not make the battle all consuming, because that can make us sick, too.

Andrea brings up *Horton Hears a Who*, by Dr. Seuss, and how she thinks it's comparable to our stories:

"I remember it was all these little Who people trapped in this bubble, and in order to get out of it, they all have to scream to be heard. The whole entire neighborhood is screaming, but they still can't hear it. They just need the volume of one more voice to be heard. And when one person at the end gives the tiniest peep, that's what broke the bubble, and they were all heard."

To quote Seuss in the book: "We've GOT to make noises in greater amounts! So open your mouth, lad! For every voice counts!"

Andrea says she is a very spiritual person, and believes she is here for a bigger purpose: "I feel like God gave me this experience to help share it and fix it. I think I'm meant to help make changes and bring awareness. And not let this make me so sad."

And just then, I think of another wonderful Dr. Seuss quote as we say our good-byes and I tell Andrea how proud I am of her.

Unless someone like you cares a whole awful lot,

nothing is going to get better. It's not.

—*Dr. Seuss*, The Lorax

9

"I Stand Behind Everything I Said"

The Children's Advocate vs. Levi's

After talking to Andrea and Don Orris, I decided to watch the Netflix documentary *Athlete A*, which Andrea had referenced in our interview. That program helped her decide to speak out about the abuse in gymnastics.

It was a shocking, infuriating, and eye-opening look at how many brave gymnasts decided to come forward about their horrific experiences in the USA Gymnastics community, and included testimonials from several of the women who helped convict their team doctor, Larry Nassar, as a sex offender.

While I was watching the film, I received a notification on my phone that a woman named Jennifer Sey had followed me on Twitter. I opened it up, and couldn't believe it. Jennifer Sey is a former USA elite gymnast who in 2008 wrote a book called *Chalked Up*, about her experiences in the world of elite gymnastics. She was also the one who initiated the making of *Athlete A* and was one of the producers. I took it as a sign that I needed to reach out for an interview to keep shining a light on this important mission.

Jen says she always dreamed of being a gold medal gymnast competing for the US national team, and then eventually in the Olympics. But she ignored her own physical and mental well-being for years, suffering painful injuries and an eating disorder. She calls it "a competition for perfection." She has been trying for many years to change things for the future of the sport and its athletes.

Our timing was also appropriate because the day before I talked to her, many of the gymnasts who were featured in *Athlete A* testified on Capitol Hill in front of Congress about their shocking, abhorrent experiences with Larry Nassar and the USA Gymnastics cover-up. It was both heartbreaking and empowering to see them sharing their stories along with the anger and crippling anxiety they've endured for years afterward.

I ask Jennifer about how she feels now, seeing some of her hard work finally resonate.

"One of the hardest things wasn't thinking about the abuse but thinking about what they and so many others went through when they first came forward. How they were dismissed and discredited and maligned."

Jen says she was shamed for close to a decade after she wrote her book, and says that for years she was called a liar and an opportunist. It's devastating to continue in the face of something like that.

Having been in touch with many of the gymnasts who came forward (many were featured in *Athlete A*), she knew their stories, but that didn't make it any easier to see them again in front of Congress.

"I kept crying at the drop of a hat. The abuse they faced coming forward, and the abuse they endured. When you finally are able to say, 'This is what happened to me,' and then being dismissed and discredited. What could be in it for any of these young women to come forward and say these things? It's so painful to have to revisit it and then abuse them all over again by calling them liars. I mean, who wants to be known for being a survivor of sexual assault?"

Jennifer admits the silencing is what is so damaging. It prevents others from coming forward. Rachel Denhollander was the first woman to publicly accuse Larry Nasser of sexual assault in August 2016. That took great courage. They called these women sluts and alcoholics; many said they brought it on themselves. But then others started coming forward, one by one. Close to one hundred women had credible stories. But it took years before anyone took them seriously.

I ask Jen where the bravery comes from. She says it probably developed over the years, and the ability to firmly root yourself in the truth even though others claim you're a liar. But it's very hard to do this while having that desire to protect people. You have to block out all the naysayers, and the mean, horrible critics who will try to take you down for doing the right thing. In the world of gymnastics and in other sports, the coaching methodology starts with total obedience, and the silencing of the child.

"And that's on purpose. It goes far beyond sexual abuse.

"The coaches are like your captors, and you believe them. When you grow up and mature and you enter this world, you can't even trust your own perception of what is happening. It's a very dangerous dynamic, and that is why children of abuse, often under abusive relationships, believe it's their fault. That's what their abuser tells them, and to break free from that and connect with your own understanding of the reality is a really difficult process."

Jennifer worries that no meaningful change has come out of this yet. USA Gymnastics wants to think it's just about one bad apple: Nassar. But there was an entire system that supported him and those around him. They chose to look the other way, and sacrificed children in the name of medals and sponsorship dollars.

"It's a culture that is deeply rotten and that doesn't get fixed with testimonies on Capitol Hill. It doesn't get fixed with one horrific case. And I think as I watched it all unfold in real time, I thought this is the inevitable outcome of a culture that disregards children. And I don't think that gets fixed overnight, even with their powerful testimony. The reckoning within the organization hasn't happened. I hope it's a turning point, but culture change is hard and slow."

The Civil Rights Act was passed in 1964, but Jennifer says it doesn't mean racism disappeared overnight. It starts with every coach and in every gym. They have to say they are putting our kids' development and well-being first.

"We need to know what's going on because these kids don't even know it's happening. They are beaten into silence. They don't know what to think or how to feel. It should connect to the broader culture of emotional and physical abuse. So many young women around the world have suffered and didn't understand why—they thought they were the weak ones. That's why they think they struggled in the sport: not because of the way they were treated, but because they failed."

Many victims don't identify the physical and emotional abuse. They are made to believe it's their own personal failure, and that's why they remain silent. We can only hope these women's testimonials are a turning point, but it will take a lot more, starting with leadership on a higher level along with coaches on the ground saying "that's not how we do it." It's also going to take athletes and parents demanding more.

I think of Don Orris and the guilt he will always feel about what he could have done to prevent his daughter's pain. Jen says it's not fair to totally blame the parents, but it's not wrong to be angry at them, either.

"I was mad at my parents for many years. I think it's hard to understand because this is a weird, closed-off culture. Oftentimes, parents aren't even allowed in the gym. The girls didn't have cell phones or cell service. He (Nassar) was the one that stayed on the campus with them as the other adults and coaches went out to eat and went drinking. He was the fox guarding the henhouse."

Jen says it's hard to understand just how little the parents know. The system was designed that way.

Jennifer's career began in 1975. She made her first national team at ten and was training thirty to thirty-five hours a week. Once she made the team, the next step was being in the top ten. The Olympics was now her dream. She begged her parents to let her go to another gym. So when she turned fourteen, she switched to a gym in Allentown, Pennsylvania.

That was closer to home, and she could go there more often. This is where she endured the worst in terms of emotional and physical abuse.

"We were weighed twice a day, and our weight was announced over the loudspeaker. We were fat-shamed constantly while being denied food. Our bags were searched and snacks were taken from our luggage. We were constantly ridiculed and shamed as garbage. You start to internalize that as a kid."

She trained on broken bones. The coach would literally lean on her to ensure that her splits were perfect, so Jennifer ended up with a torn hamstring, which she only recently realized was abusive. All the degrading, the belittling, and shaming: she withstood it for a very long time.

In 1985, at the world championships, Jennifer broke her femur—a very serious injury. She had the cast taken off early so she could continue training.

She describes the pressure coaches would put on doctor to do these things, to take the cast off too early. "I mean, the doctor was in cahoots with these coaches—he came to our gym once a month and brought his little black bag and shot me up with cortisone, and that was considered okay. We were forced to train on major injuries. We had serious eating disorders and were just constantly degraded."

Despite it all, Jen won the national championships in 1986. But she knew she had to walk away.

"I could feel it in myself that I was coming undone. And that's what happened. I did not quit, because no one quits when they've just won national championships, but that next year for me, which was my senior year in high school, was really my undoing. I just I fell apart at the seams."

Along with the eating disorders, there were undiagnosed injuries and constant pain. She was forgetting how to do things. Jennifer was depressed, and even contemplating suicide.

She finally confided in her parents, but they didn't accept it. Her mom and dad felt they had sacrificed so much and wanted her to continue—for just one more year. But one more year when you are in

intense physical pain, eating two hundred calories a day and feeling suicidal? One more year was not possible. She found the courage to stop
just a couple of months before the Olympic trials in 1988. It was a long
road back.

"Walking away was not simple, because I did feel like it was a failure, and I was weak, and that it was on me. I continue to suffer for two
decades after that, from the physical and emotional abuse."

Eventually Jen decided to write about her experiences in her book,
Chalked Up, which was an opportunity to make sense of it all. While
she does make clear that she herself was never sexually abused, she says
that behavior was rampant in gymnastics. If you talked about it, you
were silenced.

"You were told to keep quiet because you don't matter. She doesn't
matter. None of us matters."

Many came out to attack her after she published her memoir. She
had to cancel readings because there were threats against her.

"But as much as that was incredibly tough, it did sort of strengthen
my resolve, because I felt like I had touched a nerve. And while I was
very careful in the way I spoke about it at first, I grew braver with time
and pushed back, because I knew that there was something there."

With every year that passed after writing about her experiences,
Jennifer heard from others who said, "Me, too."

When other victims began coming out with their own stories, people began taking Jennifer more seriously. Suddenly she was telling the
truth, after years of being called a liar.

Her parents also came around and ended up being supportive. They
were ashamed of their behavior, but other parents needed to hear it, too.

I'm fascinated by what made Jen so passionate about helping others
even when she was up against everything, and ostracized. She was David
when no one wanted to take on Goliath. She says she had to do it, because if she didn't, who would?

Jennifer also reminds us that gymnastics is a tremendously dangerous sport. It's not like basketball or tennis or track and field. There are

women who have died. Former gymnasts are now in wheelchairs. If you find yourself disoriented, or emotionally not with it, it can be the most harmful sport in the world. If you land on your head you can forever alter the course of your life. Even the fans don't understand the seriousness.

Jen says it was very courageous what Simone Biles did during the Olympics: deciding it wasn't worth hurting herself, and walking away from some of the competitions.

"For Simone Biles to say no matter what the world is expecting of you, I can't do this; I'm not going to put my life at risk. That's immense courage. It moves you to your core."

Jennifer compares that moment to Kerri Strug's vault in 1996 when she didn't have the choice but to go through with her performance even though she was hurt. Kerri was part of the US women's gymnastics team during the Summer Olympic Games in Atlanta and severely injured her ankle after landing on it from the vault. I remember watching that moment live and then seeing it on the news and in newspapers afterward. You knew how hurt she was: you could see it on her face. Excruciating pain. Yet she went on to perform a second vault—on her injured ankle—and nailed the landing on one foot, before collapsing in pain. She was carried away by her coach, Béla Károlyi, who was the one who told her to keep going.

That performance helped Team USA earn their first gold in women's gymnastics. And we all cheered her on because it was the American Dream.

"As an athlete she was heralded as this incredible champion, and she is, but no one had the right to put that on her. To force her to vault on an ankle that could've been broken. She was lucky she landed on her feet, but it might not have gone that way. She should have been able to protect herself. That doesn't make her any less heroic or less of a champion. But she should not have been put in that position by the people in power. The whole world wanted her to do it. The whole world."

But what if Kerri Strug had said, "No, I can't do it"?

It might have changed the course of the sport.

Jennifer says gymnastics isn't the only place where this kind of torture is happening. It's in a lot of the individual sports that are set up in a weird dynamic and intense relationship between athlete and coach. And it's easier to silence a child than an adult.

I ask how we start changing things. Thank God for the brave women who told their stories on Capitol Hill. But it's not enough.

Jen says it starts with the athletes and the parents demanding that it be different and not tolerating this kind of behavior anymore.

"And I will say, there's some really remarkable coaches out there who always put the kid first or who have been willing to admit that they were wrong and reexamine their methods which were taught to them by being in the sport. It's important that coaches are empowered to stand up and say no to another coach—this is how you do it."

What is encouraging is all those who have spoken out and said this is not okay anymore. That said, there are still parents who will do anything to win, and will turn a blind eye to what may be happening to have their child get into the Olympics. So, it has to be on the parents as well.

I ask Jennifer what she tells people who want to come forward, but are terrified to do so.

"I try to get them to block out the noise and the criticism or the fear of being criticized, let them know I support them. I just try to listen and tell them I believe them. It's the truth. They were abused. That's not subjective. And maybe if I listen and tell them I believe them, then perhaps that's just enough to give them a little more strength to get them through."

• • •

A few months after my interview with Jennifer about her advocacy in the world of gymnastics, she was making headlines for being forced to leave her job of over twenty years with Levi Strauss & Co. The reason? For speaking out about school closures during the COVID-19 pandemic.

After decades of trying to expose what was happening to young gymnasts, and a successful documentary that brought her hard work to light, her employer, an American institution that represented hard work and family values, stood by her and embraced her as a hero. But when she started questioning whether schools should be shut down during COVID, and suggested that these policies could cause the most harm to underprivileged children, opinions about her advocacy began to change.

Speaking up for kids wasn't new for Jennifer, but the topic of discussion was deemed too controversial, and the bosses were getting uncomfortable. Tweets from within the company about getting rid of then president Donald Trump were okay, but wanting schools to open to help the less fortunate kids and those with special needs were not.

Despite the warnings, Jen persisted with her beliefs and even moved her own family from California, where she had lived for three decades, to Denver, Colorado, so her own children could get back into classrooms. It's also important to note that Colorado kept their schools open, and was run by one of the most liberal Democratic governors in the union. Not all of the blue states were in lockstep with each other.

The final nail in her denim coffin came when she went on Laura Ingraham's show on Fox News to talk about why it was important to get kids back to school during a pandemic. The CEO of Levi's said that it was "untenable" for Jen to stay with the company, and that's when she decided to walk out. This was a new Goliath that Jen was going up against, and so I asked to speak with her again.

Looking back on it, she and her husband were horrified about the school closures from the very beginning. If you looked at the data coming out of Italy in February 2020, young people were not being affected as greatly as the elderly. And in the Centers for Disease Control and Prevention's own pre-pandemic playbook, it is written that even in the worst possible circumstances, you should never close schools for more than a couple of weeks. Never.

"I was just baffled by that from the outset. And then seeing [California] Governor Gavin Newsom saying they would be closed for the entirety of the spring. That's when the panic set in for me, because there were no clear markers for what would help us come out of this."

In California, public schools stayed closed for almost two years. What really set Jen on fire was that private schools opened in the fall. The inequity of it was glaring.

She couldn't understand how others couldn't see this. The Democratic Party was historically supposed to care about access to public education, about children, and about equality of opportunity.

I ask if her online advocacy was the stuff that got people really upset. She says most of it did start on Twitter. She naively thought in the beginning that she would just vent and find some like-minded folks on social media, and she did. Many of them were in the medical field and were analyzing data from other countries. There were also many teachers who thought all of this was ridiculous.

By the summer of 2020, Jen started getting calls from work, saying her online activity was problematic. In the fall, her story began getting picked up on the local news, and at rallies she was initiating with other moms. Jen wrote several op-eds as well for newspapers that wanted other opinions.

When Jennifer and her family moved to a different state, she decided to use it as a moment to let others know that she was taking matters into her own hands. The main reason she moved from San Francisco to Denver was to get her kids back into school. A tweet about that went viral and led to more awareness of what Jen was advocating for. Interestingly, very few major media outlets wanted to have her on to talk about what she was doing, even though other families that had the means were also moving out of their cities and towns where public schools were closed.

"Instead, there were teachers talking about death if the kids came back. No one would represent a parent's point of view. And if they did, the narrative consistently represented that moms like us were racist and wanted Black children to die, which is so ludicrous on its face."

Jennifer decided to take her message to Ingraham's show. She knew this might be controversial, but if Ingraham said something that wasn't factually correct, or brought her down a path she wasn't comfortable talking about, she would stand her ground. The interview went well, and Jen was proud of the appearance.

"I stand behind everything I said, and I think honestly, Fox has been the only network to bring on parents and represent the issue fairly."

Jennifer says that appearance enraged people at work, and there were many complaints. Social media was picking up on it, and things began to snowball. There was a consistent drumbeat from management, asking her to think about what she was doing, but Jennifer kept reinforcing that this was an extension of her previous child advocacy work, which Levi's had always supported.

During this time, she submitted a formal proposal to some of her peers asking if the company would take a stand on school closures affecting the poorest families: the kids they were supposed to care about the most. In the past, Levi's had been open about weighing in on societal issues, including equality, gender, and race.

"And I said this is impacting all of those things. It's affecting our workforce and the kids that are being kept from school are disproportionately Black and Latino. So, if we care about these things, we should weigh in and have an impact and ability to influence as one of the biggest companies in San Francisco."

Levi's said no, we don't comment on local issues. But the fact was, many in her company were sending their kids to private schools—which were open. Those folks never had to worry about their own situation because they were "higher on the paycheck food chain."

In October 2020, Jen was promoted from chief marketing officer to president. The social media uproar was never about job performance. There was a conversation about her being the eventual successor to the CEO, but it was couched with a message that her online presence was standing in the way of a promotion.

"I felt they were using that potential job to try to get me to stop. I certainly thought about it, but I couldn't *not* care about this: There were

so many kids being harmed. And by the fall of 2021, management decided to launch an investigation into my social media usage."

She told the bosses they wouldn't find anything in the way of financial entanglements in the past, and she's never committed a crime. But
her tweets would be a bit of a gray area, and that would probably be more
trouble than it was worth. She decided it was time to leave the company.
Jennifer then wrote an essay that appeared in the online publication
Substack with the headline, "Yesterday I Was Levi's Brand President.
I Quit So I Could Be Free. I turned down $1 million severance in ex-
change for my voice."

Jen says she hears from people she used to work with, and many say
that she's missed. She worked there for twenty-three years, and made
lifelong friends. The number of coworkers whom she hasn't heard from
has been upsetting.

I ask if her advocacy about gymnastics laid the foundation for what
she's been fighting for now. When I think of what I've been doing over
the last two years, going up against a powerful leader like Andrew
Cuomo, I would not have the strength to do it without the past experiences against other powerful men. She agrees, and says it helps to
have a partner who is of the same mind. Everything she was feeling and
fighting for was supported by her husband.

"But there was also the perseverance, and the fact that I just believe in my heart of hearts that with time, and it might be ten years,
people would see this as it was: a tragic, unnecessary string of events
that would harm children for very long time. And it was completely unnecessary."

That's not to say that Jennifer never thought people would die from
COVID. We all know it is a deadly virus. The question remains: Is
closing schools going to prevent that?

"And I think the answer is clearly no, but we were unwilling to
accept that. Sadly, this was a tragedy and people were going to die, but
could we protect those more prone to the virus and still keep our kids in
school to keep their development going?"

Both lockdowns and school closures would do nothing to save the vulnerable, and Jennifer says she was lumped in with COVID deniers. But for her, there needs to be a certain acceptance that this was a tragedy, and of course, we must do everything to protect the vulnerable.

"But let's also do everything we can to ensure that we could also protect the development and the future of our kids."

Many tried to paint Jen as a right-wing loon, but in fact she's been a Democrat her whole life. I tell her that that's exactly what the Cuomo administration tried to do with me. Because I worked for Fox and I was fighting against their incredibly awful mandate of putting COVID-infected patients into nursing homes, that made me a nut despite all the science, and losing my husband's parents. Liberal media didn't want to cover my story. And here's the crazy part of it: Wasn't accusing the governor of hiding how deadly the virus was the most democratic thing you could do in 2020?

Jennifer says people would tell her she was never a "real Democrat" even after spending thirty years voting for Dems or Green Party candidates left-of-center, and giving money to those candidates.

"Like to what end? So I could bring this on the world when I turned fifty-three? That yeah, I'm actually a conservative? It's just so ridiculous and nonsensical on its face."

The other tough part of this battle is that sometimes when you fight for something you believe in, it makes you unlikable to others, especially if you're taking a stand that looks to be political. Suddenly you're put in a box. That's really hard to deal with if you've always been someone that has tried to stay away from politics your whole life.

I tell Jennifer that it makes me laugh when people tell me to stick to the weather. Or just *stop talking*! What happened to the "mostly sunny" lady? It's not your brand, they say, to go after the governor of New York. For me, I've tried to say, "Hey, I can be both of those people. The sunny weather lady, but also someone who stands up for thousands of elderly who died in nursing homes."

Jennifer says that someone has to go first and stand in the gap. That's what she stood up for in gymnastics, and for years she was attacked as a liar and a grifter out to make a buck.

Contrary to what some may think, she doesn't love being in this position.

"I have days where I just want to crawl into bed and not face the world. It's really hard."

I agree wholeheartedly. Sometimes I dream of going back to the way it used to be before COVID, when I would just do the weather and take selfies with *Fox & Friends* fans.

But then there's that fire in your belly where you know something's wrong with what's happening around you, and you can't stay quiet any longer because too many bullies have gotten away with it.

Jen says this fight is definitely harder than standing up against USA Gymnastics. She grew up knowing nothing *but* gymnastics and spent ten hours a day training. Seeing that community completely reject her was tough, but it was a much smaller group. The fight she's in right now feels like the whole world is against her. Or at least every Democrat, which is a much bigger population than the gymnastics crowd calling her terrible names.

So where do we go from here? Jennifer says we all have our own path, and for her, she's trying to be part of a conversation about free speech, and open debate.

"If you think about the last two years, there are many people finally admitting that what we did was not the right approach. That lockdowns and school closures caused undue harm. Now, had we allowed other opinions, I think we could have gotten to a very different place."

It's important to provoke and prompt all conversations. That's where Jennifer says she can add value. We have to come out of our corners, disagree, and still respect each other, because otherwise there's not a real viable path forward for us as a country.

People have asked Jennifer if she would be open to being in politics. Right now, she says it's not the time. But that's not to say it might not be an option at some point. She's working on a documentary about the impact of school closures on different states, and once she's done that, maybe another door will open.

I tell her I think that in some ways we have more power doing what we're doing now, because we're not beholden to a party. One of the greatest compliments I've received over these past two years is when others have told me they saw me standing up for what I believed in, and that gave them the courage to do the same.

We have to keep going, so it's helpful when you hear those words of encouragement from others.

I tell Jen how glad I am we found each other through this process. I don't believe it was by accident.

We share many similarities, too. We're both extremely optimistic about the future despite the battles we're up against.

"It would be totally defeatist to think, Well, here's what I believe, but I'm not going to say anything because the machine is against me. There's optimism in believing that courage begets courage and one voice can inspire others to join you, and believing you can make a difference."

The truth will always see the light, and there's always going to be the ones who tell us to stay in our lanes. "Do the weather." That kind of thing. But we have to be able to look back and learn from the past. That's what I do in my profession, the business of predicting the weather is assessing the damage from a storm and finding out what went right and, more important, what went wrong. That way we learn for the next time. From the tragedy of putting infected patients into nursing homes to how we failed our kids by keeping schools closed, we must demand accountability and investigations regardless of political affiliations. I will fully accept the reality as long as we do the work to find out what happened. It should be the same with the origins of the pandemic. We should care where the outbreak began. Because if we choose not to find out, how do we correct it for the future?

The whole Larry Nassar scandal that Jennifer helped bring to light also makes this point. It's not just one horrible man who made this happen: USA Gymnastics wanted to be able to dismiss the whole thing as just one evil pedophile. Now that he's in jail for life, some will say 'it's fine,' and everything goes back to normal. That is false.

"He was able to thrive in a culture for thirty years because they allowed it," Jennifer explains. "It was an environment so emotionally and physically abusive that by the time a young woman or child walked into his office, she was so beaten down that she didn't challenge or question what he was doing."

Jen won't let this to be dismissed as the case of one bad apple. Because then, we create another and another. The atmosphere around him contributed to it, which is why you need the inventory and the correction to make changes for the future. That means an honest reckoning.

So what does she hope to see in gymnastics? Do you want it reformed, or just to go away? She says the bottom line is that she just wants children to be in a safe environment. That's all she has ever wanted. If the system has to be burned to the ground, that's fine. The world won't be worse off for it.

Whether you're talking about COVID or protecting kids from predators, we need to acknowledge the failures of the past and fix them. There has to be a realistic assessment of where we are and what went wrong so that it never happens again. Our kids deserve a world that encourages them to thrive and learn, to be loved and accepted. Because if we don't all agree to do the right thing when it comes to our children, then what kind of world are we raising them to live in?

10

"It's That Protective Instinct. That's What Guides Us."

The Mama Bear vs. the School Board

Even though the pandemic was a really tough time for all of us, there were some silver linings that came out of it. For me, it was quality time with my two boys and my husband. I really enjoyed working from home. If you had told me in 2019 that I would spend more than a year broadcasting from a spare room complete with a green screen and equipment that allowed me to predict the weather from my house, I would have laughed out loud. But it happened in 2020, through the spring of 2021, and then again in the beginning of 2022, when COVID-19 and its variants were "spreading like wildfire" through New York (a phrase former governor Andrew Cuomo famously used to describe what COVID was going to do inside nursing homes, after he personally lit the match).

Being at home and seeing what was happening to our kids during that time was eye-opening. Remote learning took a toll on kids, including my youngest son, Theodore. He found it very difficult to be on an iPad with more than thirty other kids, competing for a microphone with no real personal interaction. There were tears of frustration at first, and then meltdowns and panic attacks. Both of my kids were in public school from the very beginning of their education, and my oldest son, Matthew, was able to handle the new world of distance learning very well, but Theodore could not. I would sit next to my sweet boy for hours to try to help him through the day. I even asked the school principal if she could send me the work week by week and I would try to homeschool him, but that was apparently not allowed. I started consulting with other moms in the neighborhood to try to come up with ideas to help. We were hearing early on about the Catholic schools still making it work and getting their students back to class pretty quickly.

Growing up, I went to public school, and when we moved to Long Island, we sent our boys to the public schools. But during the pandemic it seemed like the private schools were the ones making the effort to try to get kids back as soon as possible, safely. That became a godsend for many parents. We found the money to pay for this magic formula of teachers and students returning to the classrooms, and we have never looked back.

My point to this story is this: suddenly, because of the pandemic, many more parents were paying close attention to what was happening with their children and their schools, because they were frustrated. Some were getting active at their school board meetings and getting vocal about what was being taught in the classroom. For many communities, it was a call to action.

The "mama bear movement" was waking up from a long slumber, and one of the women behind the awakening was no stranger to using her voice, experience, and background to be heard.

Asra Nomani was born in Bombay, India, and came to the United States at the age of four, not knowing any English. She knew early on that journalism was in her blood, when she became the editor of her high school newspaper in Morgantown, West Virginia. Asra continued her passion as a reporter in college, getting her bachelor of arts degree in liberal studies. After graduation she worked at the Reuters news agency while completing her master's degree in international communications.

With an inquisitive mind, Asra began breaking stories right out of college in the world of transportation, politics, and lobbying, starting as a reporter at the *Wall Street Journal*. In 1997, she moved to New York to report for the *Journal*. After the terror attacks of September 11, 2001, she became a correspondent for *Salon* magazine, reporting in Pakistan. During that time, one of her close friends from the *Journal* came to stay at the home she was renting in Karachi. His name was Daniel Pearl. After leaving for an interview one day, he was kidnapped by local militants. They sent a message to the United States saying that if their requests weren't met, Daniel would be killed.

The investigation into his whereabouts consumed international media for weeks. Asra took on one of the biggest challenges of her life: trying to find her friend Danny.

Despite efforts to track down the terrorists, Daniel was beheaded. Weeks later, the terrorists who killed Daniel released video of his brutal murder, and the whole world mourned. His severed head and decomposed body were found cut up into pieces in a shallow grave north of Karachi.

Asra says her kinship with Danny was one of the most sincere friendships of her life. As an immigrant to the United States, she had never really immersed herself in American culture until she became friends with Daniel. Twenty years after his murder, she still replays in her mind moments of their friendship. He still inspires her. His memory is always there.

Asra's role as an activist began when she returned to the United States from Karachi, after Danny's murder, and advocated for a moderate expression of Islam, starting with the rights of women in the Muslim world. In 2003, she challenged rules at her mosque in Morgantown, West Virginia, that forbade women from walking through the front door of the mosque and praying in the main hall, demanding instead that they take a separate back entrance to pray on a secluded balcony.

She encouraged Muslim women to assert themselves in their mosques, and was put on trial to be banished.

Asra received death threats after appearing on television to talk about what she was trying to do in her community. Despite the pushback, however, she forged ahead, co-founding an organization for Muslim women and men that advocated for peace within their religion.

In 2020, I watched Asra take on a new role, one that I believe helped change an election. She was the roaring mama bear standing up for our children in schools.

A group of parents, including Asra, were very vocal in protesting the changes they were seeing in Virginia schools during the pandemic. The mama and papa bears did not like what was being taught to their children so early in their lives.

Parents increasingly saw equal outcomes replace merit-based ones, with standards continually lowered instead of raised. Gifted programs were eliminated, and Asian students were shortchanged for being "white-adjacent." Kids were taught race-based essentialism—all Blacks are like this and all whites are like this—and told it was antiracist instead of racist.

Their advocacy was getting national attention, and some government officials were not pleased.

By the fall of 2021, emails show that the National School Boards Association started working with the White House and the Department of Justice to investigate parents after hearing that they were showing up at meetings and voicing concerns. Their foes had a name for them: domestic terrorists.

As you might imagine, Asra did not react well to that label, especially after all she had done early on in her career as a Muslim woman after the worst terrorist attack on our country in history. So she led the charge and turned up the volume. The night the National School Boards Association released the letter equating parents to "domestic terrorism," Asra picked up art supplies and made shirts that said I AM A MOM NOT

A DOMESTIC TERRORIST. She posted video rebutting the demonization of parents, and it resonated with others across the country.

Asra and I started following each other on social media during the pandemic, and found a lot of common ground in our causes. We were both moms who had had something profound impact our families, and we used our experiences and passions to raise awareness and demand accountability on behalf of others who didn't have a platform.

I reached out to Asra and asked if she would talk to me about what fuels her passion to expose the truth. I wanted to know about all these paths she's walked in her life that have led her on this important journey.

Asra begins by expressing her condolences about my husband's parents. One of her closest friends had family in a nursing home in Washington State at the beginning of the pandemic, when we first heard that the elderly were dying quickly. She understood what I must have been feeling at the time in the spring of 2020: seeing our governor admit COVID patients into nursing homes, defying science. I told her it's been a long, strange trip for me, trying to fight for our loved ones who I feel were wronged. Sometimes I question this strange obsession I have to keep fighting for justice, even after all this time. I don't know what it is about my personality, that no matter what, I will never ever give up.

Asra says she knows exactly what I'm talking about. She traveled to Guantanamo Bay to look one of Daniel Pearl's alleged killers in the eye and had written about her nonstop fight for justice after the murder of her friend and colleague.

"The obsession I felt after my friend Danny's death, to know the truth, comes out of tragedy. There was a grief and a trauma within me that I didn't know how to express, so my intuitive response was to put on my Nancy Drew hat and uncover every detail about what happened. What I learned is that the pain and the grief remain, waiting to be expressed, and so it is important to take the time to express our sorrow— even as we doggedly pursue justice."

She says it starts with wanting to uncover the truth. We are obsessed because that's what it is. It's in the front of your brain. All the time.

I remember Pearl's story unfolding on the news in real time. We all felt like we were personally affected by this horrific nightmare. I ask Asra to reflect on that year, and how that experience shaped the person she is today.

They met in the Washington, DC, bureau of the *Wall Street Journal*. Asra was in her twenties and Danny had just arrived from Atlanta. They became fast friends in the newsroom.

"Danny introduced me to American culture back then. I had been living the life of a good Muslim girl and he was a breath of fresh air."

It was after the 9/11 attacks they both ended up in Pakistan as journalists. Asra was on leave from the *Journal* while Danny was still working for the newspaper. She was renting a home in Karachi and had fallen in love with a handsome young Pakistani financial analyst.

"I had decided I was going to write my great American novel in Karachi and Danny and his wife, Mariane, came to visit," she tells me. "On January 23, 2002, Danny set off for an interview. We were expecting him to be back that evening, but he never returned. He was kidnapped by Muslim extremists. I plunged into an investigation that night to try to find him."

The world found out that Daniel Pearl was kidnapped and brutally murdered five weeks later. Asra says that was the moment that transformed her and the trajectory of her life. She ended up moving to the opinion pages of media outlets to challenge extremism within her faith.

One of the biggest connections Asra had with Daniel was that they were both the product of parents who immigrated to the United States.

"We grew up and learned America. I really, really fell in love with this country. I was able to run and play freely. There was no gender divide that I had inherited in my own culture. My parents raised me with the idea that I could do anything I wanted to do."

Asra says her advocacy now is based on the boundaries being forced upon children. Instead of seeing each other as the same, we are now forced to look at each other with microscopes. The work Asra is doing today as an "accidental activist" in education is challenging these divisions and ideologies that are being forced on kids.

"It comes out of my lived experience. I believe in transcending boundaries with people, and enjoying friendships with people whose narratives are seemingly so different from yours, if we are shallow, but so connected if we understand each other deeply. That's what we have to fight to preserve in the world today."

When I heard about the "mama bears" speaking out about what was happening in schools, I had a visceral reaction. I knew exactly what she was talking about: protecting our cubs at all costs.

Asra says my inner mama bear came out when I was fighting for my husband's parents, who died in New York nursing homes.

"The spirit of the mama bear kicked in for you, and that has driven you all of these months. Just like with my friend Danny Pearl, I couldn't save his life, and you couldn't save the lives of your beloved mother-in-law and father-in-law. But you could fight for truth and justice, trying to save the lives of others."

Asra says it's the maternal instinct, that protective instinct. That is what guides us.

"There's no shame in it and no shame in being fierce and ferocious because it comes from a loving spirit. A caring spirit."

In 2021, the governor's race in Virginia was becoming a big story. Well-known Democrat and former Virginia governor Terry McAuliffe was favored to win again. But something happened in the few months leading up the election that raised hairs on the backs of mama and papa bears in schools.

Parents were seeing disturbing trends in what children were being taught in the classroom, with lessons about sexual orientation and racial issues, and X-rated books in the school libraries. Families wanted more of a say. McAuliffe responded in a September debate, just weeks before ballots were cast. When pressed about the issues families were fighting against, he responded, "Parents shouldn't be telling schools what they should teach."

That statement was the beginning of the end for him.

On election night, with 99 percent of the expected vote tallied, Glenn Youngkin had 50.7 percent of the votes compared with 48.6 percent for McAuliffe, in a state that President Joe Biden had won by 10 percentage points just one year earlier.

The Virginia parents were loud and clear, and Asra was one of the mama bears fighting to get the message across. Education was one of the biggest issues to sway the election and will be a bellwether for other states going forward in 2022 and 2024.

Asra says that these parents were vessels for the message.

"The stars aligned in our lives to be able to advocate for America's children. To tell a story to capture the imagination of folks. We wake up every day with good intention saying, 'How am I going to use these talents for good in the world?' That's what happened for me," she says.

Parents began raising their voices in the summer of 2020, with moms and dads at her son's school (Thomas Jefferson High School for Science and Technology), concerning a "war on merit" that had already been carried out against gifted students in New York City. The proposal in New York was to eliminate gifted-and-talented programs and schools and punish smart kids. Like New York, the students at Asra's son's school are about 70 percent Asian, most of whom come from immigrant families. The new "war on merit" promoted a discrimination against advanced learners, targeting specifically Asian kids.

Word was spreading through the community, and parents of all backgrounds were starting to speak up about what was happening.

"We started organizing meetings and all these parents from different nationalities were showing up. A mom named Yuyan Zhou had stood in front of tanks at Tiananmen Square in 1989 to protest communist repression. She had survived the Cultural Revolution and was now standing in front of the big dome at our school protesting the war on Asian students. We had families step forward that had transcended their own cultural imprint. In many of their experiences back in their home countries, they had to fear being shamed or sent to jail or worse if they challenged authority. They were now courageously standing up and protesting."

Asra believes education became the number one issue in the Virginia race because that was the nerve that educrats and activists pressed.

The Youngkin campaign was smart enough to see this, and seized on the momentum of parents wanting back-to-basics teaching without politics.

Then, in the fall of 2021, the unraveling of the National School Boards Association happened.

For nearly eighty years, the NSBA was a noncontroversial, bipartisan lobbying group. But, after seeing what was going on in Virginia with parents taking part in school board meetings trying to voice their concerns, the president-elect of the NSBA wrote President Biden a letter. He alleged that threatening and aggressive acts against school board members across the country might be a form of "domestic terrorism" and asked for federal law enforcement intervention.

Many of the state chapters of the NSBA pushed back against the lobbying group after seeing the letter, with seventeen states announcing a full departure from the group. The NSBA apologized, stating "there was no justification for some of the language included in the letter."

I bring up Nancy Drew again, that instinct in both of us that lets others know there's more to our causes than meets the eye.

"Yes," she agrees. "It's that innate sense that there's something to uncover. You have to keep peeling back the layers. And we don't even know the extent of the cover-up in both of our cases—yours with your in-laws, mine with the school boards. But in this time of COVID we've faced tragedy. And finding out what goes on in government during a tragedy is quite sick. It's the intersection of money and politics. That's what connects our stories, it's ultimately our motivation from a place of *good* intentions, that will allow us to prevail. I'm confident that this will allow the truth to keep revealing itself."

I know exactly what Asra means by that instinct, and it's more powerful the older I get. If what had happened to Sean's parents, dying in New York nursing homes, had happened twenty years ago, I would not have had the guts or confidence to speak out against the most powerful leader in New York. But with decades of experience seeing bullies and bosses in power behaving terribly, it's like all those versions of myself over the years have finally brought out the beast in me. Now I have kids, and I'm older and wiser. So, look out, world. It's revenge of the moms.

Asra says she thinks our awakening does have something to do with our being witness to a pattern of corruption. We saw this behavior in our twenties and thirties but we were more forgiving and accommodating. Or maybe we needed more data to act.

"Through these life experiences, we're starting to find out what goes behind an organization calling parents 'domestic terrorists.' I worked beside these counterterrorism guys when I was trying to find Danny. I know how they operate. They don't do anything without ten prior approvals. I know there had to be ten people in a room somewhere that decided that parents are now the enemy. Who were those people? You and I have walked the halls of Washington, DC. We know it's someone sitting in the office that has a friend on Pennsylvania Avenue, and they picked up the phone to call in a favor. And then there's someone that has donated money . . . and we connect the dots."

I ask Asra if she had any moments of wanting to give up. Was there a time when she was just too tired to keep fighting? Was there a point where David decided to rest or perhaps find someone else to take on the challenge instead?

Asra says one of her favorite books is *The Alchemist*. There's a line in there that says, "When you want something, the universe conspires in helping you to achieve it."

She believes this to be true, and says she's been doing this kind of work for a very long time.

For twenty years she's been chasing terrorists: looking to find her beloved friend Danny, then trying to find answers about his brutal death. Raising a son as a single parent and being a Muslim feminist who wanted to be treated fairly within her own religion has also been part of her challenging journey.

Asra tells me a story about when her son, Shibli, went off to college. She says that she felt a metaphorical postpartum depression. Feeling lost and sad, she stayed in bed for days, wondering if she had raised him properly. Should she have done things differently? Did the Nancy Drew in her interfere with responsibilities as a parent? She called on her mother for support.

"My mom told me that when I went to Tahlequah, Oklahoma, for science camp at the age of sixteen, away from home for the first time, she cried every night. She had never shared that experience with me because my mother wanted me to be able to grow and experience life and freedom. She was telling me this to give me permission to feel my grief while allowing my son to fly."

Asra also remembers back to the time when she was pregnant, and told her mother she didn't deserve a baby shower because she was unwed. Her mother reminded Asra that she doesn't live in a village somewhere. She's an American. She should never live in shame.

"You know, sometimes I'm a hero, sometimes I'm a zero. It depends on who you're asking, and when. And so, Janice, that was really the moment I became free of shame. My mother lifted my spirits and put me on this course of self-acceptance. I truly believe we were put on this earth for some purpose. And now we're realizing it, and carrying it out."

As we near the end of our conversation, I confide in Asra that over the last few months I've been asked to get into politics by several people. And truth be told, I've thought about it quite a bit. I have a message and the desire to help others. But, if I'm honest with myself, I don't think I could stomach it. Could she see herself doing it someday?

She laughs and said she would be terrible at it because she's so uncompromising.

"I think you have the same type of personality, Janice. We are civil and easy to talk with; we will talk with anyone. We're optimistic, positive people, but we're also uncompromising in our ethics and our values. And you know the deal. It seems you can't really be that way in politics."

I tell her that in some ways I think I could do the job very well, but the other part of me thinks I would be awful. A good friend of mine who has been in government for decades told me it's a blood sport, and not for the faint of heart. That makes me a bit sad, because there needs to be more mama bears like us out there in the political arena.

Asra says we need to figure out how we can best contribute to the world and be unwavering. It's hard to be a whistleblower and a politician at the same time. They both have important roles. We'd be the ones taping all our conversations in the halls of power.

"But we can make things better," she says, "and I do believe all of society is that way. I could never be a community organizer—that's not my skill set. But I can be an organization builder because I work well with other people. And that's why we have created organizations including Coalition for TJ, Army of Parents, Fight for Schools, Independent Women's Network, and scores of other groups around the country. Among this network of parents, I have found a community."

I ask if my mama bear friend is still hopeful. She says she's always been hopeful, but is a realist, too, for example, regarding the influence of money and politics. And the fact that we also have to be skeptical to see who is trying to pull the wool over your eyes.

"I do believe that progress is inevitable, and the human spirit is leading us to truth and justice. We will always have forces of corruption. They will always exist, but our optimism and our fight for truth and justice are critical to maintaining a balance in society."

I ask about gratitude, because even though people have been through the wringer these past few years it's important to find grace and be grateful for even the little things. Waking up and being able to see your kids. Taking a walk around the neighborhood on a sunny, cold morning. I find myself thanking God for that.

Asra says she finds herself looking at an old passport photo she has of Danny Pearl before he lost his life. He was a young man and didn't get to see his baby grow up in the world. Every breath we take is a gift. When she sent her son off to college she really understood the truth of how our children are also a gift, perhaps on loan in our lives for a relatively short period of time.

"There's this other quote that I love that sustains me. It comes from poetry in Sufism, which is the mystical interpretation of Islam. I was just telling it to a friend last night who's going through some tough times. It goes like this: suffering is like acidity to leather. It just makes our souls softer and more beautiful. I think that's so true. Suffering is inevitable in life, but how we manifest the lessons from our difficult times, and allow those lessons to transform us can be magical. Bringing us more depth and understanding and making us even more insightful about others and life. Sharing that wisdom is important, too. We're so lucky we get to do that, you and I."

I tell Asra that there are moments when I want to give up the fight, and then I feel a surge of energy come through me. I feel like some of that is from my in-laws. They are trying to give me signs to keep going another day, and to fight for them and the thousands of others who no longer have a voice.

Asra says she has signs from her friend Danny all the time. She remembers back to a time when she was about to give a big speech and was feeling a bit nervous about it. Right then she saw her phone buzz, and it was Danny's father, Judea Pearl.

"Dr. Pearl is such a good friend to me now, the kind of friendship that I felt with his son. He's such a funny, optimistic man, even though his family have endured so much in this world. I learn a lot from him, and I feel he was with me that moment when I needed him most. I said to myself, 'Oh, of course, Dr. Pearl, you knew that this was a big day for me, and that's why you called.'"

Asra says she is grateful for the things she has and the past that sometimes comes back fleetingly and with purpose. It happened recently when she was wandering the streets of Washington, DC, with her son and his friends. They all went to a comedy club together on Eighteenth

Street NW in the neighborhood of Adams Morgan. She was the chaperone that night because they were all under twenty-one, and she decided to show them around the area she knew so well.

Asra took them outside the building where she and her pal Danny hosted a rooftop party for her thirtieth birthday. She then showed them a picture on her phone that captured the occasion, in which she wore a pink fuchsia gown she had bought for herself as a gift. Daniel was holding the birthday cake. They retraced the footsteps of her friendship with Danny from their days in DC. Asra shared a story about a "Mid-Summer Night's Prom" that she and Danny had thrown after she told him she wasn't allowed to go to her own prom when she was younger. Back then, she wasn't allowed to date or dance with boys.

"And there I was, standing on Eighteenth Street with the photo on my phone and the rooftop above us, the stars glittering overhead, enjoying the evening with our next generation. There stood my son, whose roots are in India. Next to him was his new friend from Saudi Arabia, a student here in the US, just as cool as can be. My son's other friend has ethnicity from Panama, Ghana, and Ethiopia. And the other buddy came from the United Arab Emirates."

This next generation lives in a special place beyond divides and boundaries, in the United States of America.

"That's why I fight, Janice. For them," she says.

I ask about all those who find themselves in the battlefield against Goliath. What advice to you have for those brave enough to try?

"I tell them to think about the one voice that made a difference in their life. Just close your eyes and think about that one voice, and someone will emerge. And then there may be many people who have given you strength once you start reflecting on them."

Asra remembers her English teacher in seventh grade, Mrs. Wendy Alke. One day, Mrs. Alke gave the class journals. That was the day Asra learned to pen ideas of inspiration. Years later, in another journal, Asra wrote what her mother told her: Never to feel shame. And there were so many others who had given her strength and clarity through the years.

The ordinary people who give us extraordinary strength without even knowing it . . . like her friend Danny Pearl.

"We can each be that person to another. That's what I would encourage everyone to do. You don't have to do it on a national stage or speaking to an entire country. It's important to connect with your neighbor, a child, your parent, your friend, from a place of insight and wisdom, with kindness and compassion. This comes from a place beyond parenting and gender or place of birth. I want people to embrace their inner spirit so they can share it with others. That spirit comes from a place of humanity . . .

"And we've all got that."

11

"I Needed to Do Something That Was Long-Lasting"
The Nurse vs. COVID-19

*And once the storm is over, you won't remember how
you made it through, how you managed to survive. You
won't even be sure, whether the storm is really over. But
one thing is certain. When you come out of the storm,
you won't be the same person who walked in.*

—*Haruki Murakami*, Kafka on the Shore

I think about this quote a lot, especially after all we've all been through during the pandemic. It's important to remember what our first responders and frontline workers sacrificed in the early stages of COVID-19. They were the ones who, despite the unknown and terrifying nature of this illness, still had to go into work, risk their lives and health to do their jobs, while the rest of us could stay home.

COVID-19 became the Goliath we all were facing and had no idea how to defeat.

In March 2020, New York became the epicenter of the pandemic, with almost ten times more cases than any other state. Hospitals were overrun and there was a call put out through the nursing community for assistance from other states. Governor Cuomo called on health care workers across the country to travel to New York, which at that time accounted for nearly a quarter of all cases in the United States. Former New York City mayor Bill de Blasio said the city needed an additional 45,000 medical personnel to help with the overflow of patients.

Travel nurses like Arlene Simmons from Milledgeville, Georgia, make up a small portion of the 3.8 million registered nurses in the United States, but they were crucial when we needed them here in New York during the pandemic. She never imagined how much of a toll the experience would take on her both mentally and physically.

I got to talk to the woman many called "America's nurse."

Arlene has been a nurse for more than two decades, but she always knew she would do something in her life to help others.

"When I was younger, I thought I would be a psychiatrist. I remember as far back as ten years old, wanting to help others. We don't have any doctors or nurses in our family, but I love to speak to people and assist with things. When I looked into education, nursing was the most interesting and that's what I chose."

Arlene has lived in Atlanta for thirteen years. She's seen a lot in her career, but being in New York as the worst of the pandemic was unfolding was unlike anything she had ever experienced before. It was life-changing. She had a lot going on already in her life, with kids, work, and a grandchild on the way. But she kept thinking about all those other nurses who were probably tired, working nonstop, without a break. Arlene was no stranger to going to other states to help out during disasters, like Hurricane Harvey in Texas back in 2017, when catastrophic floods displaced more than thirty thousand people. Hundreds of nurses flew into Houston to provide relief to storm-weary medical staff over several days. Arlene says it's important work for her, and she takes pride in helping others.

After her daughter had a baby on April 1, Arlene says, she sat with him, studied every hair on his head, touched every finger and toe to keep him in her memory. She prayed on the decision, and the following week packed her bags and headed for New York. She was gone for two months that she says felt like two lifetimes. When I ask her to explain, Arlene admits it's hard to put the experience into words. She gets choked up when she tries.

"Every day I would go in," she recalls, "and there would be family members outside with pictures begging for information about their loved ones because they couldn't come in."

People would ask Arlene to remember names and try to find out about their loved ones. Many would come back day after day asking for information. It was heartbreaking. The nurses' shifts were never-ending, and without organization. Arlene uses the words "chaos" and "pandemonium" to describe what was happening inside the hospital.

"So many staff members, so many volunteers were just running around. No one had an actual schedule. We were all just going as long as we could go. Nurses were sleeping in the hallway, tired, worn out. Many would crawl into corners crying, you know it was just . . . it was very emotional to see my coworkers that way, and then we had so many patients in the hallway on the gurneys needing assistance."

It was well reported that hospitals were not getting access to the supplies they needed. Arlene says staff used the same masks over and over again. That was against CDC guidelines, but they just didn't have enough to go around.

"We had to do what we had to do. Nurses were fainting because of exhaustion. Many gave up after working days on end. They would just walk out of a hospital room, and then out of the building."

Arlene would see them leave and never come back. I can tell it's difficult for her to get through the interview. She has to stop a moment to catch her breath. Tears come easily. The biggest sadness she has is knowing that some of the patients couldn't get the assistance they needed. It was so overwhelming.

"I couldn't take care of many of these patients. They would drown in their own fluids. Their lungs just failed. We didn't have the means to get oxygen to them."

Something that would be so simple in any other time became impossible under these extraordinary circumstances.

"I keep thinking if I could've just had a suction to get into the back of their throats. A lot of them had pneumonia in their lungs. . . ."

I try to reassure her that it wasn't her fault. She was doing the best she could. Arlene says she now suffers from post-traumatic stress disorder from all those weeks in New York hospitals when people had no idea what COVID was or how to treat it.

At night when she would get back to her room, Arlene would still hear the IV pumps, the code blue alerts, the patients' struggles to breathe. It was hard for her and others to get emotional help for what they were dealing with day in and day out, without a break.

Arlene believes what she is going through now is very similar to what soldiers experience after being at war. She worked weeks with no break and no one to really talk to. There was never any downtime. She wanted to help, but in fact felt helpless.

"I wanted the connection with the nurses, but we were all overwhelmed and exhausted. When that broke down, it broke me down."

Deaths were happening regularly. Reports of body bags piling up were not exaggerations. There was nowhere to put people.

"When you have four people die before lunch, every single day, that's a lot. You usually don't get something like that in a full year."

Arlene tries to remember what it was like in the hospital, but it's all a blur. The patients all look the same. Their eyes are glassy. The lack of oxygen causes the eyes to be discolored and odd. Like zombies. They all had that appearance, and everyone had that same look before they died.

Reflecting back on her two decades in nursing, Arlene remembers the first person who passed away in her care. That had a tremendous impact on her. He had a heart attack, and she did CPR, but she couldn't save him.

"You never forget that. It's been almost twenty years, and I can remember every detail about this person and what happened, his diagnosis and everything about it. I still remember the events of that day, doing those chest compressions, everything. But in New York, I don't have that recollection of actual procedures on a certain person. Everybody looked the same, and they couldn't breathe."

When she did have a few hours off, she would drive around the city. It was like a ghost town; the streets were completely empty. She would park her car and walk while taking pictures of landmarks and statues. Now when she scrolls through those photos, she can't remember being there. It was like a dream. Or a nightmare.

"I think my brain is suppressing a lot of that stuff. And I'm hoping it doesn't come back, in a negative way, you know what I mean? Because I'm trying to move forward."

I tell Arlene that one of the things I think I've blocked from my memory is that we couldn't see our loved ones before they died. Sean's dad died alone in the nursing home. We didn't even know how long he was sick. We were unable to visit because of the quarantine, and the updates weren't coming as regularly as we wanted. One morning there was a call from a doctor saying Sean's father wasn't feeling well and was running a fever. Three hours later Mickey was dead. After Sean's mom, Dee, was transported to the hospital from her assisted living residence, there were no visitors allowed. We got updates about her deterioration, and then a call stating that she had died. The only time Sean was told he could visit her was after her death, and it would be in a different room, to look at her body through a glass window. That's really hard to think about. There were many nights I prayed for a kind nurse like Arlene to be by their side as they took their last breath. I thanked Arlene for being an angel for all those family members like mine who weren't with their loved ones during their final days, but prayed for someone like her to be close by.

Back in March and April of 2020, no one had any idea what was happening with the virus or how transmissible it was. No phones or iPads could be brought into the hospitals, for fear of germs on surfaces.

"You couldn't have anything that could carry the virus back to your room or car. I would eat in the hall or the stairwells, the fire escapes. Even drinking a bottle of water was difficult to do."

Arlene would get dehydrated because she was afraid to take her protective clothing or mask off. There was the uncertainty of what you could and could not do safely.

She found herself counting down the days, hours, and minutes when she could go back to Georgia. But when she did return, it didn't feel like home. There was still a feeling of dread, and terror that she might be bringing the sickness with her. Everything she brought to New York was thrown into the trash, and during the fourteen-day quarantine from her family, she couldn't hug or see anyone even though she was desperate for personal contact.

Arlene came down with symptoms of what seemed like COVID at the end of April. She went to bed with chills and could hardly get out of bed the next day.

Her body was aching, especially her knees and back. She couldn't walk and had to hold on to things to stand up. Dizzy, and knowing something wasn't right, she took Tylenol and ibuprofen to help with the aches but they wouldn't go away. Arlene drove out to a COVID testing site, where she came up negative, but was told she could be getting sick with SARS-CoV-2, and to be mindful of her symptoms.

Arlene turned to God and prayed for good health. She reminded Him that she was put on this earth to help, and asked the Lord to please let her keep serving others.

The next day, she says, her symptoms were gone.

"When I got up and braced myself, I felt absolutely nothing. Every symptom that I had was gone. And I just stood there and did a little dance, because I could move my legs, and I didn't have any of the issues I had the day before. And I cried, 'Oh, my God, You saved me.'"

I ask if Arlene had told anyone she was symptomatic. She says she was too afraid to because she didn't want anyone to worry. She just prayed that things would work out and the Good Lord would show her the way.

"It had to be divine intervention. That's the only thing I can think of because I prayed so hard, that night before asking God, please do not allow me to go downhill. You didn't bring me here to get COVID and have to bow out like that. So I know it had to be God's will. It had to be."

Today, after the storm, Arlene says she takes nothing for granted: "There was a different mind-set I came to after that. It was: you have one life; let's not waste it. Nothing was the same."

I ask Arlene, when she looks back, does she wonder why she was put on this path? Is this a calling?

She believes she was sent to New York for a reason. And despite all that she's been through, Arlene would still do it again. If she got the request, even knowing how hard it was, she would accept the challenge.

"I would do it again because I believe I was supposed to be there, and I was supposed to be there because the other nurses could not. And I could. I was called on to help somebody, you know what I mean?"

After Arlene arrived back in Georgia and had time to heal and rest, she decided to do some good with the money she earned working in New York.

"I looked into my soul. I searched and I asked God for a clarification on what I should do next. Where is this leading me? Let me take a step back. I focused on a path toward the future. A whole new mind-set from what I had been through. What was important in my life? What were my priorities? I needed to do something that was long-lasting, and something that will change more lives."

Arlene says her heart is with the youth. She has done philanthropy work in her community for many years, and she felt that's what her serving heart was meant to do. There were underprivileged children and crime where she grew up, so a youth center might encourage kids to get off the streets and socialize in a safe place. She found a facility and began renovating. It kept her centered and focused on doing something good.

"So while I was getting the center ready and cleaned up, I realized this was therapy for me. I decided to take my time instead of rushing. I painted and then I would sweep, and design the rooms. And during those weeks I was helping myself, and I didn't even realize it until sometime afterward. I was helping myself heal."

At Christmas, Arlene took part in one of the largest Christmas drives in Georgia, something she does every year. She says COVID didn't stop their motivation to help underprivileged kids. They made it a drive-through so people could socially distance and pick up gifts in their cars.

When COVID testing became more available, Arlene helped with drive-through locations around her area. She joined "vaccinate America" to become part of the solution, trying to end the virus, and also helped put together one of the nation's first mass vaccination sites. That was a proud moment, too. Even though it brought back memories of how tough those first few months were in New York, getting involved, helping combat the disease became therapeutic and another big step forward.

When she looks back at the last few years of her life, Arlene believes all of this is connected. But the outcome of where we all are depends on the actions we take. If you do what is in your heart, everything will make more sense. Even if the beginning was incredibly difficult to get through. Sometimes the most beautiful destinations come from the hardest voyage.

I ask where Arlene's courage comes from. Can she trace it back to her childhood or something she went through?

"I think I am a courageous person, but I didn't realize how courageous until COVID. I come from a long line of strong individuals, in the face of adversity. We grew up poor. When I say poor, I mean disadvantaged. We didn't have some of the things that we needed. So I saw strong people, who could continue on even when they're facing adversity. I also pray and believe if I do right by people that will come back."

I ask what advice she has for someone who is struggling right now. Someone who wants to do something to make a difference but is having a hard time choosing the right path.

"Fear is in all of us, and on the other side of fear, there's possibilities and there's accomplishments. So if you just keep walking through that, you'll eventually get to where you're going. If you don't walk, you can't get there. I've told people many times, if you do not take that first step, how are you going to get to your destination? If you don't move, nothing will happen."

I ask Arlene if one person can change the world.

"Yes. One person can help change the world. But to me, it's the 'trickle.' You can do something that makes the next person do something, too. It happened with me in New York. Other nurses reached out after they heard my story and said, 'I want to do that, too. You inspired me.'"

Arlene says it's important to do what your heart tells you.

"So many nurses did what I did, and that's the trickle effect. I didn't even know I made a difference or that people were watching. It went that deep, you know?"

The tragedy of the pandemic blossomed into a blessing for the kids in Arlene's Georgia community. She continues to work at her youth development center, and was able to start a foster-care program for children before and after school if they need a place to stay. Her serving heart has found its way home, for the time being.

Before we end our conversation, Arlene tells me she's grateful for this interview and happy that I wanted to share her story. She says the decision to go to New York during a once-in-a-lifetime pandemic was a simple one.

"I go where I am needed."

Because that's who Arlene Simmons is.

12

"You Help Everyone You Can"

The Chef vs. COVID Lockdowns

While I was fighting for answers and accountability from New York's governor Andrew Cuomo in the middle of the pandemic, Chef Andrew Gruel was doing the same in California with his governor, Gavin Newsom.

Andrew was the founder and executive chef of Slapfish, an award-winning food truck that he turned into a successful restaurant chain based out of Huntington Beach, California.

Chef Gruel has worked in restaurants off and on his whole life. Though he studied philosophy in school, he spent more time working in the food industry than going to class. He knew pretty early on that it would be his profession and his passion.

In 2020, Andrew had no idea he would be the spokesperson on behalf of businesses, specifically restaurants, that were struggling during COVID. He decided to post a video on social media in December 2020 listing all the ways in which the ban on outdoor dining in his area made no scientific or economic sense.

His video was viewed more than 800,000 times, and he doesn't mince words: "Here's the situation: Do we take the pandemic seriously? Of course we do. Am I saying we shouldn't close outdoor dining? Yes, I am.

"At every single juncture along the way here, from the beginning shutdown to today, we've listened to all of the advice from our government officials, only to be shut down over and over and over again, and then not compensated for the elements that we put in place in our businesses in order to protect our customers.

"We shut down indoor dining. No problem. I got a warehouse full of Plexiglas right now. Okay? We went outdoors. All right? Now that's getting shut down. I just put thousands of dollars into outdoor heaters.

"There is zero scientific evidence that proves that outdoor dining is contributing to a rise in cases related to this."

Andrew didn't stop there. He called out the hypocrisy of government officials, including Governor Newsom, for not following their own rules. Newsom was caught dining at the French Laundry, a very fancy restaurant, with others in close proximity and with no mask to be seen.

Even the *New York Times* took notice: "Flouting his own guidelines and exhortations to Californians to avoid socializing, Governor Newsom and his wife joined a birthday celebration for a friend—and prominent lobbyist—at the luxurious French Laundry restaurant in the Napa Valley. It is hard to say which was more astounding, the hypocrisy or the hubris."

Andrew was not impressed: "We're being told to do one thing, when the people telling us to do that aren't even following their own rules. Chef Gruel followed the science, and believed there was no clear evidence that eating outdoors led to a spike in coronavirus cases.

"You see the hypocrisy. Really think about this here: no one is following their own rules. How serious can those rules be if they're not following their own mandate?"

When I saw what Andrew was doing on his own, speaking up on behalf of restaurant owners, and those who were struggling to try to keep their businesses afloat, I saw a kindred spirit. He was a good example of one person raising awareness, risking his livelihood and reputation to ask for accountability. We as citizens have to speak up, and as Andrew and I both learned, we do have the power to accomplish something.

At the beginning, Chef Gruel had the same goal as everyone else.

"We wanted the 'we're all in this together' cliché and we want to make sure we can do everything humanly possible to not just help slow the spread, but to also help the community and to contribute and give back and be a part of this."

Andrew and his wife, Lauren, have always lent a hand, within their industry, but then when they started seeing data about how the pandemic was specifically tough on businesses, that's when they started speaking up. This was an opportunity to point out that being in the restaurant industry, you are inherently trained to create safe and sanitary conditions, and to understand the health protocols of cross-contamination and even social distancing before we all had to do it ourselves during a pandemic. The thing that made the Gruels' blood boil was restaurants like theirs being shut down over and over again while big businesses continued to have their doors open.

Many companies were getting rich off the backs of small businesses. It was overt and in your face.

"It was so apparent that the governments, especially the local and the state governments here in California, were picking winners and losers. There was a certain point where we were keeping all of our employees on board and we got rejected through the PPE phase. In the very beginning, we lost one of the restaurants that my wife and I had just put all of our money into. We lost that right off the bat. Eight weeks after we lost that restaurant, I get a bill in the mail for all the sales tax. And then I get bills for all the other restaurants from the state of California Tourism Board. I couldn't fight back, and originally they had said they were going to relieve us in terms of a lot of the sales tax. And then when we called the Board of Equalization, they were like, 'We don't know what you're talking about.' There was just no relief."

Every program available to try to help them was delayed. Andrew was watching businesses like his drop like flies because people couldn't even make it to the point where they were able to receive funds. Then they would be completely forgotten by the government.

"So for me, it culminated when they shut down outdoor dining, and I said, 'Whoa, this is just absolutely absurd. Four hundred meters up the road, I can go into Wal-Mart and pile on top of each other, not wear a mask while eating Burger King inside the Wal-Mart. Something's got to change here.'"

That's when Andrew got loud and started speaking out. He continued to serve food outdoors despite restrictions because he firmly believed that it was safe to do so.

Hearing Andrew talking about this reminds me of when our families couldn't have funerals or wakes for our loved ones. We couldn't see them when they were sick in the hospital or in their nursing homes. Yet we turned on the TV and watched thousands of people taking part in protests crammed altogether. It was infuriating. The politicians get to decide what's more important than your dying family.

"We were watching. It was right in our faces, and it was promoted, and that was the point. And it was then you drew the comparison of, well, what I'm doing is more important than what you're doing."

Andrew watched employees get completely taken over by debt and depression. He and his wife tried to help as many as they could by starting a fund in December 2020. He was starting to see news articles about misappropriated unemployment funds that were being distributed to fraudsters. When the government shut down outdoor dining for the fourth or fifth time in California, that was the final straw for a lot of restaurants.

"You watched thousands of employees before the holidays effectively get thrown out on the street. And then they couldn't even apply for unemployment benefits. The government's nuisance response was, well, deal with it. It's a public health crisis. We'll be able to get the unemployment benefits when the federal government refreshes our coffers sometime in 2022."

Andrew and Lauren tried to assist those who needed it the most. People started reaching out to them, saying they couldn't pay rent, electricity, or for their kids Christmas gifts.

That's when the Gruels started a fund to help raise money and distribute it to unemployed restaurant workers. They raised about $450,000, and they are still helping others to this day.

"I remember driving around two days before Christmas with my family of four, handing out checks to landlords and paying people's rent and electric bills and giving people cash to buy Christmas gifts for their children. I mean, that was how we spent our holidays. And still the government came after me, no matter what we did to try and help. I was the enemy for speaking out against Newsom."

I tell Andrew that my main reason for writing this book is to find out what motivates people to keep going even when they have the machine going against them. What makes you get up in the morning and say you have to do this?

He says it's hard to ignore when it's right in front of you. Right in your own backyard.

"Originally, we were just trying to help in Southern California. And then we started getting inquiries from a lot stricter states like in New York City, which had the same thing happen in their restaurant industry. Other states also reached out. We had thousands of applications with people telling their stories. My wife and I had to call for references to see if they were real. And they were."

Andrew says what it boils down to is a story about the government we elect not being able to help the people it represents. Instead we see examples of corrupt leaders spreading messages they themselves need in order to spread their own propaganda and help their buddies. Gruel and his wife, on the other hand, were stepping in to help their fellow business owners. That's what kept them going.

"Every single day we've got to get to these fifty applicants—then suddenly it's seventy-five applicants. How can we do it? Between my wife and myself, we were doing all of this while simultaneously running eight restaurants in Southern California with another twenty franchisees around the country. It was certainly a busy time of the year."

I ask where this comes from, this urge to help others, and that fire for the fight? He says being from New Jersey is part of it. We both get a good laugh out of that.

"It just comes from my upbringing. I grew up with two parents who worked really, really hard. They came from nothing. And I grew up in a family where they were going to work at seven in the morning, coming home at eleven at night and still teaching us principles."

Faith is another thing Andrew believes has helped shaped him. He was raised Catholic and was an altar boy growing up, learning to help others and spread kindness; that's where he says it originates.

The Gruels try to teach that attitude to their kids every day. They have four kids, ages one to eleven.

"You think they wanted to get into a car on Christmas Eve and drive around Southern California? We had just had a baby, our fourth child, and it was crazy. But hopefully they'll see that and they'll remember it when they're older and pass it on to their family."

I ask Andrew about his wife, Lauren, his partner in all of this. It was very tough on my husband, Sean, when I was advocating on behalf of his deceased parents. He's a very private person, and the last thing he wanted was this incredibly tragic story being broadcast everywhere. But I'm so glad he finally gave me his blessing to share what was going on, because had he not, I'm not sure the story would have gotten any real attention. There's a moment when you ask your spouse to trust in your instincts. It requires great faith in the other person.

"It's scary because you start to think we're going to lose it all. This is how you get canceled. We were having conversations every night. Do we back off? Do we push forward? Obviously, our language and our rhetoric weren't targeting anything or anyone in a hurtful or hateful manner. It was just, hey, here's the deal. But when you call out the situation and somebody is obsessed with the policy that supports the negative scenario, they feel personally targeted by that."

The Gruels got hate mail and threats, and people were following them. Strangers sat outside their restaurants and took pictures of them talking to guests outside without masks. Those photos would get posted on social media. Facebook groups would attack their family as COVID deniers, which they were not. It got scary and they started asking themselves, at what cost do they continue to speak out?

"The pandemic certainly polarized groups of people. It became very political and it still is political. And you can put a broad stroke across each side of this from a political perspective. But there are many in the middle who disagree with the ways in which things were being managed, and who might not agree with each other on a lot of other issues."

This had nothing to do with politics, even though many wanted to put Andrew into a Trump-supporter box. But he says that what many don't want to admit is that a significant portion of the restaurant industry is undocumented workers. They were completely ignored and left behind because they were afraid to get unemployment benefits. Those folks all lost their jobs.

"And regardless of what you feel about the issue of comprehensive immigration reform, when it's December 24 and it's a family, and they're about to lose everything, you don't think about if they are undocumented or not. You help everybody you can."

Those are the stories that help stop the division and make everybody realize it really is about neighbors helping neighbors.

I ask Andrew if he remembers a low point in all of this. Did he look at his wife and say, "I can't do this anymore. It's too much"? He says it came a few days after his viral tirade online about the outdoor dining ban. They got served a full investigation by the office of Gavin Newsome. It was a labor inquiry on some of the businesses and management companies he holds equity in. He says it was clearly a political move and the matter is still under investigation.

His wife, Lauren, was subpoenaed and there were demands about bank records. The Gruels' attorneys have asked what's driving all of this, and the investigators won't say. Andrew says they have never had a single labor law violation. They pay employees twenty to twenty-five dollars an hour entry-level with full benefits. Everyone got unlimited time off when they were sick. There was no internal spread, and the government wasn't helping one bit.

"So from the perspective of being a good employer, we are on that pedestal and yet suddenly this political inquisition gets dropped on us. And my wife was scared. When you get the subpoena from the government for bank records and employee records and she's named on it, that was frightening. We still have to spend thousands and thousands of dollars on attorneys to fight this. And there's not going to be any recourse. We're not going to get any of that money back. It's just the way in which they try and wrap you up in bureaucratic red tape if you ever speak out against the system."

I mention the story that got picked up by most news organizations during the pandemic, of Newsom going out to the French Laundry with friends. It was indoors, and they were close together with no masks. The governor was breaking all the rules he himself had put into place. How did that feel to Andrew?

He says that when the images first emerged and Newsom made his apology, he accepted it. It sounded like he was outdoors under a tent, and the event was preplanned. But then, when Newsom's excuse turned out to be a lie, it was a double-down effect. It was the straw that broke the camel's back.

"You lose all respect; that, in and of itself to me, should have been a disqualifying event right then and there. And I've said that all along, any political leader who breaks their own rules should immediately be thrown out of office. That's how serious it is, in my opinion."

And it's not just a political mistake. We're seeing it all the time— those in power not listening to the orders they make. There seems to be a different set of rules for the politicians.

The question now is, Where do we go from here? What do we do with those who were supposed to represent us and protect us? These officials we elected to office are now feeling like an enemy.

Andrew says there's a level of negligence with the way in which they're planning policy that can affect your business, your life, and your family that requires you to be proactive and put measures and protections in place for yourself.

"So that's where we go from this. We're not going to fundamentally change the system overnight, but what we can do is defend ourselves and be a lot more pragmatic with each decision that we make, by not being naive to the fact that they're not there to make the right decisions for us, but only for themselves and their cronies."

For Chef Gruel, what made this fight so worth it is the families and businesses that they have helped. That kindness caused a ripple effect through the community. They gave six thousand dollars to two gentlemen who owned a food truck, and who used that to keep themselves alive. Then that small food truck ended up re-raising the money and giving it back to the fund. That's what keeps Andrew and his wife going.

Many people have asked me: If Andrew Cuomo ever asked to meet me, would I go, and what would I say? It's hard for me to answer that question because I really don't think he would even entertain that possibility. He should have met with families who lost their loved ones in the very beginning, but he didn't. He lied, denied, and blamed everyone else. I ask Andrew if he would meet Governor Newsom if he had the chance.

He says he would, and would want it to take place at his own restaurant: "Let's talk over real food, not French Laundry, and understand how he makes his decisions. Sometimes when you're insulated by a lot of yes-men and you're hidden from the reality of the situation, it's easy to just think, I had to make really tough decisions. And a lot of times they convince themselves of that. So I think it's important that they look at the consequences of the choices that were made. And then you understand the hypocrisy."

Andrew and I have something in common: we never set out to be political in our professions. But because something affected us personally, and we decided to raise awareness on behalf of others, we were thrust into the political arena. It has opened our eyes to things that were never on our radar before: the people who are elected to lead us. I want to see people get into politics for the right reasons—not because of their name or extreme wealth or connections. It's more worthy if elected officials change things on behalf of others because they themselves have gone through something.

Does Andrew ever think about getting into politics himself?

The answer is yes.

"One hundred percent. I've always been a political geek growing up, but I ended up in the kitchen. I'm a professional dishwasher, but I say this: chefs would be the best politicians because we're trained to cut waste. That's all that we do is we cut waste, and we know there's a lot of that in the government. And food is love. Love is the backbone of everything we do. And that would create a great politician."

I ask what Andrew's advice is for his kids when they grow up. He says it's to work hard, and take risks. Make yourself uncomfortable, whether it's talking to someone you don't know, or wiping a table while engaging a customer.

Is he a hopeful person?

"Of course. I'm always positive and I think that we've got enough of a strong enough foundation in America that we're starting to see people open up their eyes to what's going on. It's going to be difficult, with bumps along the way. But I certainly am hopeful."

Chef Gruel says he's grateful for his health and family, and for those who have similar principles wanting to spread the word. He's amazed and inspired by the support that has come out of the darkness. And for those who need a little confidence right now, does Andrew have any more food for thought? Chef Gruel says, keep pushing. Juggle. Do whatever you have to do to leverage it out.

Never stop.

I thank Andrew for his passion, his determination, and his advocacy on behalf of others. We need his voice and others like him. Now more than ever.

13

"If God Puts a Goliath in Front of You, There Must Be a David Inside of You"

The Family vs. the Diagnosis

It was a headline from the *Akron Beacon Journal* in Ohio that caught my attention while I was researching stories for this book: "Baby David's Giant Battle: Family Thankful for Son Who Faces More Hurdles."

The article was published in December 2020 and documented some of the incredible challenges a child named David had faced before and after he was born. His parents, Carlla and Brad Detwiler, described their son's journey by saying: "If God puts a Goliath in front of you, there must be a David inside of you."

Carlla and Brad tell me they found out at about twenty weeks of pregnancy that their child would face tremendous challenges. Doctors told the couple their son might not make it to term, and if he did, he probably would not survive after birth. Despite the odds, though, even a slight chance of survival was worth fighting for.

Carlla remembers the scheduled checkup in early December 2018. She went without Brad because it was just a routine visit (and this wasn't her first rodeo, having had three other healthy babies). But when the doctor started the ultrasound, Carlla noticed she became very quiet and was studying the same spot on the sonogram.

"The doctor then left the room and came back to say that the baby didn't have any fluid and there was something wrong. And then she asked me if I could call my husband to come in."

The Detwilers found out that their baby was missing a kidney, and the one he did have was nonfunctioning. Carlla says a lot of people don't know this, but amniotic fluid actually comes from the baby's urine.

"Without him producing any of that fluid, he wouldn't survive birth. His lungs wouldn't have developed."

It was suggested that they consider terminating the pregnancy or carry him to term only to have a few minutes before he died after being born. Carlla says they told the doctor there was no way they would consider getting rid of their child.

"Abortion is just not an option for us. And we knew right away that wasn't something that we were going to do. The doctor also told us not to research what David had because there was only one case in the United States of a baby that survived this syndrome."

They found out that US representative from Washington State Jaime Herrera Beutler had given birth to the first baby known to have been born without a kidney; she had tried a new procedure called amnio infusion. Carlla started calling every hospital across the United States, asking if they performed the infusion, but kept getting turned down. The Detwilers never gave up, though, and one day were referred to a children's hospital in Cincinnati, about 230 miles away, that might be able to help. They got a call the next day asking if they could travel to Cincinnati. Brad and Carlla say they'll never forget the date: December 25.

"On Christmas Day of 2018, we left our kids behind. It was the hardest day ever. But we had to be in Cincinnati the next morning, starting at seven a.m. to get some testing done. So we did it."

After meeting with all of the doctors, Brad and Carlla got the news that the hospital would accept mom and baby-in-utero as patients and begin the amnio infusions.

"We drove down to Cincinnati every Friday for ten weeks, where I had a thirteen-inch needle placed right into my uterus, filling me with pseudo fluid, which was just like sterile saline. And by the grace of God, we got his lungs to develop."

David was delivered by C-section in April 2019. Most babies start crying as they take their first breath, but he never made a sound, which was concerning. The doctors took David away and intubated immediately. Brad says he didn't have a recognizable pulse. They saw him for only a few minutes.

Carlla's uncle is a priest, and came in from out of town to baptize baby David right away because they knew he might die. He was then transported to Akron Children's Hospital's intensive care unit.

Despite everything, Brad was sure his son was going to make it: "I'm speaking for myself, but I just knew he was going to live. I knew it. Now, obviously, that day was scary, but there was no doubt. They came back and said he's a lot sicker that we thought he was going to be, so there were concerns. He was in rough shape."

But the hospital and the staff gave their son incredible care. A nurse named Laurel was assigned to David and stayed by his side for several nights until he was stabilized. The situation was dire, but their son kept fighting.

Carlla says she didn't know what to think at the time, and just remembers being in so much pain from labor. She refused any medication because she wanted to see her child and hold him, be coherent enough to spend any moment with him she could have. Carlla didn't know if David would survive, but she's not surprised her husband never wavered in his belief that their son would keep fighting.

"He's very optimistic. Brad is always the one that turns my attitude around when I'm having a really bad day. And everything he was telling me at that time was so positive. That helped me feel better."

I ask Brad where that optimism comes from. He says it may sound silly, but it comes from growing up on a football field with a dad who's a coach.

"I played through college, and they always, always stressed there's only so much you can control. And the stuff you can't control, is what it is. You just have to deal with it. We couldn't control anything else other than give him a fighting chance. That's what we said from the beginning: we're going to fight for this kid."

Doctors told them David would be in the hospital for six months. But he beat those odds, heading home after just two and a half.

Brad tells me about a moment he thinks was a sign their boy was going to survive this. They were in the middle of building a house, and one day while he was in the shower, there was a tile in the wall that looked like the image of a baby's face.

"And then right next to it looked like a bigger face. It resembled Jesus. I came out of the shower and I said, 'He's going to make it.'"

What Brad saw in the shower tiles reminds me of Marian apparitions in the Catholic Church, which are explained as appearances of the Blessed Virgin Mary coming down from heaven to earth. These visuals are sometimes paired with a message that Mary wants to communicate.

Carlla says they look at those tiles all the time, and are always aware of signs from God: something to help them keep believing that everything will work out the way it is supposed to.

"There's not one day that David hasn't fought to be here," she says. "He fights every single day of his life. We just follow his lead, and then we push through. Whatever life throws at us, we'll be there to help him get through it. He's one of the strongest little kids I've ever seen."

The local newspaper and television stations have been following David's journey from the very beginning, and he's become somewhat of a celebrity in their community. Many people tell Brad and Carlla that David inspires them. If someone is having a rough time, they think of him and what he has overcome.

Watching their other kids with David has also been incredible to witness. They are all learning compassion and kindness at an early age.

Carlla says that when you see David for the first time, you have no idea what he's been through. He looks like a normal boy, but he has so many issues.

"He has severe CP [cerebral palsy]. He's blind, obviously he has kidney issues, he's got scoliosis, he has a tethered spinal cord. But you would never know it. He's the happiest little boy you'd ever meet."

Brad and Carlla both work full-time and Carlla owns two businesses. She also deals with her own health challenges: she's a type 1 diabetic. With so many things to stay on top of, there are still many doctor visits, David's therapy, and their other kids' needs. Still, they make it all work. Brad's mom helps, and Carlla's mother moves into their house during the week to pitch in. You have to take it one day at a time and not think too far ahead, because that's when it gets overwhelming.

I wonder how David's brothers and sisters are doing with all of these challenges with their youngest brother, and the toll it must take on the other family members. Their oldest son, Domenik, is nine. Daniel is seven, and Stella is five. David is three.

Brad admits Domenik is more emotional and in tune with what's going on because he's the oldest and sees the struggles, and having to spend more energy on David, and that's tough. Daniel likes to read to David and considers him his little buddy. Stella is still young but talks to him and plays with him.

"They all have a good bond," Brad explains "It's great to see their awareness towards other kids that may be disabled or handicapped. They will always make sure to include those children. That's the really neat part of it."

How does their faith play a role in all of this, and when did they decide to name their baby David? Carlla says the discussion came up as they were driving to one of their amnio infusion sessions. "And we thought to ourselves, we have to give him a fighting start. I said, 'How about David? As in David and Goliath?' Because he's going to have this big battle. And we both knew that's what we were going to name him. It is definitely biblical and it comes from that strength we wanted to give him even before he was born. It's very fitting."

Brad was raised in a Methodist family and Carlla is Catholic. When they first got married there wasn't a lot of church in their lives, but they were both spiritual. Going through something like this, made them put their faith in God even more and strengthened their resolve.

Brad says they found a wonderful church that welcomed the family with open arms and supported them all the way. "The pastor came in the day after David was born to say a prayer for him and the community got really involved bringing him home. It's just been a good group of people to be associated with."

Carlla admits there have been many times they have fallen to their knees, and faith is what gets you through the long hours. "It's all you have sometimes in the operating waiting rooms and the scary moments where he gets super sick and you don't know what else to do. You just pray, and so far, He's never let us down."

The story about how David was able to receive a kidney is quite a miracle as well. Child donors are hard to come by, because when a child passes away, it's often the last thing parents think about—to donate an organ. Doctors wanted David to grow big enough to be able to accept an adult kidney. He made the goal height and weight in the winter of 2021, and was approved and activated for a deceased donor.

Brad says they had to run tests on David, so they drove to Cincinnati to meet with the surgery team.

"At that point, we were able to start live-donor screenings, and only five people could get tested at a time. I got tested, her brother got tested, my sister got tested, even the babysitter tried to get approved, but she wasn't old enough. I didn't pass my test because our blood types weren't compatible."

Carlla says she was ineligible to be a live donor because she is a type 1 diabetic, and that was devastating. Her brother was a preliminary match, so he went on to further testing. In the meantime, Brad says, they were still open to a deceased-donor kidney. David was on the list for eleven days, but then he got sick and they had to deactivate him (remove his name from the donor list). Doctors also wanted him to get some of the required childhood vaccines before they started the process again.

Once David was back in the clear, he was reactivated on the donor list. Nine days later, at 6:30 in the morning, they got a call. The doctors asked how quickly they all could get to Cincinnati.

"It's a three-and-a-half-hour drive," Brad recalls, "and at that point, it was mass panic because we've got three other kids at home. We had to get someone here so we can leave, lining up people to get them all to school and back. We had to pack everything, but we were out the door by about seven forty-five. We got down there around eleven thirty and by three o'clock he was in surgery for a transplant."

Carlla says there were still many hurdles to go through during the operation. Only a few children in the United States have survived this syndrome, and David is also specific because he was born without a bladder, so that complicated things.

"There was a whole urology team there to figure out how they were going to get his pee out, basically. They did something super new, something they've only done with two other kids in Cincinnati, where they just bypass everything and they bring the ureter, that's connected to the kidney, up to the skin and out of it. It's super weird right next to his belly button. The urine comes out of his stomach and it just drips out into the diaper."

Brad says that up until the transplant, David was tethered to a dialysis machine for twelve hours a day. "Every night we had to be at home hooking him up for dialysis in the bedroom. That takes a lot away from the other kids. We weren't able to go out to eat, we weren't able to bring the kids to their sporting events or we'd have to leave early. There were many things we couldn't do because we'd have to be back for David."

Carlla says it affected a lot of their adult relationship as well.

"I think people didn't understand that we couldn't go over to houses for pizza and a movie or go out on dinner dates and things like that. Brad and I had decided from the beginning that he and I would be the only ones that would do his dialysis machine, in case something went wrong. It affected a lot of our lives."

I'm amazed at all of the things that Carlla and Brad are now experts in. It's almost like they've had to become doctors themselves. Not only do they have to be advocates on behalf of their son and his health, but they also have to educate themselves to make difficult, life-or-death decisions. Carlla says that when you have three healthy children, you take for granted how many things have to be so perfect for a baby to form and develop normally.

I ask about gratitude. I do find that, ironically, the more challenges we go through in life, the more grateful we become for the little things.

Carlla says they consider themselves blessed.

"Brad and I just had this conversation. We were driving to Cincinnati for my brother's wedding and I looked at him and I said, 'Sometimes I do think that people feel sorry for us because we have all of this on our plate, and we're exhausted trying to juggle everything.' But I try to explain that we actually feel so incredibly blessed. We are thankful for everything that we have—the good and the bad. I pray for David's good days and I pray for his bad days because I know that even if he is having a bad day, we still have him here. So, we're always grateful."

We can't forget about the doctors who helped David. The ones who also wanted to take chances and fight for him, too, like Dr. Shefali Mahesh, the director of pediatric nephrology at Akron Children's Hospital. Carlla says that when David was in utero, she didn't know what to do, because even if he survived birth, there was a 3 percent chance that he'd have to be on a special dialysis called peritoneal dialysis. Carlla left a message for Dr. Mahesh, who called them right back.

"Dr. Mahesh jokes about this all the time that she came to work the next day, and there's a little Post-it Note with my name on it and my son's condition."

What was happening to the Detwiler family didn't deserve to be on a Post-it Note. Dr. Mahesh called them back immediately to discuss what was going on. Carlla says that day she knew they had their most important cheerleader on board.

"She looked at us and she said, 'We're going to try to get this baby here and we're going to try to help him live.' It was the first time through this whole experience that I felt like someone outside of our family was going to fight for him."

It's so important to highlight doctors like Dr. Mahesh in the medical field. You can be the smartest MD in the room, but having someone with empathy, kindness, and the willingness to do anything possible for their patients is crucial.

Brad says they were very fortunate to have Dr. Mahesh on their team, but as a parent, you must also be prepared to be a fierce advocate for your child.

"That's the one thing Carla and I tried to stress. I mean, if we had listened to some doctors, David wouldn't even be here today. So, you have to find solutions on your own. Educate yourself and make decisions based on how you want to proceed and not just take the doctors' words for it."

I ask Brad and Carlla what they would tell other parents going through something similar. David's story is a miracle, but it's also a lesson in being resilient and never giving up. Carlla says you have to be willing to fight for your child, but also know when to let faith guide your way.

"Sometimes it doesn't work out the way that it did for David, and many might say they couldn't handle all of it. We understand that, too, and God might need your child up there in Heaven beside Him, or He might want him to be here on earth to show others the way. But just let Him take the lead because that's all you can do sometimes."

Brad reminds us to take it one day at a time. There's only so much you can control. You can't worry about things that may come up, because they haven't happened yet. You find a solution to deal with it then.

"But until that time comes, you can't worry about what-ifs, and what might be or what could be. You live in the moment, and just keep pushing forward and doing what you can to make things better for you, the child, and the rest of the family. You can't just keep looking ahead. It's day by day."

Brad's advice reminds me of the serenity prayer written by Reinhold Niebuhr in 1932. It's just twenty-five words long, and asks for comfort, strength, and wisdom.

God, grant me the serenity
To accept the things I cannot change,
Courage to change the things I can, and
Wisdom to know the difference.

During all of these David-and-Goliath stories, there seems to be that pivotal moment when someone realizes at the height of the battle that they might not be able to keep going. Carlla says she remembers feeling that in November 2020. David was a year and a half old and had been through several surgeries already when his peritoneal catheter stopped working, his dialysis ceased, and he became very sick. It was late at night. She and Brad were sitting in the waiting room while David was in surgery. His oxygen levels were dropping, and doctors came out at one point to tell them that it wasn't looking good.

"I remember thinking: Please, he has been through so, so much, if this is the way the rest of his life is going to be and he is going to be suffering all the time, then please let's just let him go. I was so weak and I was so tired and I was so sorrowful for him."

Some time passed after that, and doctors came back out to announce that David had turned a corner and was doing better. He was out of surgery a few hours later and made a full recovery, but Carlla says that was a bad night for her and she didn't know how to keep going.

Brad says that even though he can't recall a time where he felt like giving up, the fight definitely gets tiring. There are many moments where he feels bad for their other kids, because of David's situation.

"Things aren't going to go according to plan, and there's going to be hiccups. But we have to keep moving."

Carlla says that Brad is the rock in their family: "He is the one that picks up my pieces as they fall when I can't carry any more. And he keeps me optimistic when I get into a dark headspace sometimes. I'm so thankful for him."

Brad says that if it weren't for Carlla, he might not be as optimistic as he is. His wife is the one who researched all of the possible treatments for their son, runs two businesses, goes to the hospital three days a week, and gets to rehab and therapy with David, all while dealing with her own health issues as a diabetic.

"I might be the motivator, I might be the voice of reason. But she's the engine that drives this thing."

Carlla thanks her husband for the kind words, and I ask about the other family members who keep their household running. Both of their moms (David's grandmothers) are very hands-on as well. Brad's mom is retired, and Carlla's mom quit her job to help out. She stays with them several days a week.

Carlla says she's grateful for their family and those who help outside the home. Coworkers, neighbors, and friends. They have a wonderful team of helpers.

I ask what's next for David going forward. Brad says the really hard part is coming to an end. It's a lot of wait-and-see for six to nine months after the kidney transplant. From that point on, they'll focus on other things that need treatment and care. David is blind, so there's not a whole lot they can do for that right now. There's ways to improve his mobility when it comes to the cerebral palsy, and therapies to help get him to speak a little bit more. His scoliosis and spinal cord issues are also something he struggles with, but the kidney was the biggest step to keep him alive. Brad admits he does feel angry sometimes about how much one little boy has to deal with.

"He is just so joyful and happy. He is very rarely upset or sad. He's starting to want a little more attention now, and if you don't answer him, he'll start yelling, 'Mama, mama!' He's also goofy and funny. He laughs all the time. And he's learning words slowly but surely. He's just so happy. That's the best way for me to explain it. If you ever meet him, you would just smile because he's just so happy and brings joy to everybody. Everyone just loves David. He can make any bad day better."

Carlla says that if she imagines what's going on in David's mind, everything is colorful and bright. If she could look into his head, that's what she would see.

"He's very inquisitive and wants to touch everything. He wants to feel your face all the time. He wants to hold your hand. He's just a good boy."

She remembers the day so well when she saw one of David's first ultrasounds and he was moving around with a heartbeat so strong. They saw him putting his hands in his mouth, and doing things despite all the challenges he was up against. Their boy was alive, and he deserved a fighting chance.

Brad says he wants to share one more story before we end our conversation. He was at a football game with his two older boys and was sitting next to a couple who had a teenage son with Down syndrome. The boy was kicking his sons, and the mom kept saying she was sorry. Brad said not to worry. He explained he also had a special needs child, and understood that their son didn't mean to kick anyone.

"And she then said, 'Congratulations.'"

Brad stopped for a moment, thinking, Why is she congratulating me? He didn't know what to say in response. Then the woman told Brad it would be okay if he was mad at her for saying that, because someone once said the exact same words to her, and she got upset. But then she explained that having a special needs child is a gift, and should be celebrated.

"It will teach your kids way more than what you as a parent can teach them in life."

That's why she congratulated him. Brad pauses and says it's hard to finish the story without tearing up.

She then added: "I hope you get to say the same thing to another parent with a special child like ours someday. Because they are the biggest blessings in this world."

14

"I've Got All the Cards I Need Right Here"

The Firefighter vs. Congress

September 11, 2021, marked the twentieth anniversary of the terror attacks in New York City, Washington, DC, and the skies over Pennsylvania.

Our family drove into Manhattan to visit with my husband Sean's old firehouse, 40/35, right across from Lincoln Center. On our way in, Sean, who rarely talks about 9/11, explained to our boys what had happened to him and his friends that day and in the weeks that followed. He knew how important it was for Matthew and Theodore to understand this part of his history as a young fireman, and how we can't ever forget that day when thousands of families would never see their loved ones again.

When we arrived, we joined hundreds of people who came to pay their respects. The morning was reminiscent of the weather two decades ago before, when the clear blue skies blew up, and the twin towers of the World Trade Center came down.

All twelve of the firefighters who were working in my husband's firehouse died that day. The "riding list," handwritten in chalk, naming all the men who were on duty that day, still hangs on the firehouse wall, forever preserved behind glass.

Looking back, those weeks and months are a blur to my husband. He, along with the rest of the surviving members of 40/35, spent weeks and months digging through wreckage trying to find remains. What started as a search and rescue became a long recovery effort.

A few days after the towers collapsed, the government tried to assure the public that the massive plume of ash blanketing the city was "safe."

The Environmental Protection Agency chief, Christine Todd Whitman, announced, "Given the scope of the tragedy from last week, I am glad to reassure the people of New York and Washington, DC, that their air is safe to breathe and their water is safe to drink."

It took her fifteen years to apologize for her grave error.

In 2003, the EPA's inspector general found that the environmental agency didn't have the data required to make that statement about air quality and was influenced by the White House.

Many first responders knew pretty early on that the conditions in which they were working were anything but safe. One of them was Kenny Specht. Kenny was diagnosed with cancer just a few years after the terror attacks but had a suspicion it wasn't a normal type of cancer. He believed the toxic fumes and debris he dug through were causing the poison to form in his body. There were clues and whispers within the fire department, and he was one of the first to speak up about his concerns.

It took almost a decade for Kenny to finally see justice and a long-term commitment for what he fought hard for. Many told him he would never win the battle, but he never gave up. When fellow firefighter Ray Pfeifer joined the cause, he helped bring their incredibly important fight to the finish line.

When I first decided to write a book about David-and-Goliath stories, I knew one of the chapters had to be about Kenny and Ray. My husband worked with Ray in 40/35 and then several years later at the

FDNY Center for Terrorism and Disaster Preparedness, at Fort Totten in Queens.

I reached out to Joe Pfeifer, Ray's younger brother, and asked if he could talk about Ray's legacy. Joe is not comfortable doing interviews, so I knew that if he said yes to the request, it would be an incredible gesture in good faith. His best friend, Kenny Specht, also agreed to talk about being one of the first whistleblowers who knew early on that their cancer was different.

Ray was with us in spirit when we all came together on a cold January day in Joe's garage. He thought this would be the perfect place to talk about his big brother. It was filled with photos, keepsakes, and firefighter memorabilia. There wasn't a patch of wall that wasn't covered with pictures or artifacts that Ray and Joe collected from different fire departments over the years. Joe showed me a workbox of Ray's that was filled with all sorts of FDNY gear, and says Ray always wanted to be a fireman.

"He didn't go to my sister [Maryellen]'s wedding because he took the test to become a firefighter that day. And he was in the wedding party!"

We all pause when he tells us the date of the wedding day.

September 11, 1982.

"He took the test, and said to my sister, 'I'm not going to be at the wedding but I'll be at the reception. I have to take this test.' She understood. Because this was what he was going to do. He was going to be a city fireman."

I ask what it was about the fire department that made him want to be a part of it.

"It's all about doing the right thing. And the brotherhood. There's nothing better. You can count on these guys to come through—for anything. In a fire, for your family. Everything. When you go into a fire, you have every confidence in the world in the guy behind you. The guy behind you is your god. If I go down, he's going to pull you out."

Kenny joined the East Meadow volunteer fire department on Long

Island in 1987 and continued there for three years before he became a New York City police officer in 1990. In 1996 he joined the Fire Department of the City of New York, or FDNY. Kenny and Joe became friends after high school when they joined the East Meadow Fire Department on the same day.

"Joe Pfeifer was the king of the entire high school," Kenny tells me. "I look around this garage, and it's like, 'This is your life.' Ray is here, of course. But Joe is here, too. There's his 'king of the prom' trophy over there!"

Ray was already a captain in East Meadow before joining the FDNY. Kenny says Ray made him nervous, and he didn't always like him.

"He could really turn the temperature up. He was a ball breaker. I was in the volunteer fire department, and he was in the city FD. I was eighteen years old. It was tough being in the same room with him. He was going to make your life difficult."

We all laugh. What do you mean by that? I ask. Joe takes over from there: "Okay, prime example. I work construction. I come home, and I would go to the [volunteer] firehouse. I just want to have a couple of beers."

(Many volunteer firehouses have a bar/community room/catering hall where they can relax and gather. This is one of the big perks of being a "vollie.")

Joe continues: "So I sit at the bar, open up a beer. Ray's sitting there. He says, 'What's in compartment A?' Well, I don't even take a sip and I have to go out and find out what's in this compartment. I go out to the rig. I look at the thing. All right. This is this—and that's in there. I come back and I have to explain to him what's in the compartment. The next day I go in. I start drinking a beer. And he's there: 'What's in compartment B?' I'm like, this guy's a pain in my ass. I'm gonna have to learn this whole entire rig before I can ever sit down and have a beer and relax."

Ray knew the job well. He was so confident, he would grab the nozzle on the hose during a fire and go through the front door by himself.

Joe says he would push guys out of the way because he knew he could get the fire under control on his own.

Kenny says Ray was like a cartoon character. He operated the line with such force, and would drag everyone behind him.

"And then Ray walked out the back door when it was over like Elvis, got into someone's car, and was driven home."

Before Ray became a firefighter, Joe says, he was making a lot of money working in the carpenters' union, Local 608. He would run shows and exhibits from the Jacob Javits Convention Center in the Hell's Kitchen section of Manhattan.

"He was making a ton of dough. But then he decided to be fireman, where he was making a quarter of that. He didn't care about money. He just really wanted to be a part of the fire department."

To Ray, the FDNY was about friends, having a good time, and doing something fun with everyone. The company picnics, birthday gatherings, Christmas parties. For families of firefighters, these were not to be missed.

After 9/11, Ray became the coordinator of all the family liaisons in the firehouse. In the tradition of the FDNY, when a firefighter dies in the line of duty, one firefighter in the firehouse then becomes the designated contact, or liaison, to the lost member's family. Ray also helped with all the funerals, and went to every single one of them. He would carry a stack of prayer cards from all the masses he went to in his pocket. When politicians were trying to give him their business cards in Washington, DC, while fighting for sick responders, Ray would take out the photos of all his friends and say, "I've got all the cards I need right here."

Joe tells me Ray was supposed to be working on September 11. It haunted him every day because he had asked someone to take his spot so he could play golf in Maryland.

"Steve Mercado did a mutual for him. So when he got word, what had happened, he was back in New York within hours. He called me up. He says, 'Joe, we got to go find the boys.'"

Kenny's brother was a police officer, and his mom called him to say that his brother was down at the World Trade Center. They hadn't heard from him after the first tower came down. Kenny asked his captain if he could go look for him. He jumped in his car and got stopped by a cop on the Grand Central Parkway. Kenny relayed the story about his brother being downtown, and the officer told him to pull behind the other police cars that were heading into Manhattan. He spent the rest of the day and night trying to find survivors, and was relieved to find out his brother was okay.

I ask Joe if he was able to find anybody that day.

"Not a whole body. Just parts of bodies."

He says the whole experience was surreal, and you thought that at any moment you could die.

"Yeah, because you look over, and there's the Trade Center sticking out of another building. I don't know what the building was—on the West Side Highway. And you knew that was going to come out and it was going to fall. We just stayed. What are you going to do? You can't really go anywhere."

Eventually, Joe found Ray, and Ray was pissed off at him.

"He lost his shit. 'Where were you? I lost you!' I said, 'Relax, relax, relax. I'm here. Everything is good.'"

At that point the captain of Marine 9 came up asking for a chauffeur (driver for engine company/maintains pumps on rig). Ray grabbed Joe and said, "Here you go. He's your chauffeur."

One of the rigs pumping water from the river wasn't working, so Joe was able to help get it back up and running. Though he had training with pump operations in his own fire department, he didn't have any experience with FDNY engines. Still, he was able to clear away some of the dust and debris. The rigs were overheating because of all the dirt on them.

"So I'm just trying to clean the rig up a little bit. And then I was washing it down, and somebody's hand fell off of it into the sewer. I remember trying to grab it. To save it. And I was like, Holy shit, that was somebody. Someone's hand . . . Oh, my God . . ."

It was like living a nightmare, I say.

"Yeah. It's a nightmare. You just want to wash it all away. You just want to just clean the rig off . . . wash it all away. . . ."

I know at this point Joe and Kenny are reliving something that haunts them twenty years later. My husband, Sean, still hasn't shared with me all the horrors he saw and lived through. I figure many of these memories he wants to stay buried. And the survivor's guilt from not being one of the guys that died that day doesn't go away.

Joe tells me that Ray had survivor guilt from day one, and it stayed with him until the day he died.

Ray believed he should have been the one working September 11, so to try to make up for it, he made the decision to take care of all the families in the firehouse, and to attend as many funerals as he could for all the FDNY members lost.

"I used to go with him to a lot of them. I drove a lot of the families to the funerals, and I brought wives to where they were testing DNA. They have to bring toothbrushes with them from their husband to help match the DNA. Very, very personal stuff. Hard-core."

I ask Kenny if he knew the smoke and ash was toxic when he was down there. He says he remembers the color of the horizon was completely different. It was green.

"I remember driving around and it was pouring rain, and the entire area of downtown Manhattan looked like an atom bomb went off. All the streets and all of the sidewalks were just mush. I remember that moment at one thirty in the morning and seeing it."

Joe says his chest was covered in a rash for a week, but he figured it was all the insulation that was in the ceilings coming down.

"You never thought about it. And then you hear from Christie Todd Whitman that the air is fine. Yeah, I remember that. The air is good. I'm like, okay, cool. All right. So, if I feel bad, I'll put a mask on. Yeah, right."

I asked if anyone wore masks.

"No, they didn't give us anything. And they fed you down there—you never moved from that area to eat. You'd lie on the ship. They had these boats on the West Side by the marina. You had to stay there and you slept on the grimy ground. Then they brought in contractors. I remember there was a hotel that was open with massage therapists and video games and some chairs where the guys would sleep, but you had to get washed off before you could go into this hotel. The guy who washed you off with brushes was covered head to toe while I had on my regular clothes. This guy is in a spacesuit. Yup. Got it."

I ask when Ray started getting sick.

Kenny says he remembers seeing Ray at a funeral in 2012 for a fellow firefighter who died of World Trade Center illness. It was a freezing cold day in Long Beach, Long Island. Kenny hadn't seen Ray in a while, and he couldn't believe what he looked like.

"It was either the next day he went to the doctor or that week, but I said, 'You look like shit.' I remember I saw his tooth was black and I'm like, 'Do you sleep?'"

Joe says it was around that time that Ray was complaining about his hip, so he told him to go get a cortisone shot.

"I had just got a cortisone shot in my elbow, and I said, 'I feel like a million bucks.' So he says, 'I'll go today.' He calls me up a little while later and says, 'Joe, I need a ride to Manhattan. I have to get to Sloan [Memorial Sloan Kettering Cancer Center]. He was told to go to the emergency room. Right away."

Starting in his kidneys, the cancer spread everywhere. When Ray was in hospice care, he had brain cancer. It had also moved into his lungs and adrenal glands.

Kenny was diagnosed with cancer in 2007. He got hurt in a fire in Hollis, Queens, and went to Long Island Jewish Medical Center for a neck injury. The doctor found nodules on his thyroid and he was diagnosed with thyroid cancer.

He then went to the FDNY medical office and spoke to the doctor there, remembering very clearly when the doctor stressed to him he did *not* get sick from the World Trade Center.

"So the New York City Fire Department told me that I didn't get sick from the Trade Center six or seven years afterward. There wasn't a lot of talk about Trade Center illness back then. But men were dying of cancer already.

Kenny admits he's the type of guy you either love or hate because he stands for the truth. "And I am the guy that started this entire battle. One hundred percent. I told them: 'I'm sick from the Trade.' And they told me: 'You need to look at family history.' And I said, 'There is no family history.'"

Kenny put two and two together. It was clear to him that all the cancers that firefighters were getting were "filter" cancers.

"Ray had kidney cancer: a filter. A lot of the body filters are cancerous because during our time down there we didn't filter out the stuff that we were surrounded by. Instead, our bodies held on to it. I had thyroid, his was kidney. I'm not a cancer specialist, but kidney cancer is ninety-eight percent survivable if it's found when it's still in the kidney. And then it's ninety-five percent fatal when it leaves the kidney. Same thing with thyroid cancer, same thing with almost any cancer: when it escapes the place where it first grows, it becomes fatal. But if you catch it while it's still in the organ in which it started, you live. Because Ray's cancer left his kidney and mine stayed my thyroid. I found it early enough."

Kenny says that when he was told he had cancer, the second he walked into the medical office, he was ready to discuss the link between his illness and September 11. But they would quickly shut him down.

"And then I watched my friend Richie Manetta die of brain cancer. He was going to France to try a different kind of treatment. He left a message on my cell phone saying he was back and it didn't work out. And I never called him back. I never had an opportunity to catch up. And then Roy Chelsen and Billy Quick. These guys were getting sick and calling me for help. They're all dead now."

I ask if the fire department knew all along it was 9/11-related illness.

Kenny says they absolutely knew. "But, when you deal with a person from the medical field, they're going to fall back on what they've been taught. The epidemiologists are going to say, 'I don't care what you say, these things don't happen for twenty or thirty years after this type of exposure.' And then I say, 'Well, maybe we're not looking at a twenty- to thirty-year problem. Maybe we're looking at a five-year problem.'"

Kenny started banging the drum in 2008, by going to union meetings and telling people there's a problem and it is going to get worse. He found others online who were sick and linking it to the Trade Center. The message board was called "The FDNY Rant."

"There were a lot of angry guys on that rant, and it started to collect a pretty decent amount of activity. People would put in fake names [so they couldn't be identified]. I managed to hook up with a couple of like-minded guys."

A few of them decided to drive down to Washington, DC, to see if they could grab someone's attention. They paid for their own hotels and tried visiting with members of the House of Representatives in their offices.

"We didn't actually meet with anybody who was elected. We met with their staffers."

Kenny had heard about a construction worker named John Feal who was doing the same kind of advocacy, and was also trying to get lawmakers to pay attention. They set up a meeting with him to see if they could work together. Kenny says he listened to what they were trying to do, and it mirrored his objectives. But he was cautious. He didn't want to get involved with anyone for the wrong reasons, and felt it wasn't the right time.

Kenny was friends with a firefighter named John McNamara, who spent more than five hundred hours at the World Trade Center after 9/11 and was diagnosed with stage 4 colon cancer in 2006. Despite his deteriorating health, John wanted to be a spokesman on behalf of the other first responders who were also getting sick, and started doing interviews to talk about what they were going through. He looked terrible, and that's when people started to take notice.

"It was difficult to look at him and see the condition that he was in. Unfortunately, in situations like this, you have to find somebody to be the face of this illness because until you can put a face and a name to it, people don't really want to pay attention."

Kenny was taking John to chemo treatments and union meetings. Others were starting to see what was happening. When John passed away in 2009, at the age of forty-four, there was a huge crowd and television crews at his funeral. Kenny credits WPIX, a local New York channel that got involved early on.

"They availed themselves to us and they would put us on and do follow-up stories."

John Feal, the construction worker who was also advocating for sick first responders, called Kenny to check in a few months after their first meeting. That's when Kenny agreed they should work together.

Kenny was now going to Washington, DC, fairly regularly, and his efforts helped get the James Zadroga 9/11 Health and Compensation Act passed in Congress in 2011. James Zadroga was a police officer whose death was linked to exposures from the World Trade Center disaster. The bill provided for some treatment and a monitoring system, but was temporary. In 2015 they had to go back and start yelling again.

"But now, all of a sudden, the New York City Fire Department is getting federal money, and they're starting to do World Trade Center monitoring. So now it's okay to admit guys got sick in the Trade Center? All of a sudden it wasn't taboo anymore."

I ask Kenny to name the politicians who helped and the ones who did not.

"Chuck Schumer was the senior senator in DC and didn't want to be part of it," he says. "Chuck gave it to Kirsten Gillibrand [the junior senator from New York]. Carolyn Maloney from the House of Representatives was also a key ally. Schumer tried to take credit for it later, but it was all Gillibrand. Carolyn Maloney is the sponsor in the House of Representatives. Gillibrand's the sponsor in the Senate."

Republicans were not on board with helping first responders at the beginning. They only started paying attention when Jon Stewart started shaming them on his Comedy Central program, *The Daily Show.*

Kenny didn't really know who Jon Stewart was, but when his staffers asked for a meeting, and then asked the right questions, he was impressed.

In December 2010, Senate Republicans were filibustering the Zadroga bill and wanted to get home for their Christmas vacations. Kenny and his team of first responders camped outside Senate Majority Leader Mitch McConnell's office after it was revealed that McConnell was trying to block the legislation. Jon Stewart then invited Kenny and several other sick responders to come on his show for a full hour to shame them. A few days later, Congress approved the bill that helped pay for medical bills and treatment programs while setting up a system to monitor sick first responders.

Kenny says he's grateful Stewart wanted to help them and get involved. He had clout and influence, and "opened whatever doors he had available to us and let us in. To speak the way we wanted to speak and to behave the way we wanted to behave. And now the union started to care because, holy shit, Jon Stewart's involved."

At the time, Kenny reached out to Ray Pfeifer, who was in the union, to help, but Pfeifer told him his hands were tied.

"And I said, 'Ray, you're telling me the same line that everyone else is. That they're not going along with it.'"

It was Ray's own cancer, diagnosed in 2012, that made him realize his mistake.

"He said, 'You're right. You're right. These guys aren't doing a fucking thing. What can I do?'"

The day that Ray Pfeifer decided to use his illness to help others was a game changer. Kenny says he remembers the morning he was sitting in a van with Ray at the World Trade Center site, waiting to be interviewed, and a stranger with a fire department T-shirt came up to Ray and started talking to him like he was his best friend.

"It's like six thirty a.m., and I don't even know who this guy is talking to Ray."

Kenny was supposed to do a press conference with reporters, but he was exhausted, and when he saw how friendly Ray was with a stranger, acting like he knew him, he got an idea.

"I said, 'Ray, you're doing this interview today, bro. I'm done. People don't want to see me anymore. I'm tired of talking.' I asked, 'You want to do this interview today?' and then I decided, 'Ray, it's your turn, bro. Go over there just like you're talking to this guy. Make the TV cameras come out.' And there's Ray in his wheelchair."

Joe says he's not surprised by this, because part of Ray's personality was making you do things you never thought you would.

"Ray makes you do stuff. Even if you literally don't want to do it—like I'm not doing that at work now. I'm doing this. But you still do what Ray wants. That's my entire life. I did it with Ray because he convinced me to go do some shit I didn't want to do."

There was a moment when the cameras were rolling in 2015 when Kenny, Jon Stewart, John Feal, and several other first responders were hanging around the basement of the US Capitol. According to the Huffington Post, they were trying to find some of the Republican holdouts who weren't supporting some of the Zadroga health benefits that were expiring. Senator Rob Portman, a Republican from Ohio, kept avoiding meetings with the group. They spotted him, and Ray was in his motorized wheelchair, so he sped up as he saw that Portman was heading for the exit. Ray cornered him in the hallway and in just a few minutes convinced him to back the bill.

Joe says that's who Ray was: "Pushing down doors and getting it done. But I also knew Kenny had everything to do with it. Ray was working for Kenny at this point. He was working for Kenny and to try to get Kenny's word out. He was a good face. He had a wheelchair, he had a cane. . . ."

Ray said many times that he knew he was the poster boy for 9/11, but if it made people sit up and take notice, then he would play the part.

Kenny says it was the right moment. He was tired of talking to people. For years he was doing this, and now it was time to let Ray be the voice. Kenny recovered from his 9/11 cancer, but Ray Pfeifer was dying from his. And that's what people needed to see.

"We would go back to the room and the medication came out. And then the hour and a half in the bathroom and his struggle to go to the bathroom, go to sleep, get changed the next morning, put him in the wheelchair. You know, Ray went from being able to move himself to needing people to move him."

Kenny says he doesn't think he could let others see him like that, maybe because of his own vanity. But Ray just kept on going until he physically couldn't anymore.

I ask Joe if this fight made Ray more alive in some ways.

"Absolutely. Yeah, he was doing things for people all over the country. And that was his party trick. It was his last party trick. 'I'm going to help other people, not just the city fire department, but all over the country.' And that was a big thing for him. Yeah, and he knew. He knew he was the face of this. He said, 'I'm sick. They need a sick guy. I can do it.'"

Near the end of his life, Ray was going to a lot of events to raise awareness, posing for pictures with lawmakers and getting recognized for his advocacy.

I remember back when Ray received the key to the city. He was sitting onstage with the mayor and all the lawmakers and dignitaries. The cameras were on and the media was asking them to smile for pictures. There was an engine company up in the balcony, and Ray said, "I don't want to be here. I want to be sitting with you guys up there."

That's who Ray was. He didn't want all the celebrity that went with fighting a cause that was killing him. He just wanted to be a fireman.

Joe agrees and says Ray couldn't have cared less. He eventually gave the key to the 9/11 Memorial and Museum.

Then Joe says: "We need to go steal that key back." (Joe Pfeifer and many FDNY firefighters feel that the key does not belong in the museum.)

On the week of the twentieth anniversary of the terror attacks, I visited several memorials around the New York area. One of my favorites was the one Ray used to attend on Long Island at Point Lookout. A steel beam from the North Tower stands next to the names of all the firefighters who died that day, and another wall beside it lists the names of all those who have since passed away from World Trade Center illnesses. I found Ray's name right away when I was there. I ask Joe and Kenny if they are satisfied that the FDNY is finally recognizing that all these names are important, too.

Kenny says he doesn't want to be known for being down in lower Manhattan on 9/11. He was one of thousands who were working that day. He just wants their illnesses to be acknowledged.

"And with that acknowledgment, I want the people that are sick to be able to get the medical care necessary that they probably wouldn't have received had we not fought for it."

Ray died in 2017, but in 2019, the victims' compensation funding was ending, and the number of people who were dying from World Trade Center illnesses was skyrocketing. It required another trip to DC. Jon Stewart showed up along with Kenny, John Feal, sick first responders, and widows of those who had died. Stewart was presented with Ray Pfeifer's turnout coat (a type of jacket firefighters wear that consists of fire-resistant materials), which he wore digging for his brothers at ground zero. Over the years, Stewart and Ray became very close, and you could tell this was a very emotional moment.

When it came time for testimonials, there were dozens of empty seats at the hearing, even though it was being televised on every major news network. Stewart had a prepared speech, but he ignored it and for almost ten minutes berated all the politicians who had failed to show up, blasting the lawmakers who were against extending the bill.

> I'm sorry if I sound angry and undiplomatic. But I'm angry, and you should be too, and they're all angry as well and they have every justification to be that way. There is not a person here, there is not an empty chair on that stage that didn't tweet out "Never Forget the heroes of 9/11. Never forget their bravery. Never forget what they did, what they gave to this country." Well, here they are. And where are they? And it would be one thing if their callous indifference and rank hypocrisy were benign, but it's not. Your indifference cost these men and women their most valuable commodity: time. It's the one thing they're running out of.
>
> —*Jon Stewart, House Judiciary Committee testimony, June 11, 2019*

The next day the bill was passed to extend the 9/11 victims' compensation fund benefits for seventy-one years. The House vote was 402–12. The Senate vote was 97–2.

Kenny reminds us there was a time when the September 11 health issue was a number one subject in the country. Every news station carried the story. We all have differences of opinion, but the bill that passed for first responders' health care was something everyone was rooting for.

"I mean, short of maybe declaring war against Japan in World War Two. I don't think you'll ever see that again, those numbers."

The bill was later renamed the Never Forget the Heroes: James Zadroga, Ray Pfeifer, and Luis Alvarez Permanent Authorization of the September 11th Victim Compensation Fund Act. It extends the claim filing deadline to October 1, 2090.

I ask Kenny how he knew back then that his cancer was the start of something much bigger. How did he find others?

He says he found guys on the Dark Web talking about what was happening. Guys being told the same thing who also had worked at the

Trade Center site. These are the people he rallied to go to Washington, DC, for the first time.

I ask what he would tell other people who see something that's worth raising their voice for. He says the first step is to find like-minded people. And do research. And don't give up.

"There's never been a grassroots movement like this, ever. We didn't just go and prove something once. We had to do it several times. And you deal with so many different ideals and ideologies but this was a tragedy that affected people throughout the nation."

Kenny says that when he looks back on the last twenty years, everything that happened from that day on unfolded the way it was supposed to.

It began with that moment in the medical office when the doctor told him his cancer was not from the World Trade Center. That was the moment of truth.

"If they just treated me, then I would have went on my way."

Looking around the garage that Ray helped build with memories, Joe tells me what it was like growing up with Ray. He was his best friend. They were ten years apart in age, and he was number six on the food chain of seven kids. He suddenly remembers a story when he was ten years old. He was asleep one night and Ray came in, woke him up, and asked if he wanted to come out with him to see something.

"It's two o'clock in the morning. I put my sweatshirt on, and my sneakers, but I still have on my pajamas with the feet. We get in his pickup truck and we drive down to Mitchel Field [a historic air base on Long Island]. Hangar one was on fire. And there's water everywhere. It was the best thing ever. Ray had an F-100 pickup truck with a blue light. He says: 'Come on, let's go!' He knew everyone there."

Joe says they hung out for hours. When he got home his parents were a little upset. They asked where the boys had been.

Joe said, "I was with Ray. I was all right."

I ask what Ray would be doing now if he were alive today. Would he be in some kind of leadership role?

Kenny says, absolutely not.

Ray wanted to be the guy in the rafters. The fireman helping everyone's family. Bringing his fire truck to parties. And being a proud grandfather. That's it.

Joe says Ray was the guy you called to figure things out. He would hear your story and tell you his opinion, and then he'd leave the room.

Kenny says that after all they went through, if he was still around Ray would still be his first phone call.

I ask Joe what Ray would say knowing he had his first grandchild on the way. His son, Terence Pfeifer, who also became a firefighter, recently got married and his wife announced there's a baby on the way.

Joe pauses for a moment, looks up at all the pictures around him, the firefighter gear and equipment. All the memories and moments that still surround us.

Without a pause he says, "He would be very happy. Yes. He would be so happy."

15

"Do the Best with What You've Got"

The Warrior vs. the IED

Aaron Hale likes to say that pain thrives in darkness. If we bring it out into the sunlight, and we face it, those scars can heal.

When it comes to David-and-Goliath stories, being a soldier is the ultimate fight, against the giant of war.

And for those who get injured or endure emotional scars, that battle stays with them for the rest of their lives.

Aaron has been up against several Goliaths in his life. Most of them he's battled against and won. For him, no matter how bad the outcome, he wouldn't change a thing.

At twenty-one years old, Aaron enlisted in the US Navy. He was a cook, serving on ships for eight years. He's been cooking since he could reach over a countertop. In the Navy he got to cook for the top brass, and was a culinary specialist.

Being a chef is something he feels he was born to do. It would eventually be his saving grace.

But, after 9/11, Aaron decided it was time to do something different. He wanted help fight the war on terror, joining the Army and taking on one of the most dangerous jobs in the service as a member of an Explosive Ordnance Disposal (EOD) team.

Those are the people who disarm bombs.

On his second tour in Afghanistan, his unit was on a call about a roadside improvised explosive device, or IED. Like so many other times before, he defused the bomb. He began looking for other explosives. There was a second one, but this one was hidden.

It detonated and blinded Aaron, breaking every single bone in his face. Not long after that, he would lose his ability to hear.

The incredible thing about Aaron is that he doesn't think about these tragic moments as challenges. To him, they are an opportunity to learn, and to become a better human being.

I talked to Aaron just a few days after Joe Biden suddenly decided to end the war in Afghanistan. Both Republicans and Democrats saw it as a chaotic withdrawal that left US citizens, residents, and Afghan allies stranded as the Taliban immediately took over.

Aaron says this decision was a travesty: "I think it's an absolute shame and the manner in which we pulled out and abandoned so many of our own people. So many of our friends and allies. It's a failure of leadership and it's absolutely terrible."

Aaron believes it was the government's myopia that led to such a mistake. There was plenty of information and no doubt in anyone's mind about what would happen once there was a pullout. And yet there were many other ways it could have been planned, instead of just handing the country over to terrorists after two decades of protection. Not to mention all the billions of dollars in war-fighting equipment that was gifted to the Taliban. He says we're now worse off than we were twenty years ago after the 9/11 terror attacks.

I ask why Aaron thinks President Biden decided to do this. He believes it's a legacy issue. But, he adds, the legacy is not going to be the one Biden wanted.

Having spoken to many of his "comrades in arms," Aaron says they are all of the same mind. Their service, despite this tragic outcome, was not in vain. But he does think their efforts were wasted.

"We spent twenty years keeping the terrorists at bay, preventing further attacks upon the United States and keeping Afghanistan more or less free from Taliban and Al Qaeda activity. It was an ebb and flow over the different administrations and years within that country. However, we denied them the ability to create major training camps and now they can go on the offensive towards us again."

Aaron thinks the pullout will create turmoil all over the world, though it won't happen overnight.

"This emboldens not just the Taliban, Al Qaeda. ISIS is back on the rise. The Chinese are emboldened as well. You will see more activity in the South China Sea and towards Taiwan. The Russians are everywhere you look, and in North Korea. We don't stand up to our word and we won't defend our friends in a time of need."

Even though what happened in Afghanistan is a travesty for all those who fought so hard for stability in that country, Aaron says that now more than ever we need stronger leadership and for the right people to offer to serve. Administrations come and go, but the military is still beneficial on a personal level.

"That's good for our nation and those who are willing to stand up and give that pledge. It's exactly what we need in this time."

I ask Aaron what made him enter the military. He says it was for less-than-honorable reasons. According to him, he grew up as a world-class, all-American slacker.

"I had just enough natural talent and ability when I was younger to not really have to put a whole lot of effort into just getting by. I could talk my way into and out of most trouble. And I got good enough grades to pass."

But the lack of ambition and a strong work ethic really caught up to him in college: "My grades reflected that I needed to find new goals, and a path forward. I needed to develop better values, and the military provided that. It's where I chose to direct my course."

After he was suspended from college in Ohio, Aaron moved out to live with his dad in California. He worked odd jobs but wasn't able to save much money. He felt he was going around in circles, without a plan. He needed to find a purpose in his life. Little did he know that thirteen years later, despite all the incredible challenges he would face, military service to his country is where he would find it.

I ask if he felt it was a calling for him. Aaron says he believes it might have been divine intervention or fate. Regardless, it was the best decision he ever made.

"What I've gained is so much more. I am a stronger person. I appreciate everything in my life to such a greater extent, and the people and the experiences I've gained through those friendships and relationships. Without a doubt, my military service, and I'll say it again, was the greatest decision I think I've made in my entire life."

Aaron knew he had a dangerous job: to neutralize and dispose of anything that explodes, especially IEDs. Often they would get to a scene and have to conduct post-blast analysis. That's after the land mines or the IEDs have already done their damage. Aaron has seen some of the worst that battle brings.

Sharing his story has brought catharsis to his own pain, and it's been helpful for others who are experiencing their own difficulties.

"So now it's a gift in a sense that it's like bitter and the sweet of life. The black to the white, the yin and yang."

He uses that day to color the rest of his life.

Even though I've never been in battle, I tell Aaron that having been diagnosed with a chronic illness in my mid-thirties, I kind of know what he means. In some ways it was a gift for me, because before I got sick, it was all about the superficial stuff. Moving to New York, making a name for myself, money, prestige. When I found out that I was dealing with a major health issue, and after I stopped feeling sorry for myself, it really brought incredible clarity to my life about what is most important.

Aaron also says it's a stark reminder of our mortality. "We've only got so much time to share on this planet, and who knows what happens.

So I want to make every moment count. Each day I wake up and try to make it my best day ever."

Aaron tells me about the moment his life changed forever.

He had just gotten back from a two-week vacation with his family for Thanksgiving, and recalls celebrating his son's first birthday.

The last thing he remembers seeing with his own two eyes was his family. It was the final page in his photo album memory before his sight was taken.

Aaron was back in Afghanistan and his team was picking him up. They were heading to their command outpost in their battlefield area of operation. Aaron was told there was an IED on the side of the road, and was asked if they could they check it out. His crew found what they usually did: a vegetable oil jug connected to a nine-volt battery and a couple of pieces of plywood, a pressure plate. Simple and effective. His robot took it apart, and then they picked up the evidence. He jumped out of the truck and started to make his way with an evidence kit to dispose of the rest of the materials. What he didn't realize was that a secondary device had not been detected twenty to thirty meters away from the original bomb. The explosive device went off and the blast hit him in the head. Aaron was knocked into the air, untouched from the neck down. He was still conscious but the "lights had gone out." He checked his functions. Fingers and toes seemed to be in place, but he couldn't see.

Aaron describes his next move: "So I reached up to adjust my helmet, which I thought had gotten pushed over my face, just to find out that the helmet was completely gone. And the first thing I thought was, Oh, no, this is bad. The Army is going to want that helmet back!'"

Aaron says it's crazy that that's the first thing he thought about, but in traumatic situations, your brain works in funny ways as a coping mechanism instead of confronting the worst-case scenario.

"My team came out and dragged me back to safety. The medics got to work on me. The medevac chopper was there in minutes because we weren't that far away from Kandahar Airfield."

Within forty-eight hours Aaron was in a hospital bed at Walter

Reed National Military Medical Center in Bethesda, Maryland, in his words "learning how to be a blind person."

The blast had taken one of his eyes and had cracked his skull. He was leaking spinal fluid out of his nose and there were multiple cuts, burns, and bruises.

The doctors at Walter Reed attempted to save one eye. The other one was completely gone. After a couple of surgeries, it couldn't be saved. They patched up the cracks in his skull, which would lead to more complications down the road. Aaron says he remembers being on the bed stunned and trying to figure out the rest of his life. He was angry and disappointed in himself. Mad that he was hit with such low-tech warfare because he had trained so hard and was better than that. He had always been prepared. Over and over again, he was an expert with this stuff. And after so many times that he had succeeded, they, the enemy, had scored. He felt like a complete failure. That's what leads to the mental demons and the downward spiral for so many.

He tried to convince himself not to accept defeat: "I was still an active-duty soldier. A team leader. A husband, father, son, and brother. I had these roles to play no matter what the difficulties."

Aaron loves General Jim Mattis and what he says in his book, *Call Sign Chaos*: that in the Marines, the fact that things were hard was never a good excuse for mission failure.

"So, I think this is a hard thing to do now, but that's not an excuse. I still have to get out of bed. I am still going to perform my duties with all those hats that I had to wear. So, I realized if I was going to be blind, I'm going to be the best blind guy I could be."

Those cracks in his skull came back to haunt him years later, because either they were never completely patched or they reopened. There was still a spinal fluid leak through his sinuses. But being able to tell others what happened helped Aaron get through the hardest moments.

He decided that nothing was going to get in the way of achieving his goals. There were mountains to climb; whitewater kayaking, and running the Boston Marathon.

After coming home from one of his speaking engagements, Aaron recalls feeling awful; he was fatigued and dizzy. He lay down for a nap and when he woke up, he had the mother of all headaches.

He remembers it felt as if his head and brain were being crushed.

"I called 911 and it was actually a little funny. An operator asked what was the nature of my emergency. And I said, 'Ma'am, I have a very, very bad headache.' And to her credit, she said, 'On a scale of one to ten, how bad is the pain?' And I said again, 'Ma'am, I've never felt pain like this in my life and I've literally been blown up before.' She said, 'The ambulance is on its way.'"

Aaron was taken to the hospital and was there for many days. When he finally woke up, his mom and girlfriend were there by this side. He found out within a couple of days that he would soon be completely deaf due to bacterial meningitis.

Because of some incredible technology, Aaron is now able to hear from a cochlear implant. He describes how it works: The processor, the external part, sits on the ear, kind of like a hearing aid. But there's a tether that attaches it right up behind the temple and on the skull above the ear. It's connected by a magnet and sends a signal into the actual implant, which has an electrode attached to the auditory nerve. The electric signal bypasses the inner workings of the ear, so your brain has to learn how to translate this electric signal. Aaron says it took some getting used to for the first year or so, because you've got to go to an audiologist who fine-tunes the implants for the processors.

Mapping is what they call it, where your brain is trying to decipher what it's getting.

Before the cochlear implants, Aaron was completely deaf and blind. He says it was like being trapped inside his own body because he couldn't get messages in or out. His girlfriend (now wife), McKayla, stepped in and started tracing the letters of every word she wanted to say in the palm of his hand. That was the only way he was able to communicate for six months, until the first cochlear implant went in. It took seven or eight months before he could finally speak to someone and hear their response.

I ask if Aaron went into a dàrk place when those challenges got to be too much. He says the demons were there, especially during the first year and a half.

"The what-ifs and the why-mes thinking, you know, when is enough, enough? Why have I been chosen twice to go through such turmoil, such trauma, such struggle when this soldier repaid his fair share and his dues? But that's all self-defeating. It doesn't get me or anybody anywhere."

Thanksgiving was coming up, and he wanted to throw a big dinner, inviting family and friends from across the country. He asked some EOD students to join them, since they sometimes get stranded at school during the holidays and don't have enough money to get home. For a few weeks in advance, he was making desserts and freezing them. This new project was making him more outward-focused and bringing back his passion for being in the kitchen again.

Having a project took away the pain and suffering, and McKayla said she noticed a few things going on.

"She saw something she hadn't seen in many months: a smile on my face. And the other thing she noticed? The fudge was piling up."

There were so many desserts that his wife started giving them away to neighbors and friends. Then the neighbors and friends began coming back and asking if they could buy them. The capitalist in Aaron said, "Of course they can buy it!" That's how the next chapter of his life began: making and selling candy from his own kitchen.

However, getting to this point in his life took time. And patience. Aaron felt helpless in the beginning. When he came home from the hospital, and the bacteria in his inner ear took his sense of balance, he had to be put in a wheelchair. He then tried using tracking poles that people use to climb with. That got him to the mailbox and back, which at first was an exhausting endeavor. Eventually, after pushing through the pain, he got back on the treadmill and started walking again.

"I would start with half a mile an hour (on the treadmill) and then I hit the arrow button to go faster. Eventually I was jogging again. Two years from my first Boston Marathon, I ran it again."

Through it all, McKayla was there helping nurse him back to health, buying the groceries, taking care of the bills, and helping him get his life back. He says she was the angel sent to him by God.

Aaron has three kids: one from a previous marriage, and identical twin boys with McKayla. He tells me he is so grateful for the family he has been blessed with.

I ask him if there's anything he can't set his mind to doing. What was the biggest challenge he's had to overcome?

That's when he admits that everything that has been difficult up until now, he has looked at as an opportunity.

"After running my first marathon, I wanted to run the next one faster, and then once I got my speed goal, I wanted to go further. So I ran a twelve-hour race and made about fifty-two miles. Last year I ran an ultramarathon. Each one gets harder. Learning how to hear again was definitely difficult. But each day gave me a purpose to get better. To challenge myself and become a better person. Become a better father and better husband."

I ask what he tells people to motivate them. He loves telling a story about his days in the Army. Every team is composed of three people—a leader and two team members. They are given a huge shipping container full of tools and equipment for the job, from bomb service to hazmat kits and robots, power tools, you name it. They have to have a whole arsenal of gadgets when it comes to explosives on the battlefield because there are hundreds of thousands of types of munitions out there, and they have to render them all safe and dispose of them securely.

During the exercise, soldiers have to decide which tools they can keep with them, but they have to leave a few behind. In Afghanistan, most roads are just dirt trails and you can't drive on them, so they have to dismount and be on foot. That means leaving almost all your tools behind, except what you can carry on your back. In other words, doing the same job without a lot of help.

"So here I am without a couple of tools: my hearing and my sight, but I still have a job to do and I can't worry about what I had to leave behind. I have to adapt and overcome. And I encourage everybody to take that kind of perspective. Don't worry about what we can't change. Don't worry about what you don't have at hand. Assess the situation and do the best with what you've got."

Just like David. He had only a sling to take down the most powerful beast.

But when it comes to Afghanistan, sometimes the good guys can't win the war.

That doesn't mean people like Aaron aren't thankful. Quite the contrary.

"I'm grateful for all the experiences in my life. I'm grateful for the people that have graced me with their presence and grateful for my children and my wife and my incredible parents and my brother and my sister. Now I'm grateful for having a story like this to share. I'm grateful for second chances every time I wake up. I'm grateful for every day."

He's also grateful for the country he was born into. The military service and the ability to serve. Grateful to be a citizen.

Aaron also wants his kids to grow up with those values.

"I want them to be good people, and to chase their dreams and pursue careers that fulfill them and add value to this world. If that's joining the military, I'd be absolutely proud, and if not, I'd still be proud. As long as they live their lives to the fullest."

Aaron also believes one person can change the world. Individuals are doing it every day. One opportunity at a time.

He says it all goes back to the right state of mind in attacking each day. Once you realize that you can do something you previously thought was impossible, it makes every other day a little bit easier.

16

"I've Been to the Abyss"

The Green Beret vs. the Taliban

After speaking with Aaron Hale about his time in Afghanistan, and thinking about the scars he lives with both physically and mentally, I couldn't get our conversation out of my mind. Especially after the news of President Joe Biden deciding to end the twenty-year war the United States waged there. Those images of Afghan citizens at Kabul Airport in August 2021, desperately grabbing onto a US Air Force plane taking off kept replaying in my head. They were unable to hang on, and many died trying to cling to freedom. Even if it was just a few seconds in the air before falling to their deaths.

We also can't forget one of the deadliest days for American forces there, when thirteen American service members were killed in a bomb attack just days before the deadline for the last US troops to leave Afghanistan. Islamic State militants claimed responsibility for the suicide bombing, which was carried out during the massive evacuation following the inevitable Taliban takeover.

I think most people will agree that the enormous task of getting

Americans and allies out safely was not planned very well, and the fallout of this decision could be very big in the decades to come.

It's hard to see a lot of silver linings in this story, but I found one man who made it his mission to bring as many of our Afghan allies to safety as possible. That is certainly a beautiful light trying to shine through during a very dark time in our history.

Lieutenant Colonel Scott Mann is a retired Green Beret commander who joined a team of people trying to rescue his comrades and their families who were running for their lives.

Operation Pineapple Express was run by a volunteer group of US veterans, including Scott, doing whatever they could to help those who helped us over the last twenty years in Afghanistan. It's called the Pineapple Express because Afghans were using pictures of a pineapple as a rescue signal.

According to a report by ABC News, the first news organization to follow their mission, Task Force Pineapple worked with members of the US military and the US embassy "to protect hundreds of Afghan special operators, assets and enablers and their families by bringing them inside the U.S. military-controlled side of Hamid Karzai International Airport" in Kabul.

Some have said these efforts are greater than the commitment on the battlefield. Scott believes their mission together is the absolute definition of David and Goliath.

I start our conversation by thanking Scott for his service and asking him a bit about his history. He spent twenty-three years in the US Army, eighteen of them in the Army special forces, otherwise known as the Green Berets. He remembers meeting a Green Beret when he was fourteen years old and being fascinated by the work they did.

"They were different than the SEALs and the Rangers. Those are great folks, too. But what Green Berets do is they head into places where there's no trust and where there's chaos. They go in and they form connections. They build relationships in a very Lawrence of Arabia kind of way."

Scott says the Green Berets are combat multipliers. They learn foreign languages, forging relationships and social capital, and then mobilize people. That's what happened with the horse soldiers at the beginning of the war in Afghanistan. On October 19, 2001, Captain Mark Nutsch and a team of eleven other Green Berets were brought to Afghanistan as the United States began its effort to liberate the country from the Taliban and destroy the terrorist group Al Qaeda, which had found a home there and launched the 9/11 attacks. The Afghan tribes provided the horses, and many of the soldiers had never been on horseback. It's quite something: this kind of response was a throwback to how wars were fought with cavalry instead of using tanks and trucks.

In 2011, a bronze statue called *America Response Monument*, often refered to as the "Horse Soldier" statue, was created to honor those twelve men. "De Oppresso Liber" is also the motto of the US Army Special Forces, meaning "To free the oppressed."

It stands at the base of One World Trade Center.

Scott worked in Central and South America with the Green Berets in the 1990s, during the drug war. After 9/11, he spent most of his career in and out of Afghanistan. He wasn't part of the initial invasion but says it's a point of pride that when the terror attacks happened and America responded, it did so with less than a hundred special operators. Those soldiers who went in under cover of darkness and in less than one hundred days mobilized the Northern Alliance and various Pashtun tribes to drive the Taliban and Al Qaeda out of the country. They did it from the grassroots level, from the bottom up.

"A lot of us believe that had we stayed with that approach, we probably would be having a much different conversation about Afghanistan right now."

For many of us who watched this war unfold over the last twenty years, it's alarming how quickly and seemingly unprepared the United States was to suddenly leave the country in 2021. What happened? Scott says he worked around Afghanistan under four most recent US administrations and found them all to be "magnificently underwhelming" in their understanding and command of the Afghan War.

"Now, to understand what Joe Biden did, you have to understand that just before him, President Trump put together a peace deal that completely excluded the Afghan government that we had worked with for twenty years. If you were in that government, how would you feel about dealing with the US? So, when President Biden came into power, the fix was kind of in on a really bad deal. I mean, the Taliban held all the cards."

Scott says a conditions-based exit was going to be very difficult, but Biden put the final nail in the coffin: "He owns the catastrophe that is the Afghan withdrawal. But if you look at his history, if you look at comments that he's made about Vietnam when he was a junior senator, it was the same thing. He did not feel one ounce of obligation to anything other than getting American citizens out."

In April 1975, as many South Vietnamese were asking for help to leave their country, then senator Biden reportedly said in a Senate speech: "The United States has no obligation to evacuate one, or 100,001, South Vietnamese."

President Gerald Ford tried to remind Biden that Americans have always welcomed refugees, especially when it comes to war, but the Delaware senator didn't agree.

In a Senate Foreign Relations Committee meeting, Biden was quoted as saying, "I will vote for any amount for getting the Americans out. I don't want it mixed with getting the Vietnamese out."

Scott believes that since there was no commitment to get Vietnamese refugees out back then, why would there be remorse for Afghans?

"So it's really not surprising if you look at his history. He was right on point with what he does, and has not wavered. He has not given one ounce of consideration to at-risk Afghans, and he won't."

I ask Scott what he would have done differently.

He says, start by listening to military officers on the ground. "I have it on high authority that General Mark Milley, who was the senior NATO commander on the ground, and other senior commanders were telling the president and his administration in March [2021] that if you pull away completely out of Afghanistan, the whole thing is going to fall like a house of cards. So, that's the first thing I would have done: listened to the men and women on the ground who were prosecuting the war."

Scott says he also would have left in place a counterterrorism force, which was highly recommended, and kept building a force of Green Berets like we've done in the Philippines and Colombia, to keep working with the military, the commandos, and the Afghan special forces. Keeping those units on the ground would make a lasting impact.

"And the final thing I'll say is I certainly would have kept Bagram [Airfield] open longer. I would have kept Kandahar Airfield open. Put more priority on these places and green card holders getting out. There should have been more priority on lives who had their paperwork in."

If Scott had been in charge, he would have doubled down when the State Department asked what they needed to get all of this done. It should have been a priority.

"And then I would have worked to fly people out of Bagram and Kandahar and not just Kabul International Airport, which was a disaster. Those are the big things I would have done," he says.

I tell Scott the image I have seared in my memory is of those Afghan people at Kabul Airport literally dying to get out of there by grabbing on to the plane that was taking off and heading to America. They were so desperate, and it was heartbreaking. He says a lot of those folks would rather have fifteen seconds of freedom than fifteen more years under the Taliban.

He tells me, "When I hear people saying the Afghans didn't want democracy, the Afghans didn't want freedom, they didn't believe in fighting for it? Well, many that came together in Pineapple to help get out, they fought to the last bullet. They were calling us saying, 'The generals have fled. What do I do? Do I keep fighting? Do I hide my weapon?'"

There is plenty of blame to go around, but let's not forget that Afghanistan has been at war on and off for thousands of years. So, to think that in just twenty years we're going to help get them back on their feet is not realistic. But for Scott, and others who have skin in the game, this is nation building. It's in our best interest to maintain long-term partnerships and work with them over the long haul.

If you look at Operation Pineapple Express or any of the other veteran-based organizations, that's what's at play. These groups of people, combat veterans, look at a situation and say, "No one is coming for them, so I'll do it."

That's what leadership looks like.

"I take so much courage from that and so much heart from that, and I hope other Americans do, too, because our country needs that right now. More than ever. Our kids are watching us. They are looking at us, asking what are you going to do? Sit in the bleachers? Are you going to get in the arena? That's my biggest metric: knowing that my three boys are watching me."

I ask Scott to talk about how Task Force Pineapple came to be. He says it started with his Afghan special forces friend Nezam, whom he met in 2010. He had been trying to get Nezam a visa for years, and he was on the run, living in his uncle's house like Anne Frank. It was obvious that if the Taliban found him, he would be killed on the spot. He was known to every bad guy, and had already been shot in the face and wounded six times. There was no way he was going to be allowed to live with their retribution campaign.

"So for me, it was like, you can either sit here and watch another friend die, or you can do something. And it was clear that no one else was going to do anything. Nobody else was coming. I called up some other Green Beret buddies who knew the country, and knew Nezam, and I was like, he's got to move across the city and he's got to do that undetected. If we can get him close to the gate, we can probably build one of our relationships and get him out of there."

His friends agreed to help, and they became Nezam's eyes and ears, using Signal Messenger encrypted chat rooms to communicate. They knew the territory, with years of experience and relationships they had built, and started trying to get him out. It was not easy.

"Trying to move across the city with no real plan, your phone is running out of power and you have no money . . ."

They found a diplomat who was a former Green Beret and came up with a code word: Pineapple.

Scott will never forget the day they got a selfie of Nezam on the other side of the wire. "And that became Task Force Pineapple. But then, suddenly other SEALs, Rangers, and special forces guys were hearing about what we did with Nezam, and all of a sudden, they had people they wanted to help get out, so 'Can you help me?'"

Task Force Pineapple now has a safe house program and a humanitarian corridor of six thousand people. It costs about $15,000 a day to do something like this. The money they've raised is all private, and the effort is far from over.

Scott tells me this kind of work is not something new: "I know an eighty-seven-year-old Green Beret still pulling Montagnards tribesmen out that he fought with in Vietnam, and he's not going to stop until he dies. That's just how it goes. And I think the Biden administration and all these bureaucrats and generals completely misjudged the American people. They sure as hell misjudged the veteran population because we're not going to let this go. Ever."

Although the task of getting folks to safety is a herculean one, what happens when they come to the United States with nothing but the clothes on their back? They need everything from clothing to food to income.

Nezam, for example, left his country with his wife and three kids under the age of eleven. They only had a backpack. They left everything behind and spent 150 days in refugee camps, from Qatar to Kosovo to Fort Dix. They were all traumatized. But people stepped up to help.

Scott says his Tampa Bay, Florida, community came together and sponsored Nezam and his family. They raised close to $60,000, and an entire house was donated, along with furniture, food, and clothes. Nezam was overwhelmed by this outpouring of love and kindness. He's now working with Scott's nonprofit, teaching Afghans when they come to the United States.

"He may choose to get a different job in six months," Scott says, "but the thing is, for six months to a year, they've got a nice landing where he can get his feet on the ground. He speaks wonderful English. He's a great leader. He's going to really contribute to American society. But if we just put him in a hotel and he gets a job as a cabdriver and lives on welfare, that's a different outcome. Unfortunately, the latter is what's happening the most."

Nezam's story is one of true resilience and overcoming some of the worst challenges a human can face. He was born at the end of the Soviet era. His father was an Uzbek freedom fighter and was killed by the Soviets. The next day, a bomb was dropped on their village and everyone fled the house where Nezam and his family were living. He was only four months old when he was left in his crib. Their house was destroyed, but when his mom went back to try to find her son, they pulled Nezam from the wreckage. He was alive, without a scratch on him.

"And that began the journey of this young man who was very hard to kill."

After Nezam's father was murdered, his mother was sold to an older man and brought into a new marriage. Her son lived as a servant, slept in the barn with the animals, and joined the army at age seventeen. He became a commando by the age of eighteen, and by the time he was twenty-one was one of the most feared commandos and special forces guys in the inventory.

When Scott met Nezam, he had been shot through the face in combat. He's small in stature, under five feet tall, and when you meet him and get to know him, he has a sweet disposition, kind, with a bright smile and big laugh that you never forget. Scott says he became a brother to him, and when the United States started pulling out of Afghanistan, one of Scott's first thoughts was to get his buddy Nezam out.

"He's part of our regiment, he's part of who we are. And through all of that trauma that he's endured, his attitude is so positive. He's grateful for everything that's happened in his life, and he's grateful to be here. He's going to be an amazing leader. I can't wait to see what he does because I think when he really gets his voice and he starts telling his story, people are just going to be in awe of what this guy brings to the table."

I ask Scott if, through all of this, he is still optimistic. He says that to some degree he is, but he's also a realist in the sense that he spent most of his adult life as a Green Beret, and was in the most trust-depleted, dangerous places on earth. He thinks that right now we are on a path of tribalism, and the sad part about that is the individual is the one that suffers, because if tribalism flourishes in a society, the individual no longer has relevance. Having said that, Scott also believes that our country has an amazing amount of resilience, mostly because of the people he works alongside.

"I have a lot of faith in our combat veterans. I think that's who we should be looking to right now for what leadership looks like. I believe we should point at things like Operation Pineapple and realize that's what we should be doing more of."

Scott says that's his main focus: being a motivator at a grassroots level during a really tough time in our country. His mission is to inspire what he calls "rooftop leaders" who get up on the rooftops like the Green Berets did to rally Afghan farmers to fight alongside them.

"And that's what I'm after: inspiring people to just take a stand in their own arena. And it doesn't have to be Afghanistan. It can be the school board, the PTA. The issues you know are right or wrong. Step in there and take the microphone. I mean, that's what the country actually needs.

I ask Scott about his boys. What do you wish the most for them in this life? His oldest son is an infantry platoon leader, his middle son wants to be in federal law enforcement, and his youngest son is a baseball player who also has aspirations to go into the military. He tells them that regardless of what you choose to do in life, your greatest responsibility is being an American citizen.

"Being a citizen to me is one of the most daunting, difficult jobs in the world. You have to be a steward for your society when nobody's looking. You have to trust in something that's sometimes hard to believe in and fight for and protect it. Being a great citizen and a protector of the Constitution is one of the most noble things a human can do. It's an honor, and no matter what occupation you have, it's still your job to be a citizen."

Scott also strongly believes that one person can make a difference. Just look back at what they did in August 2021: Starting with nothing except an Afghan comrade in duress and three Green Berets who wanted to help. That was it. Now they've raised $7,000,000, sustaining six thousand people in safe houses. Scott hasn't had any special training other than being a Green Beret, and didn't come from money or influence.

"You have to imagine that it's possible, and then you have to work at it. It's difficult work and it's underappreciated and you get about eighty spears in your back every night. But yes, I absolutely believe that one person can make a difference, and it's probably our only way out of this."

I ask Scott if he can remember a time when he felt like he couldn't do this anymore. Was there a point where he said someone else needs to take over, and it's too much? Was there a moment he almost gave up, but then someone or something told him to keep going?

Scott says it's happened a few times, but the one, pivotal moment was when he first got out of the service. "I looked around at the country in 2013 and was so disgusted with what was happening. I felt like I was completely irrelevant, and I had lost my voice. I didn't have a purpose anymore. The country was just chewing itself apart, and I didn't want to be a part of it."

He was doing contract work with the government and it wasn't rewarding. The PTSD and survivor's guilt were setting in.

"Within eighteen months, I was standing in my bedroom closet holding a 45-millimeter. So, yeah, I've been to the abyss, and had my son not come home that afternoon unexpectedly, I don't think I'd be here."

Scott says there have been moments that were about as dark as it can get, but what helped was talking to other veterans. He realized that it was helping him and others.

"I started to really see that I had a relevant purpose again, I had a role to play and I started really doubling down on that at a very interpersonal level."

Most recently, just a few months before the anniversary of September 11, Scott felt like he had taken on too much, trying to get all these people home from Afghanistan. He hadn't slept in days, and even though they had gotten many out, there were so many others left behind.

"I was sitting at the kitchen counter with Monty, my wife, and I was almost in tears. We've put our own money into this and we were running out of money, and I'm like, I can't do this anymore. And then right about that time, I got a text and it said, 'Scott, it's [General] Mark Milley. Call me.' And that started a dialogue with leaders in the Pentagon to try to keep this thing going, and to try to find ways to solve this problem."

Scott says his whole life has been punctuated with examples like that, and it's usually in that time of the greatest struggle, the darkest moment, that a sign will come, and you have to decide to keep moving.

"That's the resistance, and it usually means that you're on the five-yard line. You just can't see it through the fog."

I tell Scott I'm so grateful I've met him and heard about his incredible journey. I believe that all these stories can help people realize that there is light at the end of the tunnel. You just have to keep moving to finally get there, no matter how painful and how dark. That's where the healing begins, too.

"I think in our country right now, what we need to be doing is sharing more of these stories. If we would just pay attention to the words of others, really listen from a place of discovery. Try to be an empathetic witness and see the miles a person walks. If we did that, we would have such a shared perspective, and a lot of this other stuff would fall away."

Scott thinks this method of storytelling in the veteran population should be expanded into civilian society as well. Instead of looking to leaders we vote for, keep reminding Americans we have a great batch of true leaders who are here among us. All around us.

"Look to them and they'll show you the way," he says.

17

"Just Doing the Job"

The Weather Reporter vs. the Storm

A lot of people like to dismiss those who do the weather. I've heard it all.

"Hey, it must be nice being the TV meteorologist! It's the only job you get to keep even if you're wrong most of the time."

When I was challenging Governor Andrew Cuomo after his reckless and deadly mandate to put COVID patients into nursing homes, the one piece of ammunition his office thought they had was to demean me for my career as a broadcast meteorologist. "The weather girl." Their official quote from disgraced Governor Cuomo's spokesperson Rich Azzopardi was "Last I checked, she's not a credible source on anything except maybe the weather."

What people conveniently forget is that when it comes to alerting the public, weather forecasters are the ones who have to deliver the news that can potentially save lives, and we take that job very seriously. It involves scientific study and an understanding of how the atmosphere works, which is not something required in covering general news or politics.

There are many examples of weather that shaped a crucial decision or moment in history, including in times of war.

The American Revolution could have been a whole lot worse if it weren't for some foggy conditions that helped save patriot troops. After a week of fighting the British in Brooklyn, New York, General George Washington decided to cross the East River to withdraw. It was a long process, happening at night and into the early hours of the morning. Had the British seen them, they would have been captured or killed. The fog also helped cover their movements, and the soldiers lit bonfires to make it look like the whole army was still there. By the time the sun came up, the low clouds cleared, winds changed direction, and the Continental Army was gone. If they had been seen during a clear day, the war might have turned out very different.

The 1930s Dust Bowl changed America's population forever. The name came from the drought-plagued Plains during a dry period that lasted on and off for several years. Severe storms blew dirt and dust, which swept through states stretching from Texas to Nebraska. People and livestock were killed, while crops were lost. These extreme weather conditions, combined with the devastating impact of the Great Depression, forced families to move west to look for work and better living conditions.

The most famous forecast of all was the prediction of a clear day for D-Day. As the story goes, there were three teams of military weather forecasters from the US Army Air Corps, the British Royal Navy, and the British Meteorological Office.

Group Captain James Martin Stagg was the chief meteorologist and the one who convinced US General Eisenhower to change the date of the Allied invasion. Stagg not only helped predict a storm on June 5 (which delayed the invasion by a day) but also made the incredible forecast that the weather would quiet down just long enough the following day (June 6) to allow Operation Overlord to go ahead.

Captain Stagg felt there was an opportunity for a small ridge of high pressure to bring clear skies for a short period of time and give them a very big advantage over the enemy. There was also the additional help of a full moon to assist the plane and glider pilots with visibility the night before. Low tides gave them more room to go around obstacles.

Meanwhile, the German meteorologists were predicting gale force winds and stormy weather arriving on June 5 and lasting for several days. The Germans were so bold in their decision that many soldiers left their posts for military exercises in France instead of anticipating an attack. German Field Marshal Erwin Rommel was so confident that the weather would keep the Allies away, he went home to Germany for his wife's birthday. He reportedly bought her a brand-new pair of shoes for the special occasion.

On June 6 the weather started off less than ideal, with rough seas, high winds, and cloud cover. It was challenging for paratroopers and boats to move in, but by noon, conditions improved just as Stagg had predicted, and the Germans were unprepared.

More than 160,000 Allied troops were able to storm into Normandy, France, on that brief, clear day of June 6, 1944. But without those incredibly smart meteorologists, the invasion of Europe would have been delayed for several weeks. By then, soldiers would have had to deal with a beast of a storm, one Prime Minister Winston Churchill described as the "worst channel storm in forty years."

A few years later, during the ride to the US Capitol for President-elect John F. Kennedy's inauguration, Kennedy apparently asked President Eisenhower why the invasion had been so successful. He replied, "Because we had better meteorologists than the Germans!"

That's the story I've always known, that is, until a couple of years ago, when I learned there was more to it, and it had to do with a young woman from Ireland named Maureen Flavin Sweeney.

Miss Sweeney was the one who took those important weather readings at Blacksod weather station on Ireland's west coast.

The *Irish Times* wrote:

On June 3rd, 1944, Maureen was the very first to help forecast the massive storm at a remote lighthouse and coastguard station at Blacksod Point, county Mayo, Ireland.

The barometer at the remote weather station showed pressure was dropping rapidly, indicating a major Atlantic storm was due to arrive and blow right across western Europe. Based on Ms Flavin's readings, US general Dwight D. Eisenhower postponed the D-Day landing by 24 hours.

Today, her son Vincent Sweeney is the lighthouse keeper at Blacksod Point.

He says that his mum was proud of the dispatch's service and "happy that she got it right."

At the time, she was completely unaware of her David-and-Goliath forecast. Despite its size, Operation Overlord was a well-guarded secret. That small ridge of high pressure was the vulnerable spot David discovered before taking out Goliath.

She was just doing her job, and her readings were the first to point out there was a storm on the horizon, which later helped open the window of opportunity that Eisenhower and the Allies needed to launch their invasion and change the course of history.

I talked to Vincent about his mother's incredible forecast, and his family's legacy there. He tells me about his travels all over Ireland. He's worked offshore on the lighthouses before they were automated. Right now, he says he's "shore based" and lives a good life. Vincent joined the service in 1974. His other two brothers, Gerard and Ted Jr., were also part of the Lighthouse Service. Ted was a marine engineer and took care of all the lighthouses around the coast, bringing fuel and water. Gerard was also a lighthouse keeper, and Ted Sweeney Sr., their dad, worked in the lighthouse from 1933 until 1981, when Vincent came ashore and took over.

"The sea is in the blood," Vincent announces.

His mother is still alive, and lives in a nursing home in Belmullet, County Mayo. Maureen was honored in a ceremony in June 2021, marking the seventy-seventh anniversary of D-Day and the role she played in helping change the course of the invasion. Her name is now listed in the US Congressional Record for the now-famous weather report she delivered that "ultimately saved countless lives."

US Representative Jack Berman, from Michigan, a retired three-star Marine Corps general who holds the highest military rank of any current member of congress, wrote on the seventy-seventh anniversary of the D-Day landing that he was honored to recognize the service of Maureen Flavin Sweeney.

"Her skill and professionalism were crucial in ensuring Allied victory, and her legacy will live on for generations to come."

I tell Vincent that I always knew the significance of the D-Day forecast, but I didn't know his mom was the one delivering the information. He tells me that years went by before the Sweeney family learned how that weather report was an important turning point.

In 1956 the weather station where Maureen took her observations was moved from Blacksod to the nearest sizable town, Belmullet, twelve miles away. The government set up the station so meteorologists could run it.

"It was during that transfer that the top dogs from the Meteorological Service in Ireland mentioned the incredible significance of that forecast," Vincent says.

His parents were shocked to find out how critical their work was to quite literally the history of the world.

The Sweeneys' contribution wasn't really publicized or written about until the fiftieth anniversary of D-Day, in 1994. Brendan McWilliams, who worked with the Irish Meteorological Service, had a daily column in the *Irish Times*, called "Weather Eye." That's when the story grew legs and created more interest.

McWilliams wrote:

Light winds, good visibility and calm seas were essential if the attack was to be a success; military planners selected 5 June as the best day for the invasion to go ahead.

On 3 June, 1944, reports started coming in from a weather station at Blacksod Point in County Mayo in the west of Ireland of the approach of an active—and totally unexpected—cold front.

The small weather station was manned by the Sweeney family, who also ran the local post office. The weather reports sent to Dublin were passed on to London.

A cold front would be over the invasion area bringing rain and strong winds.

Sure enough, rain and winds affected the English Channel around the time for which the invasion had been originally planned.

By 6 June, however, the depression had lost much of its intensity, the cold front had passed the battle area, and the weather was sufficiently good not to interfere with operations.

The rest, they say, is history. Vincent says that after that column ran, there was much more interest in his mom and that famous weather report, including a documentary and many TV and radio reports across Europe.

Vincent says the award his mother received from the US House of Representatives in the summer of 2021 was incredibly special.

"And only now," he tells me, "just in her ninety-eighth year, you could say it's the recognition she deserved. I'm happy for her and for those who worked together during the war to give those forecasts."

He pauses and adds, "Because Mom is still alive. She's the only one left from that moment, you know."

I ask Vincent what his mom was like growing up.

"She was a good mother and she worked hard to educate the family. And Dad worked very hard because in those days there was no 'free education.' Gerard and I were sent to boarding school, which you had to pay for."

Ted, the eldest brother, went to an engineering school in Cork and trained as a marine engineer. Emer, their sister, studied to become a nurse and lives in New York.

He recalls his mother being very straight in how she dealt with things, and strict in their upbringing. She had a tough childhood. Her own mom died when she was just twelve, and her sister passed away in 1970. She was on her own.

"People tried to pull the wool over her eyes, but there was no way they were getting away with that," he says.

He pauses.

"She was strict. But always fair."

I was struck by how Maureen spent many years in school. Back then, for a woman to put an emphasis on her studies was quite rare.

Vincent agrees. "Absolutely. Yes. She did her five years in the convent boarding school, and then did her final exams. We call it here the leaving certificate. She did very well. She was very good at math. I remember her working in the post office, and there weren't calculators at the time. She never needed one. She could do it in her head. As long as her pencil was sharp, she would say—and would always use a pencil because you could erase it and start again."

I tell Vincent how much I love his mother's story and wanted to include it in this book because Maureen really took her job seriously. She challenged herself and took on something that was out of her comfort zone and stuck with it. I remember what it was like studying to become a broadcast meteorologist. You have to have a level of confidence in your experience because a mistake in your warnings can literally mean life or death. Being in the middle of a war brings it to the next level. Vincent says that during the dark winter nights when she was completing her weather observations, if she heard an aircraft overhead, she was afraid.

"She always thought the Germans were going to invade, with paratroopers coming in by sea. That was scary because there wasn't much radio communication then. There was no way to receive information. And the BBC wasn't going to come out and just spill the beans on everything."

Vincent is also someone who has to rely on the weather to make informed decisions during his work. He's on call 24/7, 365 days a year

at the lighthouse. They have a refueling base for search-and-rescue he-
licopters and air ambulances that have to be at the ready.

"We are always watching the weather charts. It's part of us," he says.

One more extremely positive thing that came out of Maureen's work
is how she met Ted, her future husband and Vincent's dad. Ted is the one
who checked her weather observations to make sure they were correct
before sending them out.

"They got to know each other while working in Blacksod Post
Office and the weather station. They got married in 1946, and lived in
Blacksod for many years, raising a family of four."

He pauses, and then concludes:

"It worked out for them. That's what happened."

And they trusted each other.

I ask if Maureen ever told stories about the war to her kids. He says
she would remind them about how poor everyone was. He remembers a
lot of talk about rationing coupons.

"She loved her cup of tea," he recalls, "but tea was rationed. She knew
food couldn't be wasted. She saw that people suffered during the war and
learned to appreciate the good things in life when the war ended."

That was instilled in Vincent's upbringing as well.

As we chat about the war and life back then, I am reminded that we
all just went through something very big, too—living through a pandemic.
Still, even though this is an extraordinarily difficult time in our history,
we aren't part of a world war. Vincent says he's always been interested in
history. The influence of the D-Day forecast inspires him to this day.

"Omaha, Normandy. There are over nine and a half thousand Americans buried. My God," he says, "I just could sit there for hours thinking
of the sacrifice that these men and women made for freedom, all the
Allied forces that fought. It's very emotional."

Vincent says he has visited many graveyards, and it's devastating to
learn about all the young lives that were lost in that war.

"But I take my hat off to America. Europe would have been lost
without their help," he adds, "It's great. Freedom. Freedom, democracy.

I thank all those troops who sacrificed their lives. Both the men and the women."

I ask Vincent if he thinks his mom was proud of her achievement. Or, did she just say it was something she was supposed to do, not really knowing how profound that experience would be?

"Yes," he replies. "She did say, 'I was doing my job. Just doing the job.' But she was also a responsible, honest person. Even at the post office. At the end of the day, she had to count all the cash, and balance the books. If she was a penny out, she would find that penny. That's how conscientious she was. She was diligent and she was clever. So clever."

Maureen is still alive, and is living in a wonderful nursing home in Belmullet, County Mayo. They take good care of her.

I tell Vincent about my husband losing his parents in the spring of 2020 during the pandemic. It was so incredibly tragic not being able to see them before they died. Vincent tells me he knows our story because his sister Emer lives in upstate New York, in Poestenkill, about half an hour from Albany. She works as a nurse in a nursing home, and Vincent explains that he spoke with her after I requested an interview.

"She told me, 'You must speak with Janice!' Because she knows what you've been through, she watches you all the time, loves watching your show, and sees your fight on the news. So, I have no problem talking to Janice Dean," he says.

I get a bit choked up after hearing this. I suddenly feel an emotional and personal connection to Vincent and his family despite having never met them.

I ask if Vincent gets to see his mom regularly now. He says rules were very strict during the pandemic in Ireland as well. "We go see her three or four times a week. She's being well cared for, but the COVID lockdown was tough."

When they had the restrictions, they would have window visits with his mother, and that was difficult. Being on the outside looking in. They had a microphone set up in the facility by which they could try to talk to each other. But it wasn't the same.

"You couldn't shake hands or give her a peck on the cheek when you greeted her. And of course we had to wear masks when visiting."

I tell Vincent how glad I am that he can see her. They're now trying to get their sister Emer back to Ireland from New York. She's just been able to do phone visits via WhatsApp.

I remember what it was like finally getting to see my own mom, Stella, who lives in Canada after almost two years from being apart. I took a picture of my boys Matthew and Theodore hugging her in our kitchen after she walked through the door. I can't even put into words how emotional that was for all of us.

I end our conversation by asking about the lighthouses Vincent knows so well. There is something so soothing about them. I think of them as a symbol of hope and guidance in the lives of others.

Vincent knows exactly what I'm talking about.

"A lighthouse is the guiding light," he says. "It helps to steer you home. It's like life, isn't it?"

Vincent says that some of the pilots who have to go out and do search-and-rescues sometimes have to travel hundreds of miles off the coast to find others. There are also sometimes medical evacuations, and when they are on the way back, in the distance, they see the lighthouse.

"They go out in the depths of winter night on the ocean," he tells me. "And then they see the light; and there's a sigh of relief because it's there. They always tell me it's a comfort. It's always there and shows them they are close to land again."

I tell Vincent that in times like these, we need to be lighthouses for each other. His family's story is so powerful. How a young woman delivered a forecast that helped guide the way for Europe's liberation, and changed the history of the world.

I would love to meet his mom someday. To tell her thank you for her hard work, and to give her a hug. There is no doubt in my mind that one person can make a difference in this world.

And delivering a weather forecast is very important work.

Don't let anyone tell you otherwise.

Epilogue

I remember first starting out in broadcasting over thirty years ago. Those nervous butterflies were with me every time I went on the air. Believe it or not, the little tummy flutters still show up from time to time, and they can be a bit unsettling. But it's a reminder that, after all these years, I still care about doing a good job and getting it right.

When I decided to speak out publicly about the deaths of Sean's parents, it was a different kind of nerves. Instead of coming from a happy, excited place, the message I was delivering was coming from sadness and frustration. I remember texting my sister-in-law, Donna, a few minutes before going on the air and asking her to pray that I would be able to keep it together. I wasn't used to unveiling this side of my personality to the audience, but I needed to use the platform I was given to speak out about an injustice that had happened to our family. I can never go back and watch those interviews again because it brings me right back to that incredible pain and anger. That's what fueled me for all those months without stopping: the storm that was strengthening inside of me. It was that kind of energy that kept me going, and led me to find others with similar journeys.

When I began writing this book, I was still upset and distraught. Yet as I sit here, finishing it a year and a half later, I'm at peace knowing I wasn't alone.

I think about my friend Shelly driving though a blizzard to bring awareness to the opioid crisis. A pregnant Carlla leaving her kids at home on Christmas Day to get treatment for her unborn son. My friend Ray, dying with cancer, cornering politicians with his wheelchair, shaming them to help sick 9/11 survivors. And nurse Arlene, watching countless people die from COVID and promising she would try to make the world a better place afterward.

Lieutenant Colonel Scott Mann says we all must listen to the words of others from a place of discovery, where we can open our minds to situations we may find ourselves in someday. I found that writing this book was a wonderful place to amplify these incredible true stories. There will always be bullies in the world and injustices done; that's never going to change. But hearing about good people fighting against the odds brought hope and encouragement. As Coach Andrea Orris says, "Sometimes it just takes one more voice."

You might remember the story I shared about my son Theodore who was badly bullied at school. Recently, he told me that things were getting better. After weeks and months of tears, anxiety, and fear from the kid who would make him feel bad about himself, Theodore one day found the courage to fight back after witnessing the bully targeting one of his friends.

This past year, Theodore was in a different class, but he would still see the mean kid in the hallways and at recess. I would ask once in a while if the bully was still bothering him.

He told me that he wasn't afraid of that kid anymore, and that even if he did say mean things, he would try to stick up for himself or someone else. After a trip to the town pool one day, Theodore admitted that the bully was finally being nice to him.

I told my son to be on his guard, because you never know when the mean kid might resort to his old behavior. But, I admitted, this was certainly good news. On one of their last trips before the school year ended, Theodore mentioned that he and the bully were starting to become friends. I smiled and said sometimes people change, and that maybe Theodore helped make that happen.

There's a wall in my office at work where I post pictures of my family. There are dozens of photos of my kids in various stages of missing teeth. There are also images of my mom with her grandkids and Sean fishing with our boys on Lake George. A few months ago I decided to put up a photo that was taken at a rally a few years ago. I'm speaking at the podium with grieving family members holding up signs of their loved ones who died in nursing homes. I keep it there to remind myself whom I'm still fighting for.

Just because the dust has settled almost three years later doesn't mean the battle for justice and accountability is over. It's part of who I am now. We all weathered something extraordinary these last few years: living through a once-in-a-lifetime pandemic, and we're all still fighting to get out of it.

What I've learned is, we all have it in us to inspire change. The storm is within all of us. And we can use it to do better.

Together.

Acknowledgments

I had no idea there would be another book in my future. When the nursing home scandal began to get attention, there was certainly a chapter to write about, but not enough to fill over two hundred pages. I started looking for others with similar journeys, and that's when I realized we were on to something. There are people standing up for themselves and others all over the place. From the young boy in the schoolyard against the bully to the Green Beret moving heaven and earth to get his friend home from Afghanistan. The pages wrote themselves, and every one of these chapters could easily be its own book.

I had a lot of help finding these amazing humans, and that's where my friend and colleague Kelly May comes in. She did some incredible investigative work, wrote emails, made calls, and set up the interviews. At one point she suggested a podcast, which then came in the summer of 2022. Everyone needs a friend like Kelly May.

Thank you to the Fox News Radio Crew, who helped record all the interviews (which Kelly helped transcribe). You all made the Dean's List.

To the families who lost loved ones in nursing homes across the country, thank you for your prayers and encouragement. I've read hundreds of emails, letters, and Twitter messages. This will be my mission for a long time to come. It may take a lifetime, but I won't give up, I promise. We deserve answers and accountability. The angels are on our side.

To Daniel and Peter Arbeeny. Through tragedy, we found each other. I'm so grateful for your friendship. I know your father, Norman, is so proud of you.

Thank you to my Fox family, Suzanne Scott, Lauren Petterson, Jay Wallace, Gavin Hadden, Tami Radabaugh, Dianne Brandi, Irena Briganti, and so many others behind the scenes. Your support and trust mean the world to me.

To the folks at HarperCollins, especially Eric Nelson. You're a terrific editor, but you make me laugh, which may be more important. Thanks to James Neidhardt and Hannah Long for your hard work putting it all together.

To Bob Barnett, for your council and kindness.

My sister-in-law, Donna, and niece, Danielle, and the whole Johnson family. We couldn't have gotten through these last few years without you.

To Mickey and Dee, I know you're watching over us.

My mom, Stella, thank you for always being there. You're the strongest lady I know.

My sweet boys, Matthew and Theodore, being your mama makes me the happiest. You are my sonshines.

To my husband, Sean. Our love story is the best one of all.

About the Author

JANICE DEAN is the *New York Times* bestselling author of *Mostly Sunny* and *Make Your Own Sunshine* as well as a series of children's weather books, starring Freddy the Frogcaster. She serves as the senior meteorologist for Fox News and is the morning meteorologist for *Fox & Friends*. She also hosts the *Janice Dean Podcast* and has covered historic storms and some of the most iconic American events, including the Kentucky Derby, the Westminster Kennel Club Dog Show, Groundhog Day, and the Nathan's Famous Hot Dog Eating Contest. Janice lives in New York City with her husband, two children, and their dog, Lola.